Itchy Feet
&
Bucket Lists
A GLOBAL ADVENTURE

www.darmatravels.com

Itchy Feet & Bucket Lists by Emma Scattergood
© Emma Scattergood
Edited by Emily Riches

The information in this book is true and complete to the best of our knowledge. All recommendations are made without guarantee on the part of the author. The author and publisher disclaim any liability in connection with the use of this information.

1st Edition 2021
ISBN: 978-0-6453070-1-6 paperback
ISBN: 978-0-6453070-2-3 ebook

Also available as an ebook from major ebook vendors.

Itchy Feet
&
Bucket Lists

A GLOBAL ADVENTURE

Emma Scattergood

Contents

Itchy Feet
The strong desire to leave a place and travel

Bucket List
All the things you want to do or see in your life

(Collin's English Dictionary)

.

PROLOGUE

*O*UTSIDE, rain splashes miserably against the train's grimy windows, and from our starkly lit compartment, there is nothing to see of the dark Croatian countryside – just the reflection of my disappointed face. Darryl, sitting across from me, is once again buried deep within a sudoku. He bought his book of absorbing puzzles in late October, days before we embarked on this adventure and already, six weeks into our journey, it's worn and beginning to fill. Watching him confidently turn another page throws me back to our recent train trips where squares were laboriously filled and puzzles successfully completed as we shot across China, meandered around Mongolia, slogged through vast Russia, slept through Belarus and passed through Poland. And it makes me realise two things. One: it's incredible how well his body is handling our rigid itinerary, the ceaseless onward travel. And two: he will most certainly need a second sudoku book before we arrive back in Australia. Before we finish this circumnavigation of the world. Before we conclude – our second global adventure.

In 2017, Darryl and I undertook what we thought was a 'trip of a lifetime.' Using ideas or destinations on a coveted 'Bucket List,' we spent seven months traversing Asia and Europe, seeking culinary delights, childhood dreams and, in Darryl's case, health. Still in the throes of depression following a life-changing accident in 2011, our overland journey from Australia to Europe by ship and train was precisely what Darryl needed at the time. It tested his endurance, dispelled the frustrations brought about by an inability to work and cast aside his despair – something medication hadn't been able to do.

Returning home, what we hadn't expected were the after-effects of this life of travel: the realisation that a once-in-a-lifetime adventure is not good enough, that this nomadic existence is great; therapeutic and

1

informative, you want – even need – to take off again, to scratch that itch. The online Collins dictionary example sums it up quite nicely and succinctly: "The trip gave me itchy feet and I wanted to travel more." Coming from a family used to travel and growing up with a desire to explore the world so great that during my teens, I had created my own Bucket List and even laminated it, the seven months spent ticking the items on this worn piece of plastic, blogging our journey and organising our travel was something very difficult to abandon once we returned to everyday life. Writing a memoir, *Bucket Lists and Walking Sticks*, helped; we were able to relive our adventure. But unfortunately, it wasn't enough. We had both well and truly developed 'itchy feet.'

In late 2018, understanding that this itch wasn't going to go away and aware of the benefits of travel on our mental health, the joy brought about by just moving onwards, I decided to again hunt out this list.

"My father always dreamt of catching the Trans-Siberian Express," I say one morning to Darryl over my avocado on toast, my laminated list on the table beside me. "As a child, I remember hearing about this train journey that spanned the length of Russia cutting through Siberia, and how incredible it sounded. But dad died at 61 and never got to realise his dream. And your mother. She had her adventures cut off at 63. It would be good, while we still can, to do some more travel. To take off again."

"We *are* only in our *fifties*," Darryl laughs.

"I know, but who knows what's down the track," I reply. "Whether your body will hold up. Whether we will be able to travel later. Whether Trump blows up the world. Climate change? Who knows?"

"Where did you have in mind?"

"I've pulled the Bucket List back out. Amongst what's left are the Trans-Siberian Express, the Terracotta Army, the Swiss Alps and the Panama Canal."

"Which one were you thinking of?"

"All of them."

"All of them?"

"Yes. It could be our second 'global adventure.'"

It takes a year to organise and, as with our last journey, I love every moment of putting together an itinerary that becomes harder to control than an excitable puppy, an itinerary that leaps and grows, refusing to be mediocre. Already plush with our Bucket List items, each great new experience that is added seems to suggest another.

It's possible to commence the Trans-Siberian Express in Beijing, China. This leg, called the Trans-Mongolian, traverses Mongolia, so how about we stay a night or two in the freezing desert in a ger, a traditional tent? The Trans-Siberian journey terminates in Moscow, so let's spend time exploring Putin's city. Auschwitz has long exerted a strange pull, so let's visit Poland. Croatia looks incredible and is cheap, so let's go there. And if we are touring the Swiss Alps, let's ride the Glacier Express. And the Golden Pass Line. Let's have a rum in Barbados, a coffee in Guatemala and guacamole in Mexico.

After 12 months of joyous battle and intense organisation, what eventuates is a four-month, 57,000-kilometre journey crossing China, Mongolia, Russia and greater Europe, arriving in England for Christmas. The New Year sees us continuing the journey onboard a cruise ship that will take seven weeks to deliver us back to Australia via the Panama Canal, America, and the Atlantic and Pacific Oceans. In all, we will be traversing 20-plus countries utilising a score of trains, one ship and two planes. It would have been preferable to forgo the planes and achieve the journey solely by land but time constraints, combined with a desire not to repeat Asian train routes covered in our youth has us flying from Brisbane to Beijing in late October, 2019.

As on our last adventure, I organise most of our travel myself. I book our accommodation through Booking.com, purchase Eurail passes through Raileurope.com.au and use Russiau.com to help with the convoluted Russian visas we require. I organise fee-free credit cards from Citibank and order a variety of currencies from Travelex. I purchase three sim cards through Simcorner.com for China, Russia and Europe, arrange ESTAs which authorise us to travel to America and organise flu, tetanus, typhoid, hepatitis A and B shots. Disconcertingly, I discover that even though we will not be stepping onto Belarusian soil – our train will merely be passing through – visas are still required, and unbelievably, they can only be obtained personally in Moscow. I push aside the disturbing thought of what will we do if we fail to obtain these visas; the entire itinerary hinges on each leg going to plan.

I do get some help with travel through China and Russia. China is cagey about foreign visitors, so ChinaTour.net helps me with letters of introduction for our visas, the airport pickup and internal excursions. They book our tours to the Great Wall, Forbidden City and the Terracotta Army; everything else, including accommodation and internal train travel, we organise ourselves. For our Trans-Siberian journey, we consult Monkeyshrine, a company recommended by train-travel expert The Man in Seat 61.

The Trans-Siberian is the world's longest railway journey. Spanning 9,289 kilometres from Vladivostok in the east to Moscow in the west, it crosses Siberia, runs alongside the great Lake Baikal, across the endless Russian steppes and over the rich Ural Mountains.

The Trans-Mongolian is a 7,621-kilometre journey that leaves from Beijing in China. It enters the Gobi Desert, cuts across Mongolia then merges with the Trans-Siberian line in Siberia. It is, some would argue, the more interesting of the two journeys.

Both the Trans-Siberian and Trans-Mongolian Express are not one train journey each but instead routes along Russia's massive rail network. You can catch several different trains of varying grades that travel the routes. Although possible to book cabins ourselves through pass.rzd.ru, it becomes easier, given the considerable paperwork involved, to use Monkeyshrine.

Wrestling with such an extensive itinerary, I do make plenty of mistakes. I have us booked into accommodation in Warsaw ready to visit Auschwitz, when in fact, we should be staying nearly 300 kilometres away in Krakow. I have to rearrange our whole Switzerland itinerary once I discover the Glacier Express closes each year for a month's maintenance – the month we hoped to be aboard her. Booking late, I just manage to secure the last sleeper cabin on the Jadrolinija ferry between Croatia and Italy, and I learn that you must purchase an actual seat reservation with a Eurail pass and that there are limited online sites where you can buy them.

I book train tickets from Budapest to Zagreb and realise that these tickets cannot be printed online; they must be posted to us. Unfortunately, we will have left Australia before they arrive – they will have to be sent to our Moscow accommodation and fingers crossed, they turn up. And knowing we will be in London while the Premier League is playing, I leave it up to Darryl, a keen West Ham fan, to secure tickets and ask him on the eve of our departure.

"Have we got seats?"

"Um no. I was hoping you could look into them?"

But perhaps my biggest mistake, although I do not know this at the time, is to not adequately insure Darryl for any pre-existing injuries. Using the free travel insurance attached to our credit cards, we will both be covered. But when it comes to paying any extra to cover Darryl's numerous ailments, on Darryl's bidding, I unfortunately decline. A decision that will later cause me much angst.

Despite the mistakes, I do have some good wins. I purchase a new iPhone to replace my old one which is slowly dying, knowing I will be able to claim back any GST at the airport before we fly out. And I manage to secure a great deal on the cruise ship that will return us to Australia, a cruise ship we are familiar with.

"It's the Arcadia," I mention to Darryl. "The ship we sailed on to England last time."

It's surprising how quickly those 12 months pass, how well the itinerary comes together, how ready we are to once again take off, to scratch the itch. Whereas last time, it was our children's travels that ignited our travel bug, this time, both Pierce and Paige will be remaining in Australia. Pierce, currently in his third year of an electrical apprenticeship with a Byron Bay electrician, will be looking after our house.

"Yes mum. Of course, I'll keep it clean."

Paige, with her nursing studies complete, is presently looking for a graduate position while working at a Woolworths in Brisbane. Our little water dragon-chasing dog Jordie has sadly passed away.

On the eve of our departure, knowing that we will be missing the long, beautiful Australian summer, I take my usual early morning stroll along the Brunswick Head's breakwall, scanning for dolphins and enjoying the sunrise. I won't be doing anything like this in the wintery northern hemisphere. Local Geoff, another early morning walker, greets me as I approach.

"So, tomorrow, is it?"

"It is. We'll stay tomorrow night in Brisbane before flying out Monday morning."

"And you will be away for four months? Travelling around the world?"

"We are."

"Why?" he asks simply.

It's a question that I need a few seconds to answer.

"Because there's more to the world than the Byron Shire and we want to see it. Because we only have one life to make the most of. Because we still have Bucket List items to tick off."

I'm satisfied with my answer, but Geoff looks unconvinced. I continue.

"Because you can gain so much by travelling through a country, a town or a place. Because everyone should know about the joys of travel. Because when we return, I'll use my notes to write a book and you'll be able to experience the joy and hopefully learn something from our journey."

CHAPTER 1

Singapore

*O*NCE upon a time, I remember the experience of arriving at an airport and departing Australia as being quite stressful, but this morning, it's all quite straightforward. Following a great night's sleep at the Brisbane Comfort Inn, it's merely a matter of using their free shuttle service to access Brisbane's international terminal. Once there, we self check-in using a convenient machine, flash our new ePassports at customs then look for our Singaporean plane. The most stressful part is claiming back the GST on my new phone bought specifically for this journey. There's a long snaking queue full of well-accessorised Instagram girls holding fistfuls of receipts in front of the Australian Border Force office. By the time I hand over my lone chit, it's time to board: no time for coffees, let alone duty free.

We are flying Singapore Airlines because, instead of flying directly to Beijing, we have organised a 17-hour layover at Singapore Airport. With his spine full of shiny metal and his ceramic hip, Darryl finds sitting for extended periods difficult. Breaking a long-haul trip into manageable chunks helps, meaning our 14-hour direct flight has been reduced to two seven-hour flights. The time spent at the Singapore Airport Transit hotel will allow Darryl time to recover before our onward journey.

It's a beautiful day, perfect flying weather, and I am pinching myself that this journey has begun. Whereas once I used to enjoy flying, my older self is not such a great fan, so I appreciate today's conditions: the vast cloudless blue sky embracing us, the interminable sunburnt length of Australia drifting far below. This is helping with some of the little worms of doubt that for months I have managed to ignore, but now that we are on our way, are beginning to make their presence felt. With Pompeii now on our itinerary, I'm starting to question whether Darryl, with his dodgy foot and walking stick, will be able to manage the rugged Amalfi coast. Whether his painful back will be able to handle the hours sitting on uncomfortable trains, his energy levels the stamina to complete this epic adventure? I'm also starting to doubt myself and my organising abilities. Can I handle sitting once again on a claustrophobic train 75 metres below the English Channel? Or through the 116-year-old leaking Albula tunnel in Switzerland that the Glacier Express passes? How cold will it get in our toiletless Mongolian ger? What will the bathrooms be like on the Trans-Siberian trains? What happens if we cannot obtain Belarus visas in Moscow? What happens if something goes wrong?

At lunchtime, the few turbulent bumps that signal our mainland departure, our flight now travelling over the small stretch of sea that separates our continent from the Asian one, are the perfect excuse for me to put aside these doubts and scrutinise the miniature console in front of me. It's currently displaying a picture of the world map and, inspecting it, I can't believe that our upcoming four-month journey will have us travelling its entire circumference. We'll be visiting countries only ever dreamt about, travelling through places never heard. Leaning forward in my seat, I place my finger where I think Brunswick Heads is, then trace a journey north-west through Singapore, China, Mongolia and Russia.

"This is our route," I interrupt Darryl.

With my finger still on the screen, I continue onward: Poland, Hungary, Croatia, Italy, Switzerland, France, England.

"Then after England," Darryl prompts.

Madeira, Barbados, Curaçao, Panama, Guatemala, Mexico, then upwards to San Francisco in America.

"Now the last leg." And my finger moves through the vast Pacific Ocean – Hawaii, Samoa, Tonga, New Zealand, Sydney – then finally stops again on Brunswick Heads: home.

"Once again, it's turned into a huge journey, an epic adventure," I grin.

"Of course it has," Darryl grins back.

Travelling backwards in time, it's a little after 2 pm local time or 5 pm Australian time when we gently touch down at hazy Singapore Changi Airport. Although we have a room waiting for us, there is little point in accessing it straight away. Transit hotels work differently from regular hotels, generally offering a six- or 12-hour allotment. To make the best use of the 12 hours we have booked, we have decided to leave check-in until later, around 6 pm. This way, we will not have to depart at some unreasonable hour of the morning once our 12 hours have expired.

Surprisingly, these waiting hours pass easily and quickly. Singapore Airport is considered one of the best in the world, and after visiting its movie theatre, its large, vibrant sunflower garden and its moist butterfly garden full of languid flying insects, it's easy to understand why. A dinner of roti prata, an Indian bread served with thick vegetable curry, is devoured at one of the many excellent food places we stumble upon.

Our second flight and it's an uneventful trip, memorable only for the rerun of *Friends* playing on the screen in front of me, the bulky neighbour sitting beside me and the turmoil of my thoughts inside me. Unlike Monkeyshrine, the agency assisting us with our Russian travel which came recommended by a reputable website, ChinaTour.net, the company helping us with our China leg, was simply plucked from the internet. They were a gamble we had to take if we wished to book cheap airport pickups and even cheaper internal tours. They have organised to meet us in the arrivals area of Beijing airport and, if no one is there, then it will mean that we have been scammed and a good percentage of our China explorations will collapse. It will be an expensive mistake, and a nightmare to fix. Understandably, I am nervous and instead, try to turn my attention to more positive thoughts.

I have long wanted to visit China. Documentaries showcasing its ancient ruling dynasties, its stunning scenery, bicycle-loving people and incredible infrastructure have cast an appealing lure for years. I have been eager to visit the place where the calendar, gun powder and magnetic compass originated. And hungry to learn more about the country that in four quick decades, went from complete social failure to the worlds' second-largest economy. From a place with little infrastructure to the country with the largest ports on the planet. From an agricultural society to a powerhouse of industry. Today, I want to see the new Beijing carved from the wreckage of Mao Zedong's failed policies and talk with the locals who lived them. Please let there be someone waiting for us.

CHAPTER 2

China

A s to be expected, Beijing Capital Airport is heaving with arrivals when we eventually touch down. Queues fronting customs wind like spaghetti around the tightly secured area. It's a tense moment when it's our turn to front the officers; I'm doubting our paperwork, but eventually, passports are frowningly stamped, security cleared and we are free to enter the even busier arrivals hall.

With Darryl searching the huge crowds on one side and myself on the other, tension rises when, 20 minutes later, we have failed to locate a sign bearing my name.

"Can we contact them?" Darryl anxiously questions.

"My phone has data only. No credit," I reply. "I could try and WhatsApp them but I'm not confident. Just keep looking."

As we intently scan the huge building, my stress levels skyrocketing, I'm desperately thinking of all that will need rescheduling and kicking myself that we have been duped when Darryl, tentatively, points towards a small, faded sign bearing what could be his name, not mine.

"Over there, do you think that's us?"

"I think it is. Yes – thank goodness. But no wonder we didn't see it earlier. It's tiny and in your name. Why yours? Everything was booked in mine."

Darkness has fallen when we eventually reach the Howard Johnson Paragon Hotel, our home for the following few days. It was an illuminating journey characterised by crazy traffic, a lunatic driver, polluted skies and, most surprising of all, abundant greenery. With beautiful trees lining entire streets, Beijing is proving to be one of the greenest cities we have visited.

Although hungry after a long day, we are both in no mood to go searching for food and Darryl's suggestion of room service sounds good. There's a menu worded partially in English beside the phone, which I use to place our order. Unfortunately, it's an unsuccessful attempt with neither of us speaking the other's language.

"I suppose we should have expected that," I say as I hang up the phone. "No English is something we are probably going to have to get used to."

Not really sure of what to do, I head out hoping I may find a café or vending machine somewhere. I'm reluctant to leave Darryl and the security of our room but happy when I eventually stumble across the hotel's restaurant. It's short-lived happiness as again, none of the staff speak any English. Tired, ready to admit defeat and go to bed hungry, I do have one last idea. Pulling out my iPhone, I bring up the Google Translate app (something I will get used to doing), adjust it to translate into simplified Chinese then type in chicken and rice. Surprisingly, my message is understood, and it's strangely rewarding to return to our room and, 20 minutes later, have two steaming bowls delivered.

One of the most enjoyable aspects of international travel is the breakfast buffet. Usually consisting of numerous trestles groaning under the weight of great food, it's something we always look forward to. With the hotel's restaurant cold and dark, it's still night outside, I'm happy to discover this morning's buffet to be the usual eclectic mix of Western and Asian: cornflakes and noodles, warming bacon and dumplings, green tea and dire coffee. At 7 am, while Darryl quickly returns to our room to collect some of the hotel's complimentary water, I head to reception in search of our tour guide.

I find him waiting in reception, jumping up when I approach.

"Ni Hao. Great Wall?" I ask him.

"Shì de – yes," he replies.

Darryl joins us shortly after, and together the three of us make our way to a tree-strewn carpark not far from the hotel.

"Private car!" I whisper to Darryl. "That's great. I thought we were getting a minibus with others."

Unsure as to why we now have our own private car, we shrug off any apprehension and instead sink back into our comfortable leather seats.

Outside the car windows, it's still dark but despite the early hour the Beijing arteries are clogged with traffic. They are still like this when, 10 minutes into our journey, our guide's phone rings, and a long conversation ensues.

Although spoken in Chinese, it's clearly a heated discussion, our guide becoming increasingly agitated. This is confirmed when, hanging up his phone, he turns to us and holds up a sign.

"Is this you?"

"No," we reply.

"No?"

"No," we repeat. "Those look like Asian names."

It eventuates that he has collected the wrong passengers; we have found the wrong guide.

Too late to return to our hotel as our minibus would have already left, I hand over the phone number I have for our tour and trust this driver can sort something out.

"I drop you here," he says after another intense conversation. "Your tour will pick you up soon."

Although worried – he is, after all, dropping us off in some entirely foreign location in an alien city, and we have only his word that our tour will find us here – we have no option really but to get out of the car.

"I'm sure it will be all right," I say confidently to Darryl.

It's an agonising 10-minute wait, stranded on a narrow footpath heavily buffeted by the belching passing traffic. But thankfully, a minibus does pull up.

"Ni Hao – hello. My name is Paul," sings our guide cheerfully.

"Ready for the Forbidden City?"

Adding to the mornings' mayhem, it turns out that today's itinerary has been changed. Today we visit the Forbidden City and Summer Palace. Tomorrow, hopefully, we'll find the Great Wall.

Situated in the centre of Beijing, not far from Tiananmen Square, is the world's largest imperial palace – the Forbidden City. It took over a million workers 14 years to complete the behemoth, with construction finishing in 1420. For 492 years, the palace was home to 24 Chinese emperors and their families, the last forced to abdicate in 1914 following Sun Yat-Sen's republican rebellion. Surrounded by a 10-metre wall, which is itself surrounded by a 52-metre moat, are over 980 buildings with over 8,700 rooms. For many years the political centre of China, these days the Forbidden City is visited by 14 million visitors per year with a maximum of 80,000 visitors per day.

Paul is a happy guide with excellent English, and time passes quickly as our minibus weaves through narrow crowded alleys, traverses avenues as big as airport runways and dodges rickshaws and roadworks before eventually arriving at an instantly recognisable red-brick and double-eave building. Known as the Meridian Gate, it's the main gate to the Forbidden City. Waiting to enter, we can see, are a good proportion of those 80,000 daily visitors.

One of the few benefits of travelling with a tour group is the ability to skip queues, and with Paul, it's easy to make our way straight to the head of one of these massive ropes of bodies, where our passports are heavily scrutinised and permission is granted to pass through some notably impressive gates. Inside and despite the heaving crush of people, it's immediately evident that we have entered a remarkable place. Towering red brick walls, ornate gardens with ancient, gnarled trees, vast areas of white marble paving, cobbled courtyards and thousands of rooms fronted by startling statues and intricate carvings. It's grandeur on a scale that we have only ever seen once before, albeit a different type of grandeur, at the Palace of Versailles in France. It really is enough to take your breath away.

"I had no idea it would be like this. So vast. So impressive. Look at those massive brick walls. All these buildings. It really is an entire city within a city."

"It is," Darryl agrees. "It's easy to understand now how some people lived their entire lives within these walls."

Left to our own wanderings, but all the time taking a direct path through the heart of the complex, it takes a little under two hours to see the Forbidden City. And while we cannot enter any of the buildings we pass, such as the Palace Museum, the Palace of Earthly Tranquillity, the Halls of Supreme Harmony and Preserving Harmony, we do stop, admire and take plenty of photos.

During one of these photo stops, I am approached by two Chinese ladies appearing to want their photograph taken. Thinking they wish me to take a photo of the both of them, I go to grasp their phone whereas, laughing, they clumsily mime that they want me to be in the picture as well. It's surprising, although Paul, when later questioned, advises that this is normal.

"Many Chinese from rural China have seen few or no white people, especially with hair the colour of yours. They like to take a photo with you and show their friends and family when they return home."

It had been interesting to discover when organising this journey that booking a tour within China wasn't as straightforward as in other countries. Each tour company I had approached appeared to offer two prices for their excursions, a price with 'shopping stops' and a price without. As I enjoy shopping and it brought the cost of our tours down significantly, I had no problem with booking them with 'stops,' although Darryl had been less than impressed. Not long after departing the Forbidden City, we stop at today's first shopping stop, a pearl factory full of gleaming, fat pearls. While no one buys any pearls, a few of us, myself included, do purchase some luminescent face cream made from the crushed mineral. Although happy with my purchase, the limited toiletry space I have in my baggage will cause me misery when packing at many later dates.

Over the past decade, Australia has become a popular destination for visiting Chinese tourists, most travelling within the confines of a tour group. One characteristic of these tours is the sheer quantity of places visited, usually at an exhausting pace. As the hours pass and our minibus continues to weave through Beijing, stopping at numerous sights, it becomes easy to empathise with these tourists. At the UNESCO-listed Temple of Heaven, where gods were worshipped and prayers said for a good harvest, Darryl sits as the rest of us labour up exhaustive flights of stairs. While at the Traditional Chinese Medicine Factory, another shopping stop, tolerance is taxed as we combat wily apothecary touts.

"Your liver is not healthy… these tablets will help. Your kidneys are not good… this medicine will help. Your digestion could be better… this remedy will help."

It takes a strong person to ignore their persistent pitch – or someone with little room left for anything else in their luggage. Therefore, while Darryl and I thankfully manage to escape the fleecing, others are not so lucky.

"Did you buy anything?"

"Yes," is the glum reply. "About $1,000 American dollars' worth!"

Situated somewhere in the northwest of Beijing and rumoured to be the best-preserved imperial garden in the world is the Summer Palace. Late afternoon and tiredly stepping from our minibus, it appears that we have arrived at a truly beautiful place, an ancient wonderland. Comprising a vast collection of landscaped gardens, pavilions and temples surrounding the immense but tranquil, man-made Kunming Lake, it was to here that, in summer, former emperors and their families would flee to escape the Forbidden City's suffocating heat.

Revived by its beauty and given an hour to wander, we use the time to walk around the lake's curving banks under weeping willows, to take photographs from the impressive stone, arched Seventeen-Hole Bridge and to watch as families fly the quintessential Chinese centipede kites. Again, as at the Forbidden City, I am approached by some local women, and again I have my photograph taken alongside them. As we leave the Summer Palace, I can't help thinking that we have just experienced fairyland, an ancient wonderland found only in Chinese fables.

Today, I awaken feeling unexpectedly excited. In a few hours, we will be visiting China's Great Wall, and it feels incredible that shortly we will be standing upon a structure we have been conscious of most of our lives, an edifice nearly everyone on Earth has heard of.

This time we ensure that Chris, today's tour guide, is there for us and not someone else before boarding a minibus. We are the first to board, and over the next hour, as we meander throughout various Beijing suburbs, we collect more passengers – an elderly British couple here, two very large Canadians there, a single chic Parisienne. The Canadians are the last to board and do not look happy to be left with the two remaining narrow single seats.

Although not explicitly planned, we have discovered that today's 70-kilometre, hour-and-a-half journey will be taking us to the Mutianyu section of the Great Wall of China.

We have learnt that from Beijing, there are numerous parts of the Great Wall that we can visit. Mutianyu is the best-restored section, Jinshanling the most beautiful and Jiankou the most perilous, to name three. What makes Mutianyu so appealing is that a chairlift has been built, allowing people with disabilities, such as Darryl's, access to the battlements.

The traffic leaving Beijing city is horrendous. It's pretty bad most of the time, but today it's even worse due to an earlier accident. As I gaze out at the congested streets, Chris's voice rings out.

"Beijinger's drive at an average speed of 22 kilometres an hour... Their average daily commute time is 1.3 hours... Twenty years ago, 80% of Beijinger's rode bikes, now it's less than 25%... There are 1 million new cars on the road every month in China!"

Eventually, as the effects of the earlier accident start to wear off and we find ourselves further out of the city, I begin to see beyond the build-up of traffic and what I see both surprises and awes me. Surprised because many of the roads and side streets are spotless; there is a vehicle regularly sweeping away any rubbish, another hosing down any dust. Awed by the beauty that is starting to reveal itself the further from the city we travel. Wide, peaceful rivers, their banks full of those beautiful weeping willows, fruit orchards full of peach, pear and persimmon trees, acres of forests full of pines, oaks and larches.

Out here, the air also appears to be a little less polluted and, with the temperature reaching a kind 17 degrees, the sun beaming overhead means our cumbersome winter jackets have been gratefully discarded.

Like yesterday, today comes with its unavoidable shopping stops, the first a large jade factory.

"We will be stopping here for 40 minutes," Chris informs us. "Chinese jade is very special. It does not shatter like the jade found in other countries. Jade is also very lucky to the Chinese, and you will have a chance to purchase some very beautiful pieces."

While we all leave without purchasing some 'lucky' jade, the restrooms do come in handy as well as teach me an important lesson.

"The toilet paper is kept in the main area outside the toilet cubicle," I say when I return to Darryl. "You have to grab it before entering. I didn't realise but luckily, I had a heap of tissues on me. I won't do that again."

Commencement of the Great Wall of China occurred in 221 BC-206 BC during the Qin Dynasty, and contrary to popular belief, it can't be seen from space and it was not built to keep the Mongols out – the Mongols did not emerge until around 800 AD. Nearly everything built back then is now little more than a mound of dirt, and the majority of what exists today is the battlement stone structure built by the Ming dynasty around 500 years ago.

Immaterial as to why and when it was built, the Great Wall, measuring over 21,000 kilometres in its entirety, is recognised as being one of history's most impressive architectural feats.

It's hard to put into words the emotions that flood me when, through the scrubby trees on the steep hills above, I get my first glimpse of the well-defined, whitish-grey brick structure: the mountain's own long, perfect stone spine. I am definitely aware of being in the presence of ancient history, one of the wonders of the world.

"For a wall over 500 years old, it's in great condition," I eventually remark.

"That is because this section was fully restored in 1986," Chris replies. "The chairlift and toboggan came later. If you would like to take the chairlift to the top or catch the toboggan back down, tickets are not included in this tour, but I can organise them for you. You have 90 minutes to explore the wall before meeting down here for lunch."

While Chris's words do jar – restored section? Chairlift? Toboggan? – it doesn't matter. What we are gazing upon looks too impressive, too incredible, to be anything else but amazing.

With our feet dangling and our eyes continually sweeping the landscape around us, it takes eight minutes for our chairlift to travel the 723-metre uphill journey. The terrain is steep and craggy, the foliage thick and scrubby, and we are both incredulous as to how such a long snaking stone edifice could be built here. Constructed by soldiers, forcibly recruited peasants, convicts and prisoners of war, it must have been a backbreaking task.

Once on top of the wall, it's even easier to see just how extensive and how remarkable this structure is, with its perfect watchtowers, its steep crumbling steps and its long, wide battlement that stretches far in either direction. Choosing to take the least strenuous path, we slowly negotiate the thigh-killing stairs, linger gratefully at the lookouts with their breathtaking views and unsuccessfully try to avoid a party of overactive school kids who swarm like picnic ants. At some stage, I leave Darryl behind and make my way further along the wall's ridge, negotiating more steep steps, my thigh and calf muscles rebelling. Finally, fully aware of what a privilege it has been to visit here, it's time to go, and I gleefully board a toboggan while Darryl sedately makes his way back down using the chairlift.

"The toboggan was brilliant," I cry when we meet back up again. "I wish it had been twice as long."

China is not only the largest producer and exporter of tea in the world, but it's also their national drink. It is not surprising, therefore, that a visit to a tea factory has appeared on our itinerary. In search of this factory, the passing scenery has everyone captivated as we delve further and deeper into the hills that characterise this outer region of Beijing. With steep wooded bluffs rising austere and beautiful on either side and easy-to-navigate roads, we find ourselves tracing the route of a broad, near-empty river that lines the valley floor. Eventually, we enter a long tunnel and emerge on the other side to a flatter, more cultivated landscape. Here, the land is rich with fruit orchards. I am unsure what sort of countryside I was expecting before I arrived in China; I do know I wasn't expecting it to be as noteworthy as this.

Entering a nondescript, wooden building, a confident young Chinese girl sits us at a long trestle table. In front of us are five tiny, delicate, bone china teacups. We use these dainty vessels to sip various types of tea as our host regales us with information. We learn that tea originated in ancient China nearly 5,000 years ago. Some tea leaves from a wild tree 'apparently' blew into Emperor Shen Nung's pot of boiling water and, interested by the pleasant scent created, he drank some. We learn a little about the different types of tea: black, oolong, green and white, how they all come from the same plant – the *Camellia Sinensis*. The difference is how they are treated after harvest. We learn that herbal teas such as peppermint and camomile are not teas at all;

instead, they are tisanes. In all, despite the constant prompts to "buy, buy, buy," I find the whole experience interesting and pleasant and a good precursor for today's final stop – the Ming Tombs.

Burial place of 13 of the 16 Ming dynasty emperors and reputedly still full of unearthed treasures, Chris falls back into tour-guide mode as we trek their substantial grounds.

"Many of the Emperors had their concubines killed or buried alive alongside them… This is the Ghost Gate – it's the gate departed emperors who still roam here use as their main door to the other world. You are not advised to walk through it. You are also not advised to take any photographs of this gate or area."

Just before leaving the tombs, I ask Chris to help me negotiate the purchase of a single, delicious-looking peach from a small market stall set up near the site's entrance. Picked from a local orchard, the fruit looks incredible, a notion quickly dispelled when later that night I share it with Darryl.

"Yuck," he spits. "It's completely rotten inside."

Friday 1 November marks the end of our three-night stay in Beijing. Today, we board one of China's high-speed bullet trains to undertake the five-hour journey to Xian, location of the Terracotta Army. We will be returning in two days for a further few nights, but for now, we are looking forward to moving on. Using the ChinaTour.net website, our bullet train tickets have been booked; we just have to collect them from Beijing West train station before boarding. Unfortunately, they cannot be printed.

Unlike Australia, China has invested heavily in its train network. The past 30 years have seen a virtually non-existent system evolve into the world's most extensive high-speed travel network. The country is, in fact, the creator of more high-speed rail routes than the rest of the world combined, with trains capable of speeds up to 350 kilometres per hour. Being train travel lovers, we have for years heard stories about this legendary network and are incredibly excited to soon be about to shoot through the countryside on one of the fabled bullet trains.

Organised while checking out, our taxi arrives promptly and shortly drops us at the edge of a vast multi-laned, traffic-congested road. By a series of miming and pointing, the driver indicates that we are to use a nearby pedestrian subway that heads towards what could be a large railway station.

"Train station?" we anxiously question.

"Shì de."

Resurfacing in front of this sizeable austere building, we find it swarming with bodies with no English signage visible anywhere – just a confusing jumble of Chinese characters.

Also, unlike most train stations we have previously encountered, there is no obvious entrance into the building.

"Can you see how to get in? There's a picture of what looks like a ticket machine and an arrow pointing upstairs, but I can't see how we get up there."

"I don't see an entrance," Darryl replies. "And I also can't see any lifts or elevators nor someone who may speak English to ask."

Constantly aware of our train's departure time, conscious of how fast time is ticking, terrified of the repercussions, the following 40 minutes are excruciating as we nerve-rackingly search for an entrance into this building, frustratingly deal with security and unhappily struggle through X-ray. No one speaks English. No one helps us, and with Darryl's observations correct, there are no lifts nor elevators; we have no option but to scale large flights of stairs with our cumbersome bags – in vain, before clambering back down again. It's with indescribable relief that we finally locate the single English-speaking counter from all the dozens that exist, gladly retrieve our tickets and thankfully board our train.

To be expected in China, our carriage is designer-sleek, modern and comfortable. With oversized fold-out tables and surrounded by solitude, I find it easy to work away on a blog while Darryl tackles his sudoku. At times, we both look up to just stare at the passing smoggy world visible through the train's large, slightly grubby windows. Although forewarned of the development that has occurred in this country over the past 20 years, we are unprepared when out of the gloom they slither and we view them with our own eyes: clusters of concrete high-rise buildings either still under development with large cranes aloft, or finished and sitting there empty. Known as China's 'ghost cities,' and built for a population that hasn't yet arrived yet, this must be where a high proportion of Australia's iron ore has ended up. Every 20 minutes or so, these clusters appear and continue to do so for most of the five hours it takes to reach Xian.

It's overcast and raining when we eventually pull into the spacious, 2011-built Xian North Railway Station. We have organised a driver and we spot him quickly, the signage again in Darryl's name. Making our way to the Ramada Bell Hotel, we notice that Xian, although much smaller than Beijing, is still large and sprawling with many modern high-rise buildings. The roads are wide, the traffic sparser. Our overall impression through the rain-smeared windows is of many large new buildings tacked onto an older, smaller city.

One of the after-effects of Darryl's 2011 accident is tiredness. It is usually remedied by a lie-down, and as he rests in our comfortable room, I set out to explore Xian. It's still raining, and with the temperature noticeably colder than Beijing, I don my heavy-duty winter boots, bought for the upcoming snow of Siberia, after having worn my lightweight Skechers for the past few days. Walking the city streets, browsing the brightly lit shops, it doesn't take long for me to become aware of just how out of place I look. I see no other westerners and the locals all appear very well-dressed. At one stage, I enter a shoe shop where my bulky boots are openly stared at, and I exit feeling quite self-conscious. It's an experience I have never encountered before, but happy to find the shops very well-priced, I eventually overcome my unease and open my wallet. My most successful purchase is two enamel mugs complete with secure fitting plastic lids – they will be perfect for our Trans-Siberian journey.

It looks like it is going to be a lovely day, when promptly at 9 am we meet up with David, today's guide, who directs us onto a minibus. The sun is out, the rain completely gone. Also on board for the 30-odd kilometre journey to Xianyang, the ancient former capital of China and location of the Terracotta Army, is Chuck, his wife Barb and their kids Mindy and Colin. They are an American family living in the Chinese city of Wuhan.

"Chuck works in Wuhan," Barb tells me in her thick American drawl. "He's been here for the past year. But we have only just arrived. I've bought the kids out for a few months."

"It's great," Colin interjects excitedly. "We are living in a suite at the Hilton."

"What does Chuck do?" I enquire.

"He works for an American company that makes glass for TVs and mobile phones."

It was over 20 years ago that I first heard about the Terracotta Army. A documentary was shown on Australian television outlining how another giant pit full of terracotta statues had been excavated in Xian. It then went on to show footage of the current pit along with footage from previous excavations. Staring at the television screen, I had been amazed and awed at what they were televising, the sheer magnitude and historical wealth of the place. To visit and see for myself became a Bucket List item.

The story goes that Qin Shi Huang (259-210 BC), the first emperor to unify the Chinese nation, had an enormous tomb built to achieve immortality. Alongside this tomb, a vast army made from terracotta clay and estimated at 8,000 strong was also constructed to defend the emperor in the afterlife. Placed in battle formation and hidden underground, this mammoth 'ghost army,' complete with horses, chariots, infantrymen and weaponry, was never meant to see the light of day.

In March 1974, a farmer digging a well in this dry and scrubby province unearthed fragments of a clay figure – the first evidence of what was to become the most stunning archaeological find of the 20th century. Since then, archaeologists have discovered four pits covering a six-acre site. Of the four pits, three are easily accessible and form the four-acre Museum of the Terracotta Army, opened in 1979 and today's destination.

Before disembarking the bus, David provides a little more information.

"The actual tomb of Emperor Qin Shi Huang is still sealed. Inside, there are many precious artefacts which could be ruined if the tomb is opened."

"Do you think it will ever be opened?" someone questions.

"There are no plans at the moment, but I think one day it might be."

David continues to impart information as we make our way towards the museum's entrance.

"It was very lucky that they (the Terracotta Army) were found at all. If the farmer had been digging just a few metres away, then he would have missed them." David demonstrates by scratching a rectangle on the ground and marking one outer corner. "The well was dug just here. But it was not so lucky for the farmer and the villagers. The Chinese government made all the villagers move so that they could create the museum. The farmer, Yang Zhifa, received 5,000 yuan (1,000 Australian dollars) for his land."

Approaching what looks to be a recent build, David continues: "This is the new entrance to the Terracotta Museum, where the army is housed. With so many visitors now, the Chinese government upgraded this area just a few years ago."

We are standing on the outer edge of a vast concrete expanse sectioned with rope barriers and guarded by vigilant security officials. Far ahead in the distance, accessible by foot or shuttle, are three large, elongated structures – the actual museum.

"How many visitors do they get each day?" Barb asks in awe. "This area is huge."

"The maximum permitted each day is 65,000," David replies. "Those three large buildings you can see up ahead are where we are going, but first we will visit the old entrance and ticket office. Yang Zhifa, the farmer who found the Terracotta Army, will be there. Many years after discovering the statues, he was given a job by the museum. He signs autographs, and you can have your photo taken with him. He has had a photo with Bill Clinton."

"The actual first farmer who found the Terracotta Army?" Chuck challenges.

"Yes. Yang Zhifa. He is mostly retired, but he is still there some days."

While there is some doubt in our minds that this is the actual person who found the Terracotta Army, his photo alongside Bill Clinton and numerous other celebrities does seem to confirm David's story. While we are content just to say that we have met the person who discovered the Terracotta Army and shake his hand, Chuck and Barb take the opportunity to have a photograph taken alongside him and purchase his autographed book.

The following hours it takes to explore the contents inside the three vast buildings pass quickly. It is so unfathomable that something of this intricacy and size could have been built at all, let alone over 2,000 years ago. When discovered, nearly every statue of the Terracotta Army had been damaged, most reduced to rubble. The work involved in restoring them, the delicacy, the tediousness, is beyond belief. In one pit, we view long columns of reassembled warriors standing in formation, while a second pit demonstrates how they appeared when found – some upright, the majority toppled and crushed. The third museum building includes examples of the best-restored items: models exhibited the world over. At the end of our tour, as we make our way on foot to a nearby restaurant for lunch, my mind is reeling with all that I have just seen. I am totally in awe of what lies here, what has been done to showcase what's here and so very grateful to have made the effort to visit here. My words to Darryl, when asked, try to do the place justice.

"It was totally incredible. Spine-tingling. Definitely worthy of any Bucket List."

With only one full day allocated to visiting Xian, the following morning finds us once again cocooned within a silent carriage as with eerie ghost cities flashing past; we shoot back to Beijing aboard a high-speed bullet train. With no driver preorganised for our arrival, it's an awkward search for a cab which eventually takes us to our new accommodation, the Penta-Hotel located within Beijing's World Trade Centre. Monkeyshrine has suggested this hotel as it is situated nearer to Beijing Main Railway station: our Trans-Mongolian departure point for the next leg of our trip.

While the hotel's location appears to be more favourable than our last, with many more restaurants and shops, our room turns out to be less appealing. It's impossible to turn off one of our lights, meaning it's difficult to sleep and the bathroom drains, we discover that night as we shower, stink. While Darryl manages to mitigate some of the stench with a wet handtowel, the smell never completely goes. Fortunately, the hotel provides an excellent hot buffet breakfast the following morning with copious good coffee, giving us enough energy to tackle our day.

This day will be our last in Beijing, and with no tours planned, the sun struggling against a smoggy sky and back in my Skechers, it's ours to explore. We know Tiananmen Square is a manageable 20-minute stroll from our hotel, so after breakfast, we head there. While sections of our walk occur alongside noisy, busy roads, other parts take us along wide easy-to-negotiate footpaths strewn with elegant, golden Siberian elms, glorious, blazing Shantung maples and staring locals.

Nearing Tiananmen Square, we notice a long snaking queue stretching far ahead.

"I think we may need to pass through security to access the square," says Darryl.

"I hope we don't need our passports?" I reply. "They are back in the hotel safe."

While we attempt to enter Tiananmen Square using our Australian driver's licenses, unfortunately, they are not suitable. Refused entry, we have no option but to trudge the 20-minute return journey to our hotel. Armed now with acceptable credentials, we start again, but this time we walk via Wangfujing Street, one of the most famous shopping streets in Beijing, and even China. Here, to my delight, I am successful in purchasing a black silk shirt from one of the large silk shops that China is known for.

This time, our attempt to enter Tiananmen Square is successful. Although somewhat macabre, the main reason we are visiting here today is to see where the infamous events of 4 June 1989 occurred, notably, where "Tank Man" defied the mighty Chinese government. The picture of a lone man, shopping bags in either hand, confronting four sinister-looking tanks resonated with me, and, I know, most of the western world.

As we explore only a tiny part of the stark 44-hectare paved site, it's hard to envisage what happened here only 30 years ago. How the military opened fire on students calling for an end to state-wide corruption. How snipers rained down bullets and troops bayoneted the survivors. How tanks crushed the final dissenters.

"And you know, no one knows what happened to Tank Man."

That afternoon while Darryl rests, I go in search of supplies for the first leg of tomorrow's Trans-Mongolian journey. While there should be a buffet car, we can't eat all our meals there, so in a small, dusty yet well-stocked convenience store (we haven't found anything like a supermarket), I stock up on packet porridge, soup and noodles. I also throw in some water, packets of biscuits, baby wipes and a few sad-looking apples. In each hotel we have been staying at, we have appropriated the tea and coffee sachets, so do not need to purchase those items.

Although hoping to find a couple of plastic plates I am unsuccessful, and thus my final purchase is a tin bowl. "It's a dog bowl," Darryl complains to me later when I show him my purchase. "Was it full of water and sitting on the footpath?"

"It's all I could find, and it is not," I indignantly reply. "I thought, seeing as this is China and everything is usually 'made in China,' that I would easily find a few plastic plates, but no. None anywhere."

With so many eateries nearby to choose from, dinner is an easy choice as we visit a great-looking dumpling café located next to our hotel. I love dumplings and have fun choosing a large selection, while Darryl enjoys a massive dish of noodles. Surrounded by feasting families over steaming laden plates, we begin the first of many casual conversations and observations on the places we are travelling.

"I was a little apprehensive about visiting China," Darryl announces. "I had no idea what to expect. I didn't realise there would be so little written or spoken English."

"I agree. Thank goodness for Google Translate. It would have been difficult to get around without it. It's been a funny visit. We haven't really been able to speak with or meet any of the locals. Usually, you would get to talk with a taxi driver or hotel staff member and get a feel for the place but with no common language, this hasn't been possible here."

"And everything is bigger than I was expecting," Darryl continues.

"Yes," I laugh. "How big were the Forbidden City and Tiananmen Square? But the most surprising and impressive thing for me has been the greenery. Who would have thought that Beijing would have so many trees?"

Back in our hotel room, the sewer smell emanating from the bathroom drain has become even more potent. It's too late to complain, and it means that when I awaken sometime during the early hours, sick and shaky from what can only be a case of food poisoning, I have to endure this stench. I cannot escape its cloying stink as I vomit and expel diarrhoea repeatedly, for hours, until there's nothing left and, exhausted, I crawl back into bed.

With our train departing Beijing Main Railway Station at 7:20 am, and our driver organised to meet us at 5:50 am, it's an uncomfortably early start to our final day in China. We have prearranged breakfast packs, and with these, we step out into the dark, drizzly morning where we are relieved to find our Monkeyshrine representative waiting alongside our driver. This representative is holding the three tickets required to deliver us from Beijing to Moscow, and it's a relief to have them so near at hand.

At Beijing Main Railway Station, and this time it feels so good to be chaperoned by someone well-versed in negotiating Chinese stations and helping tourists onto trains. He is obviously well-known to the station officials, and we pass through security quickly and effortlessly. Before long, we find ourselves waiting in the station's departure lounge. I'm feeling fragile after last night's food poisoning, so it's good just to sit and let someone else do all the talking.

At 7 am, our guide insists on taking a photo of us standing in front of the train before helping us find our compartment. Just before bidding us good luck and farewell, he hands over the tickets for each of our upcoming legs. This is it; we are about to commence the first leg of a journey I have been aching to do since I was a teenager, a trip that will see us nearly 8,000 kilometres later arriving in Moscow, a journey worthy of any Bucket List.

"Look. A private bathroom!"
One of the downfalls of train travel is the quality of the bathrooms. Usually sculpted from chilled steel and smelling of urine, these small closets are shared with everyone else in your carriage. While I had read that a few Chinese trains did have private bathrooms, it was unlikely you would get one. I feel incredibly fortunate, especially given last night's events, that for this leg, at least, we have our own toilet and shower.

Quite clinical and cold-looking, our compartment has a set of bunks on which sit some folded damp sheets, a shallow cupboard for hanging clothes, a hot water thermos and a large streaky window. The gap under the bottom bunk is the only space in which baggage can be stowed.

Living up to its punctual reputation, at 7:20 am to the minute, the Trans-Mongolian, without fanfare, slowly pulls away from Beijing Main Railway Station. For the remainder of the day, as I slowly recover and Darryl either does a sudoku or uses his iPad, we make our way north towards Mongolia. Initially, the landscape is rocky and mountainous with spartan waterways, numerous tunnels and many lower hills covered by thousands of solar panels. These mountains, the Yanshan mountains, eventually give way to barren fruit orchards and farmlands of corn and millet. Much to Darryl's pleasure, we spy sections of the Great Wall's crumbling spine visible in the distance. At some stage, the land becomes harsher, scrubbier, more difficult to farm, and the small separate houses give way to walled community compounds.

Searching for the obligatory samovar – a Russian hot water urn found at the end of each train carriage – to enjoy a cup of tea, I meet a fellow Australian, Di. She tells me that she will be travelling throughout Russia for the following month, that she is 70, that she is travelling alone and has left her husband at home.

Climbing ever northwards and stripped down to shorts and t-shirts, the temperature, while warm inside the train (too warm), steadily drops outside. By nightfall, the 17 degrees of earlier has fallen to 7 degrees, and although I have only eaten oat biscuits and sipped tea or water throughout the day, I am still loathe to attempt the dining car. Instead, we make do with more biscuits and noodles.

Around 8 pm, with our sheets still feeling damp, we tuck ourselves into our single narrow bunks using only the scratchy blankets provided. The pillows are at least plump and comfortable.

The night proves to be quite disruptive. A little after 11 pm, an acrid smell permeates our carriage enough that we need to open our door to clear the air. Here, a passing guard disconcertingly advises that there is a fire in the train's undercarriage. He doesn't seem to be all that concerned about it himself, and so eventually, we close our door and fall back to sleep. It feels as if we have only been asleep for a short while before we are again woken. We have arrived at the Chinese border town of Erlian, and this time, it's the noisy clanging and banging of the train's bogies being changed that has woken us. Bogies are the name for each set of train wheels that need to be changed when crossing from China into Mongolia, where the gauge of the tracks differs.

Falling again back to sleep, it's with resignation that we awaken a third time, this time for the obligatory immigration checks as we pass from China into Mongolia. First, it's the Chinese officials who inspect our passports and clear them from China, then half an hour later, the Mongolians who ensure our visas are correct before stamping our passports and welcoming us to their country. By 2:30 am, it's thankfully all over, and we are free to try once again to get some sleep.

CHAPTER 3

Mongolia

*A*WAKENING a little after 7 am and outside, it's startling to find a different world. Stretching far into the distance are the endless, coarse, caramel-hued plains of southern Mongolia. Home to the two-humped camel and a region with some of the world's most extreme weather conditions, this is the vast Gobi Desert. Above, the boundless blue sky is noticeably and refreshingly smog-free after polluted China. Following yesterday's bout of food poisoning I'm feeling better, and with the samovar providing crucial hot water, I use my tin bowl to eat my packet porridge and the tin cup I bought in Xian to drink my morning coffee, all while gazing at the compelling scenery. As the day progresses, I continue to sit mesmerised and watch as the arid, gravelly Gobi Desert gives way to the central Mongolian steppe, the grasslands that transition our journey between the Gobi Desert and Siberia. Defined by a sweeping bronzed ground, I see hazy hills on the far horizon while here, near the track, the terrain is pancake flat. A never-ending concrete and wire fence follows our progress. Also snaking alongside us is an endless power line, the feet of its poles shod in heavy concrete shoes as protection against the frozen winter ground.

Any signs of civilisation we pass appear to be designed for the extreme weather conditions that thrive in this region, where it can range from −40 degrees in winter to over 45 degrees in summer. The naked houses, many painted in pastel hues, are sturdy concrete blocks with small windows, tin roofs and definitely no cooling verandahs like you'd see in Australia. Most of them are grouped within a protective walled compound. The few cows and horses we see are stocky with good, hairy coats.

Every now and then I call to Darryl, who intersperses looking out his own window with watching downloaded Netflix programs.

"Look at all the plastic caught in the fence. Even here, in the middle of nowhere, there is plastic rubbish laying around."

"Look at that stockman on his horse herding his sheep."

And finally, "I haven't seen a tree all day."

Twenty-seven hours after boarding, and shortly before 2:35 pm – our arrival time in Ulaanbaatar, the capital of Mongolia – we quickly dress in our outdoor gear, although this time I include an extra layer of thermals under my jumper and puffer jacket. Unlike Beijing, thermal underwear will be required here.

Our driver is waiting for us on the station platform when our train pulls into Ulaanbaatar's central station, and the transfer from here to our hotel, the Hotel Nine, allows us a good inspection of the city. It looks confused and disorganised like it's just been thrown together. What's also apparent is, like in so many other places, the threadbare roads were never built to handle the current traffic levels. They are potholed, heavily congested and generally in bad shape. With no subway system here thus far, unwieldy buses are the primary source of public transport which only adds to the congestion.

Around 20 years ago, Ulaanbaatar, population of around 500,000, was the sleepy capital of unremarkable Mongolia. This all changed, however, when international mining companies descended on the country and struck gold, coal, copper and uranium. Within five years, Ulaanbaatar's population had nearly doubled to 947,000 (today it's over 1.3 million), and Mongolia, whose economy was one of the fastest-growing in the early 21st century, is no longer so unremarkable.

Our hotel is situated right next to Sukhbaatar Square or UB Central Square, and after a quick shower, we set off to explore. We have no Mongolian currency, so a bank or currency exchange will need to be one of our first stops – it's unlikely there will be a handy ATM in the desert where we will be heading soon. One of the immediate things that strikes me as we stroll the sparsely populated footpaths towards what looks like a small shopping centre, is how well dressed everyone is. The women look particularly arresting in their smart winter coats and fitted jeans with their striking features. I am made to feel even dowdier than I did in Xian.

It doesn't prove too difficult to find a bank; nearly everyone we encounter surprisingly speaks some degree of English, and before long, we have exchanged our 50 Australian dollars for an absolute fistful of Mongolian tughrik. We use some of these to purchase coffees from a modern café bursting with chic patrons before exploring the area surrounding our hotel. While overall it's nondescript, there is one building that captures my attention. It's a large shop selling cashmere whose window displays are crowded with beautiful samples. Mongolia, apparently, produces some of the best cashmere in the world and I resolve to come back later for a better look.

One of the many lingering after-effects of Darryl's 2011 accident is a condition called foot drop: an inability to lift the front part of his left foot causing it to drag along the ground. It means he is required to wear a brace on that foot. The following morning after our strangest breakfast yet – two-minute noodles and boiled eggs – Darryl happens to notice that this foot brace has cracked.

"It's only a few months old," he cries in annoyance. "It shouldn't have cracked already."

"How bad is it?" I reply.

"It hasn't cracked the whole way through, but it looks like it could any moment."

Without a foot brace, Darryl will have trouble walking. It's a considerable concern that this has happened; these braces usually last for years.

"I'll have a look online and see if there is any place on our upcoming travels where we can get a new one," I reply. "Let's hope it lasts until then."

Today, we will be heading out into the vast Mongolian countryside, and tonight will be spent in a traditional Mongolian ger. Accordingly, a little after 9 am, we repack our bags and head back to reception. Not having confirmed a pickup time and not expecting a woman after our male guides there is some initial confusion, but eventually, we find ourselves back in the congested city traffic accompanied by the lovely Oyuna, our guide, and Khosoal, our driver.

We are looking forward to today's travels, and I have been both dreaming and dreading tonight's ger stay for months. I am not sure how I am going to handle the Mongolian sub-zero temperature housed in only a felt tent which also, disconcertingly, does not contain a bathroom. Oyuna can't offer any reassurance, but she can give us an indication of where we will be heading.

"If you like," she asks us, "we can make a quick stop at Zaisan Memorial Hill? The memorial commemorates the allied Mongolian and Soviet soldiers killed during World War Two. It's situated atop a hill with excellent views of Ulaanbaatar and the surrounding Mongolian countryside where we will be heading today."

With over 500 steps to reach this view, Darryl, unfortunately, can only sit talking at its base with Khosoal while Oyuna and I tackle the steep incline. From the summit, I find the view incredible albeit contradictory. The relatively small and compact Ulaanbaatar is at my feet – a city full of stunted concrete tower blocks abutting small, traditional felt gers, crumbling brick houses fronted by modern electric cars, scrubby, dirt gardens leading to beautiful, barren plains.

Our destination today is the Terelj National Park, a distance of around 60 kilometres, and as we traverse those beautiful, empty plains to journey there, Oyuna provides a little insight into life in Mongolia.

"Ten years ago, English was introduced as the second language here. It is taught in all the schools... Many of the locals leave the city in summer with their gers and camp beside these rivers," she says, as she points towards a sweeping and inviting estuary. "Mongolia was a Buddhist country for hundreds of years. Then, in 1924, the Mongolian

People's Revolutionary Party, a Communist party closely tied to the Soviet Union, gained power. During their time, they destroyed most of the Buddhist monasteries and murdered many monks. The collapse of the Soviet Empire in 1991 allowed Mongolia to form a new multi-party system and in 1992, a new market economy... As you can see, we don't have much infrastructure yet, but it is coming."

"This road looks like pretty new infrastructure," Darryl interjects – and although it is only two lanes, the highway we are currently travelling does look new.

"Yes. You are very lucky. This new highway only opened two days ago. If you had visited last week, you would have been travelling on that road." This time she points towards an unsealed, potholed road running parallel to us.

"See those car tyres lying there in the fields?" Oyuna later points out. "Developers use them as boundary markers for the vacant blocks of land that are for sale here."

While today's destination will be the Gun-Galuut ger camp in the Terelj National Park, we will be detouring via a sight familiar to us from a recent Joanna Lumley documentary: the Genghis (or, as the Mongolians prefer) Chinggis Khan monument.

Chinggis Khan (1162-1227AD) was the first person to unite the nomadic tribes of Northeast Asia. His was a brutal but successful reign and, by the time of his death, his empire occupied an extensive portion of Central Asia and China. In the early 2000s, looking for their own identity after years of oppressive Communist reign, Chinggis Khan, considered by many to be the father of the nation, captured the imagination of the Mongolians. Accordingly, in 2008, a 40-metre statue of Chinggis on horseback was built on top of a 10-metre-tall visitor's centre in the middle of the empty Mongolian plains. It is in front of this incongruous, gleaming and mammoth silver statue that we now alight.

It's still relatively early and the car park is deserted, meaning we are probably the first visitors of the day. Not far away is a tout with a caravan of camels. Spying us, he immediately heads over, and between his beseeching looks and his offsiders cajoling, it's with resignation that I find myself astride one of the shaggy, uncomfortable beasts. Feeling like a conned tourist and annoyed with Darryl who is in fits of laughter watching me, I am relieved when after a few lazy strides, the camel absolutely refuses to take another step and I can quickly dismount to enter the monument.

It's a short visit to what turns out to be a dusty, circular museum full of even dustier Mongolian artefacts. The highlight occurs when we scale a narrow set of stairs and pop out onto the head of Chinggis's horse. From here, the panoramic views of the vast, barren and golden-brown Mongolian countryside are breathtaking and unforgettable.

"It's brown and arid now," says Oyuna. "But in summer it turns green."

A ger is a portable round tent covered with felt or hide, and it's a popular activity for tourists to experience a night or two in one, either at a camp such as the Gun-Galuut or privately while visiting Mongolia. Arriving at our camp – a collection of ger's neatly lined up on what could be the surface of the moon – Oyuna advises us to leave our bags in our ger and then meet at the reception/dining area for lunch. This afternoon, we will be trekking a small part of Terelj National Park which includes a Buddhist monastery.

Our cream-coloured canvas ger, on entering through the hobbit-sized doorway, consists of three single beds tucked up against the curved wall, a couple of tiny wooden stools and a small combustion fire. Clinging to a pole that stretches from floor to ceiling in the centre of the open-plan structure are some dodgy electrical cords and a switch: our power supply. As expected, there is no bathroom nor even running water – that can be found in the reception/dining area some 300 metres away. It's basic, but adequate, and should ensure an interesting night.

Locating the dining area, we find it full of American university students. They are in Mongolia on a study exchange, and I don't know whether it's a good or a bad thing that they are sharing the camp for the night with us. On the positive side, they do imbue this middle of nowhere place with a sense of activity. On the negative, they are noisy, they eat like locusts and there is very little of the buffet left for us to enjoy.

It is eerily desolate when, after lunch, we venture further into the Terelj National Park. There's a smattering of heavy-duty houses, a lone ger or a few deserted ger camps (most of the camps close for winter), a handful of other cars. Overhead, the stark blue sky contrasts sharply against the golden but bare rocky hills. The air is crisp and cold.

As we drive, the road now gravelled and dusty, Oyuna continues to impart information.

"You must listen to The Hu when you get a chance. They are a Mongolian band who blend heavy metal music, similar to AC/DC, with traditional Mongolian throat singing."

"We will," we promise.

"You should visit the Museum of Natural History when you return to Ulaanbaatar. It showcases a lot of our heritage… One-quarter of Mongolians still live a nomadic lifestyle."

Even deeper into Terelj National Park and we reach Turtle Rock, a magnificent granite conglomeration of boulders settled into the shape of a turtle. Here we alight, stretch our legs and breathe in the pure, bracing air before continuing. The monastery, when we arrive, is situated partway up a long, steep hill. To reach it, we first trek through a wood of skeletal winter trees, cross a swinging drawbridge then spin the ubiquitous prayer wheels that mark the monastery's entrance. Standing here in this peaceful religious cloister, another incredible landscape of sand and boulders stretched out in front of us, it's surreal to think of not only how this building came to be here, but how we came to be here also.

Back at the Gun-Galuut ger camp, we farewell Oyuna and Khosoal. They will be heading back to Ulaanbaatar before Khosoal returns for us tomorrow.

A little later, as I perch on a tiny stool in the ger doorway – soaking in the stunning alien landscape with the only noise that of some of the American students kicking a football – a traditionally clad Mongolian lady comes to light our combustion stove. With my face energised by the chilling sub-zero temperature of outside and my back melting from the stove's increasing heat, I sit and watch the sky turn the most amazing hues of mint-blue, rosy-pink and copper-gold. I sit like this until darkness swallows the desert view, the students give up their game and I shut the ger door.

"Phew, it's pretty hot in here," I comment sometime later. "It must be around 40 degrees."

"Just let the fire burn for a while," Darryl replies. "Don't put any more wood in."

"It's a lot colder now," I shortly muse. "It's not really the best system, is it? You throw in the wood; the temperature rises to at least 40 degrees, which is too hot. The wood then burns, the temperature plummets and it's cold again!"

"There's nothing to regulate the temperature, and it's softwood," Darryl replies. "Softwood always burns too quickly. I don't know how it's going to last the night."

Hungry from our afternoon exertions and aware that it may be wise to try and beat the students to tonight's dinner buffet, it's not long after 6 pm that we stoke the fire once more and step out from our ger. With the outside temperature hovering around –6 degrees, we are both fully clad in thermals, boots, and jackets. While the change in temperature from inside the sweltering ger to the freezing outdoors doesn't have any effect on me, Darryl disturbingly, appears to go into shock. Seconds after leaving the ger's warmth, his body starts to shake, his teeth to chatter. It's alarming, and I am relieved when, as we reach the cosy dining area and the heat envelops him, the shaking slowly begins to subside.

"That was pretty scary," I say. "How do you feel now?"

"A lot better but still a bit strange."

"Any idea of what would have caused it?"

"Either the extremes in temperature or I'm getting sick."

Unsure which of Darryl's options I prefer but managing to have bested the students, we pile our plates with tender Mongolian lamb, mashed potatoes and snow pea salad, and try some of the local Chinggis beer. It's not the best idea – drinking a few beers before spending the night in a toiletless room, I later discover – but for now, they are very enjoyable.

Full, we eventually make our way back to our ger following the dimly lit pathway, the cloudless sky a sea of dancing stars overhead. Before settling into our narrow single beds, we again stoke the fire, and again the temperature inside the ger becomes unbearably hot. A few hours later and the temperature is now uncomfortably cold. This becomes the pattern of the night, until the early hours when the timber eventually runs out, and we spend the remaining time until sunrise shivering in our lone beds.

Desperate to use the bathroom, I awaken early and use this quiet time while the camp is still slumbering to have another look at my surroundings. As I walk the camp's perimeter, what straw-like grass still growing cracks underfoot, frozen by the nights' chill, while above the endless sky is again that mesmerising blue. There is an early morning mist that, when it dissipates, allows the golden-syrup hills surrounding the camp to reveal themselves. It is all truly, staggeringly beautiful.

Mid-morning, Khosoal returns to drive us back to Ulaanbaatar. Along the way, he is pulled over for a breath test and later we see police officers wielding speed cameras. With the speed limit on this highway only 50 kilometres per hour, it's surprising to learn how seriously the Mongolian authorities take their road rules.

Back at Hotel Nine, Darryl heads straight to bed. With a temperature and a sore throat, it's obvious he is sick, and all he wants to do is sleep. Although I feel as if I may also be coming down with something (my throat is scratchy), I am well enough to head out and have a further look around – maybe find that cashmere jumper! As I cut through Sukhbaatar Square, passing Parliament House and the Stock Exchange, I puzzle at an ill-placed large stage and some crowd control fences; they weren't there yesterday?

I find my jumper at the Gobi Cashmere store, a shop full of the most beautiful coats, scarfs and other items all made from Mongolian cashmere; it's little wonder the Mongolian women are so well dressed with such quality items to choose from. From here, I just stroll the Ulaanbaatar streets – some have footpaths that are wide and easy to navigate like Peace Avenue, others have footpaths where large potholes are hard to avoid. At the surprisingly modern UB shopping centre, I stop and purchase a sandwich for late lunch.

Back in our room, Darryl is still sleeping, so I quietly grab my laptop and head back downstairs to the hotel's dining room. Here, I spend the remainder of the afternoon and evening working on some blogs, enjoying a bowl of fresh broccoli soup and musing on how I came to be in Mongolia of all places, this Friday night in November.

Some hours after going to bed, I am awoken by the sounds of loud music.

"That's what the stage in the square was for," I mumble to myself before falling back to sleep.

The following morning, my sore throat has disappeared and, after breakfast, I head out once more while Darryl heads back to bed. Realising just how cheap my cashmere purchase had been (just 70 Australian dollars), I want to acquire one for Darryl. At the Gobi Cashmere store, I happily discover the men's jumpers are even cheaper than the women's, and after making my purchase, I do as Oyuna had suggested and head to the Museum of Natural History. Offering a rich collection on the history of Mongolia, I enjoy my visit, but – worried about time – I make it a short one.

Our train is due to depart at 3:23 pm, which means by 2:30 pm I have convinced Darryl to get out of bed, we have checked out of Hotel Nine and are sitting at Ulaanbaatar Station waiting for it to arrive. With time to spare and having spent very little of our Mongolian tughrik, I use some of it to purchase an ice cream, noticing as I do so, a blonde lady laden with a heavy backpack, a bursting front pack and arms full of plastic shopping bags. I have no idea how she is managing to carry everything; it all looks so cumbersome and heavy.

Waiting here, I also use this time to reflect on our Mongolian visit. While it has been a fleeting stopover, it has been truly remarkable. Having had no idea what to expect before our arrival, finding a city full of chic, smart, English-speaking locals has been surprising. While the ramshackle nature of Mongolia's infrastructure was probably expected, the sheer stunning beauty of its desert wasn't. Something about its vast, barren, golden beauty called to me and I would love to return. Although, noting the changes occurring here – the new highways, the emphasis on tourism – a future visit may reveal a different place. It certainly feels as if Mongolia is on the cusp of significant development. Perhaps this has been the perfect time to visit and I should leave my memories alone.

The train, when it arrives, is a Mongolian one and true to Mongolian form, it is slightly dilapidated. Decorated in what appears to be faded red velvet, I am sure our compartment once looked great, but today looks frayed, aged and dusty. Irrespective of how it looks, we are happy and excited to just be aboard for this second leg of our Trans-Mongolian journey.

"No private bathroom on this one," I say glumly.

"Yes, but no bunks either," Darryl points out.

It's true. The absence of a bathroom means more cabin space. Rather than bunks, this compartment has two made-up single beds separated by a good-sized table. As we start to find homes for some of our items, we will be on this train for the next twenty-three hours, our carriage attendant comes and greets us. Each carriage on the Trans-Mongolian and Trans-Siberian trains has its own attendant known as a provodnitsa, and ours is a proud, young Russian girl.

"Please let me know if you need anything. There is no dining car on this train, but I have noodles and chocolate and tea and coffee for sale. You can get hot water from the samovar at the end of the carriage."

"That's a shame," I say once she has left. "We didn't get to use the dining car on the first train, and now there isn't one. I hope we get one on the next train."

"And we kept all that Mongolian money to use on here," Darryl replies gloomily. "It's going to be worthless trying to exchange it."

Leaving our compartment door open, it doesn't take long to realise that the cabins on either side of us are occupied by single Australian ladies. One is Di, who we met days earlier on the train from Beijing, and the other is Bec, the baggage-laden lady I had seen while purchasing an ice cream at Ulaanbaatar Station. The following few hours pass quickly as they both squeeze into our cabin, and we trade stories.

"I often travel by myself," says Di. "My husband loves his bridge, so I just leave him at home... I'm in Russia for the following month... I managed to get tickets for the Bolshoi Ballet while I'm in Moscow."

"I'm an operations manager for BHP," Bec tells us. "I'm heading up to the Scandinavian countries before meeting my mum in New York for New Year's Eve... I spent the day in Ulaanbaatar shopping and ran out of time to pack it away, that's why I was carrying so many plastic bags at the station."

It's fun just spending time with and talking to fellow Australians, and before she leaves, Di gives me some of her freeze-dried space meals. I hadn't dreamt of bringing food from Australia with us, and Di, who's been living on these meals for the past week, is sick to death of them.

Like our previous train journey, the night does not pass without its disruptions. Around midnight, we are woken by some Mongolian officials who ask for our passports, and without much fuss, check us out of Mongolia. Shortly later, there is another knock on the door and this time, it is the Russian officials. Unsurprisingly, they are much more severe than their Mongolian counterparts. As our passports are scrutinised, non-stop questions are fired at us:

"What is your purpose for visiting Russia?"

"What are your onward plans?"

"Where will you be staying?"

A strict lady official makes us open all our bags only to give them a quick cursory inspection, while two men ask us to step outside as they complete a search of our cabin. Eventually, to our relief, our passports are stamped, the officials move on and we are free to enter Russia.

CHAPTER 4

Russia – Siberia

SOMETIME during the early hours of the morning, I am awoken by the sounds of passengers disembarking. Pushing the curtain aside, I lift my head just high enough to look through the compartment window, noting how dark it is outside. Both Di and Bec mentioned they would be disembarking the train at 6:15 am in the city of Ulan-Ude, noted for having the largest statue of Lenin in the world, and I can only assume that this must be their stop. As I snuggle back into my blankets, I feel very thankful that it's not us braving the Siberian cold this gloomy morning.

Russia is the world's largest country, occupying one-tenth of all the land on Earth while spanning eleven time zones across two continents (Europe and Asia). Due to its size, its diverse landscape is understandable, ranging from sandy and frozen desert to giant marshes and tall mountains. Much of the land is rolling treeless plains called steppes, while other parts are large, forested areas called taigas.

From the 1550s, Russia was ruled by a series of controlling Tsars until 1917, when the last Tsar, Nicholas II and his family, were overthrown and murdered. This allowed a communist group, the Bolsheviks, to come to power. Under their leader Vladimir Lenin, the Bolsheviks created the Union of Soviet Socialist Republics (USSR) which collapsed in 1991, leading to its break-up and the subsequent election of Boris Yeltsin and later Vladimir Putin under a democratic umbrella.

Siberia is a 13 million square kilometre geographical region of

Russia that spans both Eurasia and Northern Asia. Taking up 77% of Russia's landmass, it is known for its gulags – Soviet labour camps – its long, harsh winters and, as we are about to experience, its bone-chilling autumns.

When I resurface sometime later and make my way to the communal bathroom, I am surprised to find that we are the sole occupants of our carriage. Every other compartment is sitting there empty, doors wide open, ready to be cleaned by the carriage attendant. No one else has boarded the train.

"Maybe it's so quiet because we are travelling in winter," I muse.

Ablutions complete, and over our breakfast of porridge and tea, I pull out my Russian sim, insert it into my phone and am truly surprised and delighted when a service provider pops up on my screen and I can browse freely. With no sim in Mongolia, we could only rely on the hotel's wi-fi while there; it feels good to be connected to the world once more.

We are not due to arrive in Irkutsk until 2:27 pm, so after breakfast, we lay back in our beds, ready for a relaxing day. Again, Darryl intersperses Netflix with window-watching while I read one of the books I have downloaded on my phone. Eventually, the pull of the fascinating, changing landscape captures my full attention, and the phone is set aside. The sandy plains of Mongolia have disappeared, and the Siberian taiga is starting to appear.

The taiga is the forest that straddles parts of the globe in its subarctic region, the area in the northern hemisphere that lies just south of the Arctic Circle. Canada, Alaska, Scandinavia and Siberia have taigas, with the Siberian being the largest; it actually makes up the biggest forested area on the planet (even bigger than the Amazon). Full of mainly evergreens with needles that retain moisture and shed snow, it's these that are starting to appear now: spruce, pines and firs along with their deciduous cousins, the birch.

On the ground, a thin layer of snow has also started to appear, thickening the further north we travel. The rivers are now frozen at their edges.

Around midday, our route brings us alongside the southern shores of Lake Baikal, and we continue to run alongside its lapping edge for much of the remainder of our journey.

Lake Baikal is the world's largest reserve of freshwater. Created over 20 million years ago (most other lakes are a mere 15,000 years old), this crystal-clear lake contains almost one-fifth of the world's freshwater. Despite its size, in winter the lake's surface completely freezes over, allowing for ice skating and even vehicles to be driven over it.

Through my window, it's impossible to see the lake's far bank and small waves break on the land's edge. It's hard to believe that I am looking out at a body of freshwater, not an ocean. As I sit and gaze, ensconced in our warm red-velvet cabin, tucked up in my bed, I sip my tea and marvel at what this journey is conjuring: foreign landscapes, inland oceans, endless forests.

It's a landscape so alien, so captivating to two Australian travellers that it's easy to sit, mesmerised.

Like on our previous arrival into Ulaanbaatar, not far from Irkutsk Station, I prepare for the outside temperature. Long johns are pulled on under my woollen pants, while a thermal singlet, woollen shirt, cashmere jumper and puffer jacket cover my torso and arms. To complete my outfit, I put on a scarf, beanie and a pair of gloves. Darryl, whose body temperature has never been the same since his accident and is clad simply in jeans, a t-shirt and waterproof jacket, laughs at me.

"You look like a Teletubby."

"I don't care. It's –7 degrees out there."

Waiting for us on the platform is our guide Katherine, who will be accompanying us to Listvyanka, a village on the shores of Lake Baikal and our home for the following two nights.

"Welcome to Irkutsk, Siberia," she greets us. "Our driver is waiting outside, and he will be driving us to Listvyanka. It is about 70 kilometres away. We had our first big snowfall last night so there is a lot of snow around. It may take a bit longer than usual to get there."

"How long does it normally take?" Darryl asks.

"Usually it takes just over an hour, but today I think it will take us about an hour and a half."

It does take us the full 90 minutes, the roads slippery with layers of slush and ice. And while we pass through a few straggly towns, most of the journey is through undulating forests whose floor is thick with snow that spills onto the edges of the road. Always a lousy passenger, I am relieved when eventually our journey descends the tree-covered hills, Lake Baikal comes into view and we stop in front of the UD Guest House.

"We will leave you here now," Katherine advises. "I will be catching the bus back tomorrow to give you a walking tour around Listvyanka. The guest house staff will look after you and show you to your room."

Separated by a road from Lake Baikal, and alongside shuttered houses, is the guest house reception and dining room. About 100 metres away, down a slushy lane, is our room: a cosy little apartment with massive, thick pine walls.

"I feel like we are staying in a sauna," I remark on entering.

"Have you noticed that all the houses are made of wood?" Darryl comments. "I suppose it's not surprising with the number of trees we have seen."

"Apart from dogs barking, it all seems very quiet," I reply.

"Yes. I wouldn't be surprised if we are the only guests here."

Listvyanka, we shortly discover, is a small unattractive town, population around 1800, that sits right on the banks of Lake Baikal with its back towards those forested hills we have just passed through. Its central hub lines the only road entering the town with wooden shops, hotels and buildings on one side and the lake the other. Across the lake, one can just make out the Khamar Daban mountains.

Keen to explore after a morning spent sitting, it takes 15 minutes of walking alongside this road from our outlying guest house to reach the town centre. A walk made memorable by −10 degree temperatures, spying water frozen into beautiful icicles and seeing someone actually scuba diving in the frigid grey lake.

With most of the shops and businesses closed now that autumn has arrived (Listvyanka is one of Siberia's busiest tourism destinations in summer), it's not all that obvious that we have reached the centre. It's only the sight of some large, shuttered buildings adjacent to a clutch of dismal wooden stalls that makes us pause.

"That looks like a market," I point out. "Some of the stalls are still operating."

"Do you think they sell beanies?" Darryl surprisingly replies. "It's heaps colder than I was expecting. A beanie might help."

Meandering the stark wooden market stalls manned by silent, weathered Russians, it's fun to poke amongst their contents. It's all so different to home. Many are full of a dry-looking fish called omul or laden with Russian souvenirs, while others offer items made from charoite, a local purple stone found nowhere else in the world. Eventually, we happily secure a beanie for Darryl and a small wooden matryoshka, or 'stacking' doll for me.

"Why would you want that?"

"On our last trip, we arrived home with little to remind us of our travels," I reply. "I don't want that to happen this time. I want some souvenirs that we can leave around the house and will remind us of this journey. Little 'travel treasures.' A matryoshka doll is a perfect reminder of Russia."

That night, with soft snow falling, dogs barking and the only light coming from the windows of neighbouring houses, we once again don our heavy winter gear and return along the dimly lit potholed laneway to the guest house dining room. Here, in this large room, with no other customers and a cosy fire burning, our reflections are thrown back at us as we sit facing the curtainless windows. For the time it takes us to enjoy our borscht, our beef dumping broth, and to thaw out completely, we remain the lone diners.

After an eerily quiet night, we are awoken by the sound of more dogs barking. Outside, it's still dark; the sun won't rise until 8:15

am. A little after nine, we make our way back to the dining room and this time feast on yoghurt, meat, cheese, rolls and pastries. Once consumed, our host returns with large plates of scrambled eggs. Washed down with plenty of apple juice and coffee, it's one of our best breakfasts so far and should well fuel us for the day ahead.

Meeting Katherine in the reception area, she advises that it has taken an hour on one of the local buses to get here.

"The roads were not so bad this time," she states nonchalantly. "A lot of the snow has melted. It should be a good but cold day."

It is indeed cold. My phone is showing the temperature as −8 degrees or −16 degrees if you consider the wind chill factor. I have ensured that I am again fully rugged up while Darryl is now clad in his new beanie, along with the second of the two sets of gloves I brought on this trip with me.

"We will be walking alongside the lake to the Limnological Museum," Katherine continues. "Afterwards, we will visit Listvyanka."

Limnological means the study of inland aquatic systems, and walking towards this museum dedicated to its research, we learn a little more about Katherine.

"I was born in Irkutsk and have never left Russia… I have visited Moscow… I am 28, married with a young son… I studied at university… I love being a tour guide."

The Limnological Museum proves to be informative, fun, and thankfully, well heated. Our time spent viewing its clever exhibits, learning about ancient Lake Baikal and enjoying a simulated submarine journey to the lake floor allows us time to warm ourselves before once again braving the outside chill. For our return, Katherine has organised a taxi and waiting for it to arrive, Darryl gives a start and stares hard at the grey, chilly lake.

"Is that a seal?"

"Yes," I cry as I spy the fat mammal cavorting in the water. "How fantastic."

"You are fortunate to see one," Katherine advises. "You don't usually see them at this time of year."

Keen to get the most from our short visit here, later that afternoon, we do once again brave the Siberian outdoors. Our meandering walk takes us to the Temple of St. Nicholas, along pathways made from timber, through wooded forests and onto Lake Baikal beach. Finally, with early dusk descending, we return to our cosy little room, where, with no television to amuse us, I browse my phone using the free wi-fi. Disturbingly, it is full of news about Australia and its recent spate of horrendous bushfires. Many people are being evacuated, including some quite close to our hometown. I also use this time to start organising tickets to a West Ham football game while in London. I know that Darryl still hasn't done anything more about it.

At mid-morning the next day, our driver (whose name we never do learn) returns and delivers us back to Irkutsk to the Marussia Hotel, tonight's accommodation. Our room is not yet ready, but our bags have been stowed and Katherine shortly arrives.

"Good morning," is her cheerful greeting. "Are you ready for today's walking tour of Irkutsk? It snowed last night, and more is expected today, but we will be fine."

"Walking tour?" we balk. "Our information says a tour around Irkutsk by car?"

"No, it is a walking tour," she confirms.

"This should be fun," I mutter to Darryl. "Look at the temperature outside! It's –14 degrees with a wind chill factor of –22!"

Irkutsk is the sixth-largest city in Siberia, with a population nearing 600,000. It's a crucial regional business centre and a critical Trans-Siberian railway junction. What makes Irkutsk especially interesting is that the city centre is still full of wooden houses with decorative carvings on their walls and window frames that have been destroyed elsewhere in Russia. Irkutsk gives you a rare opportunity to see what a Russian city looked like 'once upon a time.'

Katherine's long, slow guided tour takes us to various city suburbs. The most memorable part is our stroll alongside the Angara River on which the city sits. Here on the near-frozen river's embankment,

51

the icy wind whipping our bodies, we experience the most bitter cold temperature of our lives.

"My lips and cheeks are frozen," I grumble to Darryl. "I can barely talk."

"Mine are as well. The cold is making my back hurt."

"It's making all of me hurt. And my nose won't stop running, and my tissues keep disintegrating," I continue to whinge. "And trying to take a photo is painful as I have to take my gloves off."

"Well, my jaw keeps locking up," Darryl counters.

Thankfully, a short time later, Katherine cheerfully advises that there's a hotel nearby where we can defrost over a hot coffee (the cold does not seem to affect her).

As we sit, sip and thaw, Katherine provides a little more information on the Siberian region.

"Over the past few years most of our tourists have come from China... The Chinese are also purchasing a lot of the property around here which they use as their second homes or turn into hotels aimed at more Chinese. It means many locals cannot afford property anymore and they are not happy about it."

Situated a short walk from the Marussia Hotel is a plethora of large Russian restaurants and a small, extremely well-heated shopping centre. That evening, we browse the shopping centre and interestingly, find it very reminiscent of our centres in Australia. Plenty of women's shoe and clothing shops, the odd chemist and a well-stocked supermarket. Dinner, consisting of two main meals, a cocktail and beer comes to 22 Australian dollars and is eaten at one of the nearby restaurants. We are beginning to appreciate how cheap the food is in this country.

"Have you noticed how threadbare the towels are in Russia compared to China?" I call from the bathroom the following morning.

"Are they?" Darryl replies.

"In China, they were fluffy and new. Here, in Russia, they are thin and ratty," I answer.

Today, the priority is to purchase supplies for this afternoon's three-day Trans-Siberian journey. Accordingly, after a hearty breakfast of bread rolls and muesli, we return to the well-stocked supermarket. Along the way, we note an overnight snowfall has made the streets even slushier and dirtier, and the temperature is a mean –14 degrees.

I have always found exploring foreign supermarkets great fun, and today is no exception. A supermarket can give you an objective comparison between your life at home and the place you are visiting along with its inhabitants. The selection of food available can show what the locals prefer, the prices, how much they can pay. Here, I find the dairy, fruit and vegetable sections scant and expensive, but the tin food and bakery areas reasonable. Despite the poor quality, we manage to secure a punnet of cherry tomatoes and a cucumber to go with a packet of crackers and two large loaves of bread Darryl insists upon. To accompany this, we throw into our trolley packets of porridge and soup, a jar of jam, cheese, sweet biscuits, more noodles and finally some sachets of hot chocolate to supplement the tea and coffee we already have.

"We will be using the train's dining room also, so this should be ample," I eventually say.

"Hopefully there will be a dining car on this train."

At 2 pm we are waiting in reception for our lift, when a message arrives advising that our driver will now be collecting us at 3 pm.

"3 pm?" Darryl questions. "Not 2:30 pm? The train leaves at 3:54 pm. It doesn't give us much time to get to the station and find the right platform."

"I know," I reply. "But that's what the message says. Hopefully, the station is nearby."

Although our driver is slightly early and we quickly jump into the car, the initial relief is short-lived.

"We stop here. You wait in car. I pick up new passenger," he states as he stops, double-parked, in front of a large hotel on a busy road.

"Stop? But our train leaves in 45 minutes."

"It's ok," he says before disappearing for 27 agonising minutes.

We are furious when he returns. "Our train leaves in 18 minutes. Where have you been? What's going on?"

It's obvious he is quite concerned as well.

"I sorry. He couldn't find bag." He gestures towards our new, unapologetic arrival.

With that, he spends the following 15 minutes hurtling us through the heavy Irkutsk traffic while we quietly freak out and our new arrival sits mute and apparently unperturbed. With minutes to spare, we pull up in front of a large grey train station, where our driver grabs our bags, pushes us through security then disappears in front of us. Desperate, we can only keep an eye on our bobbing suitcases and try to keep up. As we breathlessly reach the top of a flight of stairs leading to one of the stations' platforms, the number 1 Russian Rossiya train glides to a halt.

Too scared to even contemplate what would have happened if we had missed this train –

there isn't another for days and the future itinerary hinges on everything going to plan – I grab my bag from the driver, barely mutter a "thank you" and head for our carriage. Darryl, equally annoyed, is slightly more polite.

As we stand in front of our carriage, the carriage provodnitsa scrutinising our passports, we unexpectedly hear our names.

"Hey. Emma and Darryl. How are you?" It's BHP operations manager Bec who we met travelling from Ulaanbaatar. "I've just got off. I'm here for a few days," she tells us.

"Great to see you again," we pant. "We're having heart attacks, but apart from that, we're fine. Irkutsk isn't all that much, but Lake Baikal is great."

Minutes later, as we collapse onto our beds and our hearts return to a more even pace, the Rossiya pulls away from Irkutsk station.

"That was a bit close. We are not going to forget that in a hurry," Darryl eventually manages to say.

"You're not kidding," I reply. "But we made it! We're actually on the Trans-Siberian. And we can now say we have been to Siberia!"

We're getting into the swing of this travelling by train now, so it doesn't take us long to find homes for our food and toiletries, to stow our jackets, boots and bags, and to strip down to shorts and t-shirts. Our provodnitsa returns with gift packs of chocolate and two complimentary dinner vouchers, and offers cups of tea that, although unsure whether they are free or not, we accept. She delivers our tea in podstakanniks, a glass with a metal holder commonly found on Russian trains. Our neighbours, Fraser and Lindsay, pop their heads in and introduce themselves.

"We're from New Zealand," says Fraser. "We got on in Vladivostok."

"How long have you been on here then?" we ask.

"This is day four. We are going straight through to Moscow. Seven days in all."

"We're on until Moscow also. Are the cups of tea free?"

Laughing, they reply, "We don't know. We also had one and haven't been charged yet, but Bec who just got off had to pay for hers."

"We've met Bec," I say. "Well, we'll see what happens with the tea. The cup would make a great travel treasure."

"Did you get a voucher to use for dinner?" Lindsay asks.

"Yes, and some chocolate. We weren't expecting them."

"The food's ok. What you would expect on a train," adds Fraser.

"We are just happy there is a dining car. There wasn't one on our last train."

Generally, in Russia, the lower the number the train, the better the service. Unlike our previous two trains, the Rossiya is numbered 1, meaning it's of Russia's highest standard. Looking around, it's easy to spy the differences. This train is sleek, clean and modern, with some excellent English-speaking attendants. Our turquoise, upholstered compartment is spacious, with fresh, crisp linen lining our twin beds. Between these two beds, there is a table on which we place our tin mugs, dog bowl, water and utensils. A large window allows us to view the passing scenery. It's going to be a great home for the next three days.

Unlike our modern sleeping compartments, the 50s-era dining car is grotty and tired. That evening, we dine here on microwaved beef stroganoff, secured with our complimentary vouchers and served by English-speaking Alex, the lone waiter. Later, we obtain hot water from the stern Russian provodnitsa to use for beverages or washing our teeth and use the communal carriage toilet before settling into our beds with our phone and iPad. The rocking of the fast-moving train eventually lulls me into a deep, dreamless sleep.

Thursday 14 November and this morning, our watches go back an hour. We will, in all, be rewinding our watches a total of five hours before arriving in Moscow. Travelling through five time zones in three days really does bring home to one the immensity of Russia.

As we wash our teeth, make our breakfast and drink our coffees, the scenery outside remains the same – bleak, bare trees struggling through an endless snow-covered terrain – real Dr. Zhivago country. Sometimes, to break the monotony, we pass a cluster of untidy wooden houses with large barren yards and smokeless chimneys.

"Do you think anyone is living in those houses?"

"It doesn't look like it," Darryl replies.

"I agree. There is no smoke coming from the chimneys and no footprints in the snow. I wonder where the people are?"

"These are probably summer homes."

"Do you think so? Would there be so many summer homes?" A question to which, I later discover, the answer is yes. Like an allotment in western countries, these second homes or 'dachas' are popular in Russia.

Following a lunch of cheese, crackers and cucumber, in the early afternoon we make our way to the dining car intent on purchasing a drink and watching the eternal scenery from there. Fraser and Lindsay have the same idea, and so the four of us being the carriage's sole occupants, pass the time swapping stories. Last year, Lindsay, who has multiple sclerosis, underwent a life-changing experimental treatment

56

in Moscow and is returning for a follow-up review. When Fraser decided to accompany him, to make the most of the trip, they booked this Trans-Siberian journey. Both hail from the very bottom of New Zealand, so the cold is not affecting them as much as it is me. In fact, we first noticed Fraser on the platform back at Irkutsk; he stood out, being the only person there in shorts and thongs with a large puffer jacket on his top half.

At some stage, four sturdy Russians enter and before long, they join us. They have no English and we have no Russian, but it doesn't seem to matter. Using mainly sign language, sometimes Google Translate and with help from Alex, we manage to communicate quite well. We discover that they are all military personnel, and their names are Sergei, Igor, Alexie and Vlad. Eventually, a tattered packet of cards is pulled out, and the face of these cards is the same in both our languages; thus, our game transcends all language barriers. The hours pass as we play, communicate and all the while gaze at the passing taiga. Finally, hours after a glowing pink sun has set, we make our way back to our cabin. The first 30 hours of our Trans-Siberian journey have passed surprisingly quickly.

Earlier this morning, our watches went back two hours which means when I first open my eyes, although my Fitbit is displaying 6 am, it's only 4 am. I groan, turn over and fall back to sleep. When I awaken some hours later, the curtains are parted to reveal a grey-looking day with the same familiar scenery of yesterday.

"More snow amid the spruces, firs and birches," I call to Darryl. "And do you realise we are now six hours behind Australia?"

"Cup of coffee?" he asks.

"Yes please. I'm going to look for the shower this morning," I reply. "Fraser said it's about two carriages away and costs 100 roubles, about 2 Australian dollars."

The Rossiya is not just a train for tourists; it is also a primary method of transportation for Russian locals. Strolling through the corridors, it is interesting to note the different class of carriages. While we have gone with first class, the most comfortable option, second class doesn't look all that bad, and third class, consisting of open-plan rows of bunks, looks way cleaner and more comfortable than the third class carriages on Southeast Asian trains we have taken in previous years. The shower, when I find it three carriages further along, is surprisingly good. Plenty of hot water and a good strong flow. It feels great to wash away two days of grime, and enjoy the cascading hot water while rocking to the rhythm of the train. Returning to our compartment, I am startled to find, when moving between the train carriages, snowflakes falling upon me.

As the day continues, eyes lost in books, sudoku or simply glued to the window, we pass through Ekaterinburg, where in July 1918, Tsar Nicholas II, his wife and five children were shot and bayoneted to death. A few hours later, we pass over the Ural Mountains. These 2,500-kilometre long mountains, running north to south, form the traditional boundary between Asia and Europe. They also contain many of the richest minerals in the world, such as coal, iron, silver, gold, platinum, lead, aluminium, salt, diamonds and other gemstones. I have read that there is a sign visible from the train marking the crossing from Asia into Europe, but although I try hard, I fail to see it.

Late afternoon and with the final few hours of sunlight, I notice that the landscape is slowly changing. The taiga is still apparent, but now a little more industry is appearing, and as we descend towards the lower-altitude Moscow, the weather has started to warm slightly, the snow lighter upon the ground.

Again, our clocks go back two hours, making a total of five hours in three days. It also means we are now eight hours behind Australia. Today is all about enjoying the passing scenery as we attempt to eat the remainder of our food before our 2:13 pm disembarkation.

Outside, the taiga is still omnipresent, but now more prominent towns are appearing, many with those beautiful onion-domed churches Russia is renowned for. Alongside many of the stations, dozens of small chimney-topped sheds have appeared, although we never do learn what or who they are for

Shortly before 2 pm, our provodnitsa comes and vacuums our compartment and asks for payment of those cups of tea we enjoyed days earlier, and I reluctantly hand back my glass travel treasure mug. I have spent the past 70 hours clad simply in shorts and a t-shirt; the train is incredibly warm. But now it's time to don our layers of clothing once again. At 2:13 pm, the train pulls into Moscow's Yaroslavsky station, a 9,289-kilometre journey from Vladivostok, and it arrives to the minute. As we clamber down onto the station's platform, calling our farewells to Fraser and Lindsay, I can't help giving a little whoop of jubilation. We have done it: a life-long ambition and another Bucket List item accomplished.

CHAPTER 5

Russia – Moscow

*B*EFORE we reach the station's exit, a man approaches, my name flashing on his mobile phone: it is a convenient placard and a first for us. Introducing himself as Denis, it's not long before we are tucked into what looks like his mobile wardrobe and on our way to Arbat House, our home for the next four nights. His English is excellent, and when he tells us he used to be a lawyer, we understand why. As we travel along the surprisingly clean and broad Moscow streets, he tells us a little of his story.

"I trained and worked as a lawyer along with many others, a result of the old communist era where lawyers were seen as highly skilled, and there was enough work for us all. After 1991, with the collapse of the Soviet Union and the rise of the Russian Federation, there was simply not enough work to go around. Our wages started to decline until these days I earn nearly the same amount driving a taxi as I would working as a lawyer. As a taxi driver, I am my own boss, and I do not have the stress nor have to work the long days, that I would have had I continued as a lawyer."

The first accounts of Moscow appear in the history books around 1147 when a prince and his party, after a considerable celebration, stopped at some houses on the Moskva River, killed the owner, raped his wife and took his daughters. Not the most auspicious start for a city.

In the 17th century, much of the city was destroyed during citizen uprisings and in 1771, much of the population was killed by plague. In 1812, vast parts of the predominantly wooden city were destroyed by fire and in 1917, after the Bolshevik revolution, it was named Russia's capital, taking the honour from St. Petersburg. The dissolution of the USSR in 1991 brought extraordinary economic and political change to Moscow along with a significant concentration of Russia's wealth. After some initial years of instability, the years since have seen the city emerge as the country's most populous: its industrial, scientific, educational and cultural capital.

We have arrived in Moscow knowing this but also brainwashed with what we have observed on American television. If truth be told, I am expecting the city to be dismal, full of brown brick buildings, the people to be secretive and the streets to be unsafe. It's exciting to be here, but I am slightly apprehensive.

It takes less than 20 minutes before we pull up in front of our hotel. Inside, the foyer, although slightly worn, is lovely with picturesque tapestries lining the walls, glittering lights hanging from the ceiling and antique furniture dotted here and there. An adjoining restaurant looks equally promising. It is, however, not the décor that catches my attention, but the man checking in at the hotel reception.

"Look. It's the idiot who nearly made us miss the train in Ulaanbaatar."

"It is," Darryl replies. "He's still ignoring us."

Our room, unlike the reception area, is dingy and worn. However, it does have a large window with views overlooking the surrounding Moscow suburbs, which helps distract from its shortcomings. Having had only one shower in three days, or in Darryl's case, no shower in three days, this is the first thing we are both eager to do before organising with the hotel to have a load of laundry done; the towels are the most threadbare yet.

The following morning, over a typical Russian breakfast – black bread, cucumber, sliced ham and cheese – we reminisce about our Trans-Siberian journey across greater Russia.

"Something I have been wanting to do forever and I can believe it's over," I lament to Darryl.

"It's been an experience," he replies. "I don't think I expected Russia to look so bleak. The towns so poor. And everything to be made of wood. Although given the number of trees I shouldn't be surprised."

"It may have been because it's winter that it looked so bleak," I reply. "But I don't think so. Nearly every town or city we travelled through looked grim and grey. Apart from the churches that is. They always looked stunning."

"But then Moscow," Darryl continues, "from what I could see during our drive from the station yesterday, it looks to be so much cleaner and more affluent than the rest of the country. Usually, when I visit a country, I want to get out into the countryside. Not in Russia," he laughs.

It was a difficult decision to use Monkeyshrine rather than going it alone, which is how we usually travel. It felt as if we were cheating somehow. But sitting here in Moscow at the end of our Trans-Siberian adventure, I know I couldn't fault them nor our decision. Our organised trip from Beijing to Moscow had been perfect. To clinch it, rather than leave us bumbling around Moscow alone this first day, a final guided tour has been organised for us. Accordingly, a little before 10 am, we meet up with tour guide Stephanie in the hotel foyer. After a brief introduction, Stephanie asks us what we wish to see and where we want to go.

"You are well located here. It's within easy walking distance of most of Moscow's best-known sites," she advises.

"We would like to see Red Square and the Kremlin. Definitely St. Basil's Cathedral," I reply.

"I would like to see the Russian subway," Darryl interjects. "Apparently the stations are worth seeing."

"We also have to obtain visas from the Belarus Embassy when it opens tomorrow," I continue. "It would be good to know where it is and how to get there."

"Red Square is a 10-minute walk from here," Stephanie answers. "We can do everything you want to do. The Belarus Embassy is perhaps another 15- to 20-minute walk, or we could catch the Metro."

Red Square is where Russia's firework display occurs on New Year's Eve. It's the huge, paved area that abuts Moscow's instantly recognisable, historic red-walled fortress and centre of government, the Kremlin. It is also home to other important and distinctive landmarks such as the beautiful 16th century St. Basil's Cathedral, the mausoleum of Lenin, the GUM (pronounced "goom," Russia's foremost department store) and the stunning State Historical Museum.

As we make our way along the extensive Moscow footpaths, Stephanie slips into guide mode. "Some years ago, the footpaths were all widened which is great for the pedestrians," she tells us, "but not so great for the cars. It is why our roads here are so congested with traffic."

"It's surprising how clean the city is," Darryl comments.

"With the break-up of the Soviet Union, many of the residents of the new states such as Ukraine, Kazakhstan and Lithuania, unable to get work in their new countries, have come to Moscow. Here they form a very cheap labour force. They are employed as street cleaners and in other menial jobs. It's because their labour is so cheap that the city looks as clean as it does."

Relaxing a little further, Stephanie reveals a bit about herself, and part of the story sounds familiar: "I trained and worked as a chemical engineer, but these days there is no work for me. There are too many chemical engineers. I love my work as a tour guide. I keep my own hours; chose which days I work and get to meet people and show them my city."

"Have you always lived in Moscow?"

"Yes. I am lucky. I had a very astute grandmother. During the communist era, citizens of Moscow were provided with housing. My family were given a centrally located apartment. During the war, they were forced to move out, and squatters moved in as they did with many of the abandoned apartments. Once the war finished, my grandmother went about trying to get her apartment back and the squatters out. It took many years and 18 court trials before she was eventually successful. In 1992, the apartment was signed back over to us. Although, this being Russia, you never know what may happen in the future."

Arriving at the long red Kremlin walls, we note a crowd has started to gather.

"They are gathering for the hourly changing of the guard," continues Stephanie. "If we hurry, we can make the 11 am change."

Since 1997, soldiers of the Kremlin regiment have maintained a guard of honour at the Tomb of the Unknown Soldier here at the Kremlin. As we watch these soldiers dressed in their tall period boots and carrying their SKS rifles 'goose step' their way around the flaming memorial, it's the best indication yet that we have arrived in Russia.

Vladimir Lenin, founder of the Russian Communist Party and first head of the Soviet State, is interred (against his final wishes) within Red Square in a squat, red-granite edifice known as Lenin's Mausoleum. Mostly likely because it's the off season, today the queue to enter is short and, according to Stephanie, well worth visiting. Like the tomb of Ho Chi Minh we saw in Vietnam some years ago, Lenin's tomb is much the same: a somewhat cold-looking, slightly worse-for-wear body (he has been dead since 1924), mouldering in a glass coffin in the middle of a large, empty room.

"Interesting how Lenin has this entire huge granite tomb whereas Stalin (the Soviet Union's leader from 1924-1953) has just a simple gravesite outside," I comment, having noticed Stalin's tomb on our way in.

"Stalin was initially also interred here," Stephanie replies. "But in 1961, acknowledging the crimes he committed, the millions of deaths he was responsible for, his body was removed."

Limited to a time schedule, there's only enough time for a quick stroll through GUM, St. Basil's will have to wait, before we head below ground into the Moscow Metro. Here, for 55 rubles each (about 1.20 Australian dollars), we are free to travel its entire 381-kilometre network, to visit each of its 223 stations. While we are unable to explore much of the system, the few stops where we do alight confirm what we have heard. On orders from Stalin that these stations were to reflect the glory of the Soviet Union, they are unlike any of their Tube, Underground or Metro counterparts that we have seen. With their elegant chandeliers, marble walls, vaulted ceilings, colourful murals and, in some cases, striking bronze statues, they are more grand ballroom than sooty subway.

"A train will arrive every 90 seconds," Stephanie tells us, emphasising the point that the system is as efficient as it is picturesque.

Back on street level and with more suburbs to wander to reach the Belarus Embassy, Stephanie educates us a little on Moscow's architecture.

"Most of the buildings in Moscow were destroyed in the 1812 fire," she explains. "Learning from what occurred, almost all buildings after that were built in brick, rather than timber. They were painted in colours, many with ornate exteriors. Those are examples of post-1812 buildings," she says, pointing towards some lovely old structures painted in various shades of spearmint green, pale yellow and peppermint blue.

"This is an example of a building constructed during communist times when it was more about functionality than aesthetics," she continues, pointing towards a drab, grey concrete complex.

"And this is an example of a more recent build, a post-communist build." This time she points towards a building that, although painted a cool green, is noticeably plainer than the earlier post-fire structures. "Today, Moscow is trying to restore and improve upon the communist-era builds. Many are being repainted. A lot of improvements are currently happening throughout Moscow."

"Moscow, so far, is completely different to what I was expecting," I tell her. "I was expecting dull brown brick buildings, not beautiful colourful structures. I was expecting dirty, crowded footpaths, not these spacious, easy-to-traverse streets, and I had no idea Red Square was so big and impressive."

"Is it a safe city?" Darryl asks.

"Very," Stephanie replies. "Anyone can walk around alone at night. There is very little crime."

After noting the location of the Belarus Embassy where we will be returning tomorrow, we return to Red Square and farewell Stephanie. She has no doubt been the best and most knowledgeable of all our guides so far. Her parting piece of information is the directions to a nearby pedestrian shopping street. "Arbat Street is one of Moscow's oldest streets," she tells us. "It has existed since the 15th century. You should be able to find a place to have a late lunch easily enough."

I am getting used to our breakfasts of sliced cucumber, tomato, cheese and black bread. I've also discovered some delicious crepes on the breakfast buffet whose sweetness perfectly counteracts the savoury. I will need the energy provided by the sugar, as this morning we plan to revisit the Belarus Embassy to secure our transit visas. Having to obtain these visas has always been a worry, and we are hoping that all goes well. To add to our concerns, we also must locate some wayward train tickets. Before leaving Australia, we purchased tickets for the Budapest-Zagreb leg of our journey through the Polrail site. Time constraints had meant they could not be delivered to us in Australia; therefore, we had organised for them to be sent to our hotel here in Moscow. Unfortunately, they haven't turned up. One of the hotel receptionists, however, has been amazing. She has been in contact with both Polrail and the Russian mail service and has discovered that the tickets were sent weeks ago and are still, fortunately, awaiting collection at a suburban post office. We just have to find this post office.

Our morning walk to the Belarus Embassy takes us back through Red Square where once again we appreciate the changing of the guard, revere St. Basil's Cathedral and imagine Putin working hard in his Kremlin. From Red Square, we enter a less touristy district where flower vendors are still setting up for their days' trade, resolute commuters are making their way to work and dog owners are walking their slipper-clad dogs.

There is a small queue to enter the embassy, and each of us is buzzed through separately following a brief interrogation by a twitchy security guard. With no English signage and a lone English-speaking staff member, it is fortunate that we have brought with us completed application forms downloaded before we left Australia. Nervously handing over these forms, we hold our breath.

"You want urgent visas that you collect this afternoon or non-urgent and collect tomorrow?" simply queries the solo English-speaking receptionist.

"Urgent please," we grin, slowly exhaling. With a lot of onward travel resting on these visas, we want no hiccups; we want to hold them in our hands.

"That will be 16,900 rubles," she says, confirming the amount on her calculator.

"16,900! Wow, that much? We do not have that many rubles on us. Can we use a card or is there a bank nearby?" I question her.

"There is a bank not far," she says.

"Great. We will be back shortly."

"That is fine."

"16,900 rubles," says Darryl as we set off in search of the bank. "How much is that in Australian dollars?"

"It's about $388," I say after doing the conversion on my phone. "Expensive."

"Very expensive," Darryl agrees. "Considering we will be asleep on a train for the whole time we will be in Belarus."

"But at least we are getting them," I reply. "Imagine if we hadn't been able to."

The bank is further away than we expect, and I must consult Google Maps to locate it. It doesn't take us long once we enter, to discover that here, no one speaks English at all. Fortunately, Russians understand and use our Arabic numerals, and our withdrawal is successful using a combination of miming and pointing to our phone.

Back at the Embassy, we hand over our passports, the paperwork and the 16,900 rubles. "Come back at 4 pm this afternoon," we are told.

With the day ahead of us, we elect not to take the Metro, hail a taxi or book a Yandex (Russia's Uber): wide footpaths and bracing weather mean Moscow is a great city to explore on foot. Our ambles take us alongside the mighty Volga River that slices Moscow and by way of beautiful sweeping avenues bordered by lovely pastel-shaded buildings. I am thrilled when we pass the Bolshoi Theatre and wonder when Di, one of our travelling companions on the Trans-Mongolian, will be attending her ballet performance. Approaching GUM, we notice a Christmas ice skating rink under construction and we walk an entire street (Nikolskaya) beneath hanging colourful lights.

"Stephanie mentioned a cafeteria that served good, cheap food here," I mention as we approach GUM. "It's popular with locals and students. I'm a bit hungry. Should we find it?"

"Can you remember its name?"

"Something 57," I reply.

Stolovaya 57, located on the second story of the GUM store, is not too difficult to find and shortly we find ourselves slurping mugs of warming hot chocolate in the surprisingly empty cafeteria – it must be too early for the students. My phone rings, and it's Paige FaceTiming us. Although she has just been offered a graduate nursing position at Brisbane's Mater Hospital due to commence in January, she is thinking of declining the offer.

"I don't think I want to be a nurse. I just don't like touching the patients. I'm thinking of studying social work at QUT. I'll let you know!"

She also updates us on the bushfires currently raging throughout Australia. "People have been killed, houses burnt down and so much land destroyed. The worst part is that so many animals have been killed and their habitat lost. It's sad, and they are saying that it's going to get worse. That this will be Australia's worst bushfire season ever." She also issues a parting warning: "I'm pretty sure Pierce is not keeping the house clean."

Before returning to our hotel, we attempt to hunt down the suburban post office where, hopefully, we will find our missing train tickets. This time our stroll takes us through less affluent Moscow districts. Streets are narrower, footpaths are splattered with phlegm and the austere buildings, block-like and grey, are definitely communist-era builds. Expecting to come across a post office similar to what we have at home – an obvious shop with a post-box out the front – we are surprised to find ourselves standing in front of a residential block of grim-looking flats on a street filled with the same. Nothing looks remotely shop-like. There is simply a large wooden door, which, apprehensively, we push open. Inside, a single hanging bulb struggles to illuminate the dusty wooden floor and the large balustraded staircase, but it does shed enough light for us to notice, at the building's rear, a fully functioning post office.

Not expecting anyone to speak any English, we have come prepared and the Google Translate app on my phone is displaying exactly what we are after. There is some initial surprise at our arrival and confusion at our Google-assisted request, but eventually, much to our relief, a worn envelope bearing my name is found.

"Passport," the receptionist grunts.

"Passport?" I groan. "Our passports are with the Belarus Embassy."

"How about your English passport?" Darryl offers. "Have you got it with you? Will that do?"

"My British one? Yes, it's in my money belt."

I have a British passport because I was born in England. Before turning one, I, along with a year's supply of disposable nappies, was tucked securely into the back of a motor caravan and transported to Australia by way of Afghanistan and India – no doubt the precursor for my itchy feet. During our 2017 trip, this second passport proved invaluable and it's the same today. Removing it from my money belt, I use it to confirm my identity and, thankfully, secure our tickets.

At 4 pm on the dot, it's with great relief that we retrieve our passports, their decorative Belarus visas pasted inside. It was always a concern having to obtain these visas in what we perceived as 'difficult Russia,' and with the next stage of our adventure hinging on them, it is comforting to have them now in our possession.

While there are at least 20 kremlins in Russia, when you hear the word kremlin, you automatically think about the place President Putin presides from in Moscow. Most of this Kremlin that you see on your television, the striking red 2,500-metre-long, 20-metre-high wall and its 20 towers, was built at the end of the 15th century. The five palaces, four magnificent cathedrals and the Grand Kremlin Palace – the former Moscow residence of Russia's Tsars now split into Putin's official home and a museum, contained within these walls – all came later.

Over yet more black bread, crepes and cucumber, I broach today's plan to visit this iconic institution with Darryl.

"I've been reading a few travel blogs. It's possible to purchase your own entry tickets but it's not straightforward."

"What's the problem?"

"There are four areas in the Kremlin you can visit. But you can't just buy one ticket to see everything. If you want to see all four areas, you need to purchase four separate tickets from four separate ticket-booths. It's ridiculously Russian. The main complaints have been it's very confusing and the queues can be huge. It's recommended you purchase 'skip the line' tickets."

"Each time we have walked past," Darryl replies. "I haven't noticed any large queues. Let's risk it."

Having made this walk to Red Square numerous times over the previous days, the winding route between residential and office blocks is now familiar. And having discovered many interesting short-cuts, some underground through spotless graffiti-free passageways, it's not long before we find ourselves standing in front of a surprisingly small steel and glass building. This is the modern ticket office into the Kremlin, and it appears Darryl's earlier observations are correct. There are very few queues; travelling in winter seems to have worked in our favour once again.

"We can visit Cathedral Square, the Kremlin Grounds, the State Palace or the Armoury," I read from my phone. (It's easier to use my phone than translate the mostly Russian signage). "Most people recommend visiting the Armoury and the Diamond Fund."

"What's in the Kremlin Grounds?"

"A huge bell and a large cannon."

"I'm happy to look at anything. It's freezing today. You might be happier inside at the Armoury."

While the queues are better than usual outside, inside the small glass building it's uncomfortably crowded. Again, the signage is mostly in Russian, and it's difficult to work out which counter to front. Next to us, a group of tourists who have lined up incorrectly have had to start queuing all over again, and frustrations are high.

"This is what the websites all warn of. Why they suggest buying tickets online even if they cost more."

Eventually, and fortunately, we do manage to secure some tickets to the Armoury but give up on the Diamond Fund. "There's absolutely nowhere I can see to buy tickets," I mutter in frustration. "Imagine doing this in the height of a busy summer."

Entering through the austere Kremlin gates, inside it's an entirely different world. A completely different story. Spacious and warm, an efficient usher directs us to an enormous cloakroom where more capable staff swap our jackets for tokens and issue some portable audio guides.

"It's a shame the ticket booth doesn't operate as efficiently as this cloakroom," Darryl remarks.

As we are soon to discover, despite its name, the Kremlin Armoury does not only contain weapons but rather all sorts of treasures. From valuable European artworks, decorative royal garments, intricate ivory thrones, aged coronation dresses, priceless bejewelled royal carriages to the world's largest collections of Russian gold, silverware and priceless Fabergé eggs. Our audio guides prove invaluable as they steer us through these prized treasures and offer us an insight into Russia's complicated but fascinating history. So interested is he in one of these riches, an antiquated carriage, that Darryl leans over the rope barrier and touches it. Immediately, the sound of a loud alarm fills the room and a frowning security guard makes his way towards us.

"I won't do that again," he laughs as we quickly scurry away.

Eventually, we reach the end of our fascinating tour and make our way towards the exit. As we do so, we notice a darkened area with Diamond Fund signage displayed. Here, apparently, is where we purchase tickets to this exhibit. "Why didn't it tell us that outside?" we mutter as we pay for our admission.

Created in 1719 by Peter the Great (Russia's Tsar from 1682 until 1725, Peter the Great is credited with bringing Russia into the modern age), the Kremlin Diamond Fund is undoubtedly one of the largest and most significant collections of valuables in the world. Again, our audio guides are vital as they guide us around the incredible collection, providing us with the stories behind the displays of gemstone encrusted jewellery, enormous gold nuggets and bountiful diamonds.

"Many of the jewels were collected from private families who were forced to leave them to the state… These jewels must never be sold… This is the largest collection of gold nuggets in the world."

"No wonder the Russian people overthrew their Tsar," I comment at one stage.

"Yes," Darryl agrees. "While most of the Russian people were poor and lived in tiny wooden houses, the Tsars lived with all this."

Having viewed such blatant wealth, we depart the Diamond Fund feeling slightly numb. The Kremlin, for all our difficulties in entering, has been an incredible experience. We would have loved to continue exploring, to try another area, but are loath to attempt the chaotic ticket booth again. It's time to step back into the real world.

That real world is Arbat Street, where hungry for some familiar food, we find a pizza shop and feast on large cheesy pizzas washed down with Balika, a popular Russian beer.

Waking to our final day in Russia, we find it a wet one. Despite the weather, there are huge, hour-long queues in front of St. Basil's Cathedral, which means that for this trip, the cathedral's interior will have to remain a mystery to us. Instead, we make do with one last look at Red Square, take one last ride on the Metro and pay for our freshly washed laundry.

Three pm, and sitting in reception waiting for our Yandex which will deliver us to Leninkradsky train station, I gaze at the hotel's elegant antiques and mull over all that Russia has surprisingly revealed. An incredible train journey through desperately poor towns to a rich, vibrant capital. Little English but friendly, open people. Hearty and tasty food at unbelievable prices. Hugely qualified tour guides. Vast forests. Freezing temperatures. Strange post offices. Christmas bauble churches and, most surprising of all, safe, clean streets.

As Winston Churchill once said, Russia really has shown itself to be "a riddle, wrapped in a mystery, inside an enigma."

At Leninkradsky Station, like in China, there is no English signage. It takes some patience and the use of Google Translate to find the stark waiting room and our departure platform, both notable for their hordes of hungry pigeons and weary, waiting passengers. A little before the allotted departure time, we are allowed to board our train and settle into our overnight accommodation. This compartment is the most modern yet. All clean, prefabricated plastic panels and grey upholstery with our very own washbasin stored beneath the adjustable table placed between the twin beds.

At dinnertime, we make our way through the well-patronised carriages until we find the dining car. This carriage, with its bouquet of cigarette smoke and stale beer, is much older than our compartment, and tables and chairs have been replaced with benches where your meal is eaten standing. It's a novel experience for us both to stand eating our freshly cooked chicken schnitzels, buttery potatoes and garlicky mushrooms as the train rockets along.

At some stage during the night, our watches go back to nine hours behind Australia. We also leave Russia and enter Belarus, although we have no indication of when this occurs. Around 4 am, however, we certainly know when we leave Belarus and enter Poland. A pounding knock on our cabin door divulges an armed guard who asks for our passports and frowningly stamps them clear of Belarus. Ten minutes later, this is repeated along with a cabin search as we cross into Poland. Awake, knowing I will not be getting back to sleep before our 7:15 am arrival, I insert my European sim card into my phone and pinpoint our exact location using Google Maps. Warsaw is not far away.

CHAPTER 6

Poland

*E*DGING closer to Warsaw Central train station, I contemplate what will be required once we arrive. All Eurail passes before their maiden journey must be validated. This generally occurs at the train station you will be departing from when first using your Eurail pass and involves a simple date stamp. As we have an onward train booked for 9 am this morning, destination Krakow, we will be using our Eurail passes for the first time. Before boarding, we must find a ticket office to obtain the required validation.

To our relief, our train again arrives precisely on time. Having the whole hour and three-quarters available before our next train departs will eliminate any stress with finding the correct validation counter. It will also allow us time to find breakfast.

Unlike train stations in China and Russia, we soon realise on alighting that here the station conforms with our expectations. Electronic platform indicators are readily available, entrances and exits are well-marked. It's clear that we have arrived in Europe. While our first attempt at validation is concerningly unsuccessful – "No no, you must go to the ticket counters upstairs" – the second attempt is fruitful.

With ample time to spare, we use some of our Polish zloty, obtained prior to our departure from Australia, to purchase large coffees and even larger ham and cheese baguettes and sit munching these until it's time to board. This train, the two-and-a-half-hour high-speed express between Warsaw and Krakow, is packed with bored-looking commuters, loud families and other luggage-laden travellers. After the relative isolation and quiet solitude offered by our previous sleeper compartments, this journey feels claustrophobic and noisy.

The 300-kilometre run through primarily flat, marshy scrubland passes quickly and we soon find ourselves alighting at what resembles a large shopping mall. Krakow Glowny Train Station is connected to the well-illuminated Galleria shopping centre, and it isn't easy to see where one starts and the other finishes. Our hotel, the Europejski, is located within a few hundred metres – we simply have to stroll through the shopping centre, pop above ground, traverse a street and here we are.

It's fortunate that it is still early afternoon as the first thing we need to do is buy a new foot brace for Darryl. Still somehow holding together after cracking in Mongolia, it has been a real concern that this one would break completely. After much online searching, we found an orthotic specialist store here in Krakow that sold foot braces. No other place on our immediate travels had any such store. Accordingly, keen to eliminate this worry, we use a few more of our zloty for a taxi and shortly find ourselves negotiating the heavy city traffic.

Krakow, the second largest of Poland's cities, is also one of its oldest, dating back to the 7th century. Situated on the Vistula River, Krakow, after the invasion of Poland by Nazi Germany, became one of the most important administrative cities of the Third Reich, and its Jewish population forced into what became known as the Krakow Walled Zone: an overcrowded ghetto whose occupants were sent on a one-way journey to extermination camps. Because of its significant wartime position, the city emerged from the war as one of the few European places to have escaped Hitler's bombing. Much of the beautiful city remains as it was before the war. While it escaped the bombs, it didn't escape communism, remaining under post-war Soviet rule until the fall of communism in 1989.

Today, Krakow is cited as one of the most beautiful of all European cities, and its Old Town, Stare Miasto, was one of the first onto UNESCO's inaugural world heritage list.

Unfortunately, during this taxi ride, we fail to see any of the beautiful areas of Krakow that we have read about: the suburbs we travel through and buildings we pass are more reminiscent of Moscow's communist builds than pre-war beauties. The orthotics store is expecting our arrival, and all that is required is a fitting and adjustment before we depart, purchase in hand. Rather than return to our accommodation by taxi or tram, Darryl suggests we walk.

"If we walk," I argue. "It's just going to get later and darker. Wouldn't it be better to get another taxi or use the tram so as we can explore the Old Town near our hotel?"

"If we walk," Darryl argues. "We can see a little more closely some of the areas we just sped through."

Although not happy, I concede, and the next hour is spent revisiting Krakow's less noteworthy suburbs, trailing traffic-clogged roads and pounding the grimy footpaths.

It's nearing 4 pm when we eventually arrive at our hotel, and surprisingly, it's already dark.

"I think we wasted our time walking back here," I have another dig at Darryl. "We don't have much time in Krakow, and we are away all day tomorrow visiting Auschwitz. You haven't given us long to explore the Old Town."

Stare Miasto, which means Old Town in Polish, is Krakow's most crucial sightseeing area. Dating from 1257 onwards, this network of streets and squares surrounding Rynek Glowny, the biggest medieval market square in Europe, is packed with restaurants, hotels, antique and souvenir shops. It is also home to Wawel Royal Castle, the gothic St. Mary's Basilica, St. Florien's gate and many other architecturally beautiful buildings.

It is also, fortunately, located a very short distance from our hotel. Within minutes, we have traversed an underground pedestrian tunnel, climbed a flight of stairs and emerged into Planty Park, created during the 19th century when the moat encircling Stare Miasto was filled. From here, with no map to guide us and under the dim glow of aged lighting, we make our way alongside ancient, cobbled streets, past impressive-looking Gothic churches and regal Dickensian residences. Eventually, we emerge into a vast medieval market square. Here, a Christmas tree is in the process of being erected, horse-drawn carriages await customers and stalls selling Christmas goodies entice.

"It's only 4:30 pm and it's completely dark," Darryl says as we stand with the other tourists at the centre of this beautiful fairy-tale square. "I didn't realise how early night falls here. I also didn't realise how impressive this Old Town would be. Maybe you were right?"

It's as near an apology as I am going to get, so I take it.

"I cannot believe how quickly night has fallen either," I reply. "I have never seen it completely dark by 4:30 pm. I was hoping we could have a very late lunch, but now I am thinking of a very early dinner."

"I'm keen for dinner, but I think I may try one of those pretzels first," Darryl replies while pointing towards a cart selling obwarzanek, Krakow's iconic circular-shaped baked bread.

"What does it taste like?" I question him a short while later.

"Pretty tasteless and doughy. I don't think I'll be having another."

Spurred on by our growing hunger, we continue to explore, but keep an eye out for a suitable place to eat. With dim street lighting making the cobblestone streets treacherous and always having to skip out of the way of either a horse-drawn carriage or a sneaky car, it's not an easy search and we are grateful when a tout convinces us to enter the Tomasza 20 resto-bar. Here, in this brick, cellar-like restaurant (typical of Krakow eateries apparently), we order massive plates of delicious spare ribs. Accompanied by finger-sized chips, creamy slaw and washed down with some excellent Polish wine, it's the perfect way to finish the day.

"I didn't realise Poland even made wine," is about all I manage to groan as we make our way back to our hotel, too full to utter more.

While concentration camps had existed in Germany since 1933, acting as detention centres for perceived enemies of Nazi Germany, Hitler created 'death camps' for the sole purpose of killing Jews and other 'undesirables.' Opening in 1940, the Auschwitz complex – consisting of a concentration camp, a labour camp, gas chambers and crematorium spread over three campuses – evolved into the most infamous and largest of all death camps. Of the 1.3 million-plus people who died here, 960,000 of them were Jewish.

It's still only mid-morning when, under a grey, drizzly sky and surrounded by scrubby woodlands, our minibus pulls up in front of Auschwitz 1, the main encampment. On board with us is a guy from Melbourne, his chatty Canadian partner and an elderly Dutch couple. After disembarking, we and hundreds of other arriving tourists are quickly segregated into groups, assigned a guide and led through the infamous gates marked with the words "Arbeit Macht Frei" – work makes one free.

Although not a Bucket List item, visiting this place, entering these gates and reading these words could be. I first learnt of Auschwitz when reading Anne Frank's diary as a child and learning about what occurred here, what one human being could do to another, really struck me. It is a place I have wanted to visit but felt it didn't deserve a spot on the list. For the following two hours, as our guide gives us an in-depth tour of a place where some of history's most untold horrors took place, I am appalled but grateful that I didn't let its history dissuade me from visiting.

Consisting of row upon row of pre-war brick barracks spread over unsealed terrain, our group trails our guide throughout many of these two storey buildings. Due to the sheer number of people, it's uncomfortably crowded, but our guide's non-stop chilling narrative provides a compulsive distraction.

"It is impossible to calculate the exact number of lives lost at Auschwitz... Auschwitz is the only camp who tattooed their prisoners... This is the 'black wall' where SS guards executed thousands of prisoners..."

Crammed into one building, barrack block 10, we learn of the medical experiments performed in here by SS Captain Dr Josef Mengele – the "Angel of Death." The forced sterilisations and castrations of adults. The gruesome experiments performed on twins, infants and dwarfs. The terrible procedures done to pregnant women. In other barracks, we view huge glass display cases filled with the personal effects of former Auschwitz inmates. One glass display is full of battered personalised suitcases; another, artificial limbs; yet others, kitchen utensils, shoes and spectacles. Block four contains a model of a gas chamber used to exterminate the inmates along with the most sickening display yet: a vast glass chamber full of mouldering locks of hair

As we are herded through these buildings, under the gaze of the victims immortalised in the hundreds of photos that stare down on us, our guide continues his harrowing narrative.

"Mengele, in a study of eye colour, injected serum into the eyeballs of young children... He would also perform unnecessary amputations or inject one twin with typhus ... Above all we must never forget what occurred here."

In all, it's a very sombre group that congregate near the minivan sometime later to make their way to Auschwitz 2.

"I am glad to have visited," says the chatty Canadian lady to me, "but it was a lot worse than I was expecting and too crowded."

"It was busier and worse than I was expecting," I agree. "Way too crowded. And those display cases full of hair and shoes. They were awful."

"It *was* awful and so sad," whispers the elderly Dutch lady. "We have always wanted to visit. We have friends who lost family members here. They do not want to come, but we thought that we should, to remember, to not let their deaths be forgotten."

"I won't forget the last building, the actual gas chamber and crematorium," Darryl comments. "How they made fellow prisoners clear the gas chamber of the dead bodies and then load them into the crematorium."

"And the guide," I say as I turn back to the Dutch lady. "How important it is to him that what occurred here must not be in vain. That we must take what we have seen with us and to never forget."

Auschwitz 2, also referred to as Auschwitz-Birkenau, is a short ride from Auschwitz 1. As we park, I realise this is the camp that more often appears in the media, the one shown in most of the camp's propaganda. We have arrived at the entrance of a long, low-set red-brick building whose middle is dissected by a single set of rail tracts that disappear into the vast, open fields surrounding us. This is the rail whereby most of the camp's inmates arrived and these fields, dotted with hundreds of guard towers, are a mass of (formerly electrified) barbed-wire fences and concrete pillars. Once, a multitude of bleak prison barracks existed within these electrified compounds but they were destroyed by withdrawing Nazis seeking to hide their evil doings. Their brick footprints are all that remain.

Entering through the low-set building, we meet up with a new guide who spends the following hour showing us various sections of this vast camp, all the while continuing a now-familiar account.

"This is an example of a carriage that was used to bring Jews, Gypsies or Polish-Russian prisoners to Auschwitz," he explains, pointing to a small carriage slightly larger than a horse-trailer.

"Up to one 150 prisoners would be forced into these cattle cars, with no food nor water and maybe a bucket for a toilet. On arrival, they would be separated – the young and able-bodied sent to do hard labour, the mothers, children and elderly sent immediately to the gas chambers."

There are a few barracks still standing, and the one we enter was used to house female prisoners. Inside this cold, stark, dirt-floored building, we find three-storied bunks or "roosts," made from bricks and wood where female prisoners were forced to sleep five to a bed.

Along with most of the barrack buildings, the gas chambers and crematorium in this camp no longer exist.

"The Nazis tried to destroy the evidence of their crimes before fleeing," our guide tells us. "In January 1945, with the Soviet army approaching, they destroyed most of the barracks and all the crematoriums, then abandoned the camp and force-marched 60,000 prisoners to other locations. One in four died along the way. The Soviet troops found the remaining nearly 8,000 sick or starving prisoners when they liberated Auschwitz on 27 January 1945. When you leave, never forget what occurred here."

It's after 5 pm when we arrive back at Krakow, and another cold, dark night has fallen. Keen to revisit Old Town before tomorrow's early departure, we again use the handy pedestrian walkway. Tonight, the Christmas tree has been fully erected. It shines proudly from the centre of Main Market Square while many adjoining streets, now strewn with glowing Christmas lights, make walking easier and undoubtedly safer. Cheerful Christmas stalls selling aromatic mulled wine call to us and little do we realise, as we purchase a cup each, that these will be the first of many enjoyed as we travel throughout Europe. On the hour, we find ourselves standing in front of St. Mary's Basilica and listen as a trumpet player sounds a truncated melody.

"Did you notice how the melody cuts off mid-song?" A local

standing nearby asks us. "A trumpet player played this song once to warn of an approaching attack on the city, but he was shot in the neck which is why the music stops short now."

This morning, for the first time since departing Australia, I have time and space to do my early morning yoga. Lasting around 25 minutes, it's probably more stretching than yoga, but whatever it is, it feels good to be doing it once again. Today's nine-hour train journey to Budapest will be our longest yet, and while we would have preferred to have broken the journey somewhere for Darryl's comfort, time constraints mean this is not possible.

Although most of our zloty has gone – used to purchase doughy bread, mulled wine and pay tips – some loose notes are still in our wallets. We use these to buy food for the upcoming train journey along with a t-shirt for Darryl.

"How come you brought just two t-shirts with you?" I question him.

"I was trying to pack really lightly," is his reply.

There is not much to see as our train leaves the city of Krakow behind and winds its way through the Polish countryside. It's all too foggy. This train appears to be the slowest yet, and our fellow travellers are mainly young, heavily burdened backpackers. At one stage, my phone rings, and it's the ladies from my lawn bowls club, The Brunswick Broomstick Riders. They have gathered to celebrate a 60th birthday, and FaceTiming with them is somewhat surreal as I consider our two very different current locations.

As the hours pass, the scenery changes, as do our travelling companions. Winter-bleak Poland gives way to chilly Czechia then dreary Slovakia. At Bratislava, the capital of Slovakia, we jump down onto the windy station platform before quickly scrambling back into the well-heated train – just to say we have stepped foot in this relatively new republic. Each country we pass through provides us with a new conductor, and time and time again, our carriage completely rebirths its passengers. Backpackers give way to bored commuters who give way to grungy students or eager housewives. It's our own small traveller's microcosm.

Around 4:15 pm, with minimal fanfare, the temperature of the train stifling and outside bathed in darkness, we cross into Hungary. Budapest, our next destination, is only a few short hours away.

CHAPTER 7

Hungary

*I*T'S nearing 8 pm when our train pulls into Keleti station, the largest of Budapest's three main train stations. Between his luggage, his walking stick and the train's steep steps, it's not always easy for Darryl to alight, which means that by the time we reach the exit, the station is empty. With our room at the 7 Seasons Apartments a good 10-minute drive, we approach a mostly deserted taxi rank looking for a cab.

"7 Seasons will cost you 7,000 forints or 15 euro," casually advises a young driver, more interested in continuing his conversation with his friends than securing our business.

"Fifteen euros," we mutter. "That's steep for a 10-minute journey. Is that a flat rate or are there metered taxis available?"

"If you want a metered taxi then there is a cheaper service down that street," he replies while pointing indifferently towards a darkened alley.

"I think we should look for the cheaper service," says Darryl.

"It's late. It's dark. I'm tired," I sigh. "Although these guys may be ripping us off, I just want to get to our room. And luckily, we have euro on us."

It was our daughter Paige who insisted we visit Budapest. She had spent a few days here some years ago and loved the place.

Straddling the river Danube, with Buda on one side and Pest the other, the Budapest of today – with its beautiful, predominately 19th-century buildings, thermal hot springs and vibrant nightlife – was created with the 1873 merger of three cities: Buda, Obuda and Pest. Despite almost being named Pestbuda and a chequered history which includes a city siege that killed 38,000 citizens and its 1989 escape from communist rule, Budapest, one of Europe's most photogenic cities, has thrived and is now an international tourism destination. Other interesting facts we have gleaned on our journey here are that the inventors of both the Rubik's cube and the Biro pen were born in Budapest.

Revived by a long dreamless sleep and with plenty of room available in our modern apartment, I rise early for yoga and a shower. I emerge from the bathroom to find Darryl looking a little confused.

"I thought you said this was a fully self-contained apartment."

"It is. I booked it so as we could save some money on food and catch up on laundry," I reply.

"Well, I can see a stove top and sink but where's the washing machine?"

This is only one of a handful of places I have reserved on our entire journey that supposedly contains a washing machine, allowing us to catch up on our laundry rather than hand-wash or pay for it. After an intense search, I have to agree with Darryl; there is no washing machine. Back to hand-washing our clothes.

With its population nearing 1.8 million, Budapest is a large sprawling city full of predominately low-rise buildings, typical of Europe. To get a feel for the place and explore it as best we can in the three days we have here, we have decided to use a bus. The Hop-On Hop-Off buses have worked well for us in other cities. There's a Hop-On stop located a five-minute walk from our room, and here we purchase a two-day pass which also includes a river cruise along the Danube.

With upstairs seats perfect for viewing the city and the biting wind sharp on our faces, it's not long until we find ourselves weaving our way between a ridiculous number of impressive buildings as we head towards Heroes' Square. This popular square with its commanding statues, built in1896, is undoubtedly imposing but what interests me more is the lovely, ornate building located nearby: the Szechenyi Baths.

Budapest, also known as the "City of Baths," sits on a fault line and bubbling beneath the city is a massive reserve of spring water whose 120-plus hot springs feed the city with over 70 million litres of thermal water a day. Appreciation of this hot thermal water dates to Roman times, and today, locals and visitors alike partake of its healing properties and mineral-rich water, using Budapest's numerous thermal bathing complexes.

"There's the Szechenyi Baths. It's Budapest's largest thermal bath. I'm pretty sure that's where Paige visited and advised us to go."

"It's 10 degrees outside," Darryl scoffs. "I can't see you getting into an outdoor pool even if it is heated."

Although it is true that stripping down and plunging into water in this freezing climate doesn't appeal to me at all, visiting a bathing complex while in Budapest should be a must. It's something I quietly decide to investigate once we return to our room.

As we leave Heroes' Square and make our way towards another popular destination on the Hop-On route, the Great Market Hall, we pass the Keleti train station.

"Isn't that the train station we arrived at? The one that cost us 15 euro to get to our hotel. It's even closer than I realised – we were definitely ripped off."

The three-storey Great Market Hall is a restored neo-Gothic building that houses Budapest's largest and oldest indoor market. It's hugely popular with tourists and is another of the places Paige insisted we visit.

"I bought three pashminas there for $5 each," she had crowed. "It's stuffed with great things to buy and eat."

Alighting in front of the grand stone structure, it doesn't take us long to realise that the place is disappointingly closed – and there's a large sign advising as such.

"Open every day except Sunday," I read.

"It doesn't really matter; we've got two-day bus passes. We can come back tomorrow," Darryl replies. "It looks as if something is happening across the road. Let's have a look then walk along the river. Maybe we'll find where our river cruise departs from?"

What Darryl is looking at are several large white marquees ringed by tables of content diners. Approaching, we soon see why the patrons all appear so content: the competition for a seat so intense! These marquees are housing Budapest's answer to a Christmas Market, and never have we seen anything like it. Vat upon colossal vat of bubbling goulashes, curries, stews and ham hocks, all staffed by muscular men wielding large wooden paddles. Tray upon vast tray of sticky spare ribs, creamy potatoes, smoky grilled sausages, pork knuckles and garlicky bread. With whole fat pigs roasting in the background and wide-jawed pig heads as decoration in the fore, it's an incredible sight. Truly a feast on a King Henry VIII scale.

"I think I know where we will be buying lunch," says Darryl.

"And dessert," I reply, spying a neighbouring marquee equally stuffed with strudels, cakes, gingerbread and mulled wine. "Too bad we paid for an apartment with a kitchen. I don't think it's going to get much use."

The Danube River, whose origins begin in the Black Forest mountains of western Germany and end 10 countries later in the Black Sea, is a beautiful sight as she slices decisively through Budapest. With hilly Buda on her far side, we stroll flat Pest's riverbank until we come across the departure point of our river cruise. For the following hour, we cruise the Danube while our gruff Hungarian captain maintains a running commentary.

"This is the Hungarian Parliament Building," he states as we float past Budapest's most iconic and beautiful building. "It was built to celebrate the unification of Buda, Obuda and Pest and although construction started in 1885, it was not finished until 1904 – the architect went blind then died before completion…. In 1944, 20,000 Jews were lined up and shot just here, and their bodies fell into the freezing water. Before they were killed, they had to remove their shoes. If you look to your right, you will see a memorial to these victims."

Looking to our right, we see hundreds of assorted shoes lined up along the riverbank. Although it's not possible to distinguish from the many real shoes, there is also a selection of iron footwear, a sculptural memorial.

"To our left," our captain continues, "is Buda Castle. A castle has stood on this site since the 13th century."

Sitting on the seats alongside us during this cruise are two Poms, Rebecca and Lyle, mother and son, who are enjoying a four-day visit to Budapest.

"It's our first visit here," they tell us. "And we love it. We often holiday together, and this is one of the best yet. We leave dad at home."

"What can you recommend?" I ask.

"Definitely visit a bath house," Rebecca replies.

"Try and visit a ruin bar, if you can find one," adds Lyle.

"I've booked us into the Gellert Thermal Baths," is my greeting to Darryl the following morning. "We get to use the baths for two hours before a 20-minute massage each. I wanted hour-long massages, but 20 minutes is all that is available."

"Are the Gellert Baths the ones we passed yesterday?"

"No. The Gellert is located on the Buda side of the river."

It's fortunate we bought two-day Hop-On bus tickets because this morning we use them to return to the Great Market Hall located directly across the river from the Gellert Baths. As spruiked by Paige, the market is dripping with goods and food, and it's not long before Darryl is chewing on a massive piece of lángos (fried bread topped with sour cream and cheese) while I browse the many stores. Many are selling paprika, a spice very popular and grown in Hungary, but what I find particularly impressive, although expensive, are the stalls selling delicate Hungarian lace. Scanning the fine samples, it's easy to understand their worldwide popularity.

A little before our booking time, we make our way over the wide Danube using the ornate green-hued Freedom Bridge. Budapest has many bridges spanning this river, and Freedom Bridge is probably its most beautiful.

Gellert Thermal Baths, tucked within the Gellert Hotel building, is one of Budapest's most renowned and elegant bath houses. Opened in 1918, this Art Nouveau complex, featuring mosaic walls and floors, stained glass windows and Roman-style columns, is home to 12 pools in total. Dry and steam saunas, treatment rooms and a carbonic acid bathtub are also available.

Clad as I am in heavy winter gear, snow boots, jeans and puffer jacket, I feel a bit odd entering this stately place, slightly underdressed and unkempt. Fortunately, these feelings prove unfounded as, alongside other similarly dressed tourists, we soon secure our private dressing room keys, locate their cold whereabouts and strip to our swimwear. Our tiny travel towels brought from home are our only defence against the biting cold.

With two hours to enjoy before our massage, time passes quickly, as accompanied by cheeky cherub statues, we lazily frolic in the heavenly warm water, drip in sweltering steam rooms and dry out in pine-scented saunas. Swimming in one of the pools, Darryl is scolded at one point for not using a hairnet.

"I'm not wearing a bloody hairnet," is his indignant response.

And despite his earlier scoffing, I am happy to brave the 7 degree outside temperature, where, covered in mushroom-sized goosebumps,

I immerse myself in delicious 40 degree water under a gloomy overcast sky.

Although only 20 minutes long, our massages are exactly what is needed to finish the experience, and I leave the massage chamber feeling totally and utterly relaxed.

"That was incredible," I say as we make our back over Freedom Bridge. "Definitely worth the money."

"How much did it cost?"

"$130 for the both of us. Something like that would have cost a fortune at home."

Hungry from our watery exertion, it doesn't take much convincing for us to stop at the laden Christmas Market discovered yesterday. Here we feast on beef goulash, Hungary's national dish, and purchase slabs of cherry strudel to be enjoyed back in our room. Not surprisingly, the mulled wine again calls to us and, following our first mug, it's easy to have another.

"We may as well," says Darryl, "enjoy them while we can."

"I agree. We won't be getting them back in Australia."

One final iconic Budapest institution that Paige and Lyle, the young guy we met on our river cruise, suggest we visit are the infamous Budapest "ruin bars." Bars built within the ruins of abandoned city buildings and decorated with whatever could be gathered from the streets. Maybe it's too early for them to have opened, or perhaps we are just too tired to search hard enough, but that evening, despite following Google Maps and the drunken mutterings of a group of young lads, we fail to locate a single one. It's disappointing, but not overly so.

Our final day in Budapest is spent lamenting our unused apartment kitchen, purchasing travelling snacks for this afternoon's train journey from a nearby supermarket and visiting Buda Castle. Perched atop a commanding hill, Buda Castle provides hours of entertainment with its 150-year-old funicular, incredible views and spiralling downhill pathways through ancient castle buildings and flowering garden beds.

Unlike Keleti, our arrival train station, Kelendoe, today's station, is a good 20-minute journey from central Budapest, and our plan is to order an Uber. Unfortunately, as we are beginning to encounter more and more with Uber, many cities have started excluding them from certain districts. As we sit in our hotel foyer and pull up the Uber app on my phone, it's with frustration that we discover they are not allowed within the Budapest inner city area. Our options are either to walk to them or find a taxi. Fortunately, Anita, a helpful receptionist, notices our dilemma and quickly orders a taxi.

Kelendoe Station is a bit of a surprise when eventually we arrive. It looks old and weathered and empty.

"Is this really the station?" Darryl questions me.

"According to Google Maps and the taxi driver it is."

"Where's the entrance? It looks abandoned," he continues.

It turns out that this is Old Kelendoe Station. New Kelendoe Station is located beneath this station, and to access it, we must use a previously unnoticed lift.

Expelled into a long underground tunnel, we use our few remaining Hungarian forints to purchase cups of awful coffee from a nearby café, and as we sit sipping these coffees, I turn to Darryl.

"These are the tickets we had to search so hard for in Moscow, and I've just noticed something. Look at the departure board. Our train originated at Deli Station. Deli Station was only about 10 minutes from our hotel."

"So, we didn't need to come all the way out here?" Darryl replies.

"That's right. Maybe we're not meant to catch this train," I laugh.

Changing the conversation, I voice my impressions of Budapest.

"I can fully understand why Paige suggested we visit here. It's a fantastic city. Beautiful buildings. Gorgeous river. Great people who are definitely the most laidback and easy-going we have encountered. And cheap. I still can't believe how cheap everything is."

"Don't forget the Christmas Markets," Darryl replies.

"How could I? I doubt we'll find better anywhere."

Unlike previous trains, our seats this time are in small compartments, rather than one long carriage. The decor is old and shabby, the window and floor both filthy, but seeing as we appear to have the small compartment to ourselves, we are happy to overlook its shortcomings and soon settle down with our books and sudoku. Within an hour, night has fallen, and a steady drizzle of rain creates long channels through the window's external grime.

At some stage, as we near the Hungarian-Croatian border, border control appears and ask for our passports.

"Where are you going?"

"Zagreb then Split."

"How long are you staying in Croatia?"

"Six nights."

"How will you be leaving?"

"By ferry to Italy."

"Thank you. You are right to continue."

"No border control on our last train which passed through four countries," I muse once they depart. "And all that, just to enter Croatia."

It appears their questions are well-founded, as shortly, we hear a small commotion. We cannot understand the language, but we soon gather that a compartment of guys further along the carriage do not meet the border control requirements. They do not appear to have the answers to the questions thrown at them and are forced to accompany the border guards. The last we see of them is at the following stop where they are escorted from the train.

Around 7 pm, a few hours shy of our destination, the remnants of our cheese and bread dinner are packed away and we turn to our window.

"There hasn't been much to look at," I comment somewhat gloomily.

"Hopefully the rain has gone by the time we arrive in Zagreb," replies Darryl.

"I hope so. Thankfully, our hotel is quite close to the station, a 200-metre walk. It makes a difference travelling in winter, doesn't it? Last time we travelled I can only remember it raining once, and every train journey was by daylight. Our train tomorrow also won't leave until late afternoon."

"What time will it reach Split?"

"Around 9:30 pm."

"So, most of our travelling through Croatia will be done in the dark."

"Nearly all of it will be. I searched for trains that left earlier in the day, but this was the only direct train travelling from Budapest to Zagreb. I presume it's because it's the off season."

"I would have liked to have seen some of the Croatian landscape," Darryl replies.

"So would I. Did you catch that?"

"It was the conductor. But whatever he said was in Croatian or Hungarian. I couldn't understand a word."

"Hopefully it wasn't important. But I might see if the guy next door speaks any English. He may be able to tell us what was said."

"I'm going to look for the toilet. If I see anyone who speaks English, I'll ask them," Darryl responds.

As we have found with most of our European encounters, our neighbour does speak a degree of English, and he explains to me that for some unrevealed purpose, we will shortly be transferring to buses for the next segment of our journey.

"I do not know why. The conductor did not say. We get on buses then back on the train. We very late arriving in Zagreb now."

Despite our language barriers, I am still conversing with him when Darryl, returning, makes his way along the carriage corridor. Intent on keeping up my end of a demanding conversation and distracted by Darryl, who I note does not have his walking stick with him, I am initially oblivious to the growing change in the train's momentum, the unconscious tensing of my body. It's only with the shrill screech of metal against metal that I awaken to the fact that I am having trouble staying upright, that I am about to fall.

For what feels like an agonising age, this feeling continues until, with an awful noise, the train hits something hard, and I find myself thrown frighteningly backwards. While our neighbour and I manage to clutch successfully at nearby walls, I can only watch in shock as Darryl, arms flailing, tries in vain to secure any support. With his paralysed leg and precarious balance, he doesn't stand a chance. As the train comes to a violent, unexpected standstill, I watch Darryl fall clumsily and heavily onto the dirty carriage floor, and I can only hope that this journey hasn't come to a sudden end.

CHAPTER 8

Croatia

*E*IGHT years ago in 2011, Darryl, along with 16 others, embarked on a motorbike journey that would take them from Australia's most easterly point, Cape Byron, to her most northerly, Cape York. Not long after reaching this desolate tip, Darryl and a good mate Jeff were involved in an accident. Devastatingly, Jeff was killed outright, and Darryl spent the following five months recovering in hospital. His injuries included a broken back, hip, femur and eleven ribs. A lung was punctured, his left side seriously burnt and his brain slightly damaged.

Along with the nerve damage that resulted in foot drop, the need for a walking stick, the pulmonary embolisms and later total hip replacement, you could say his body had taken a fair beating. He wasn't expected to live. It is the reason that I am so concerned by today's accident.

Another reason I am so concerned involves our travel insurance. On Darryl's insistence, some of his pre-existing injuries, such as his hip, were not covered for this journey: "It's a ceramic hip. Nothing's going to happen to it." Seeing him now on the floor of the train, knowing that this hip has taken the brunt of his fall, I am having true nightmares. What happens if he has broken it? What do we do now?

It's an anxious few minutes' wait, and my mind is full of worst-case scenarios, but eventually, I gingerly help Darryl regain his footing. While the hip is badly bruised and the pain is excruciating, nothing, fortunately appears to be broken. As I make a note to myself to never put ourselves in this situation again, a guard approaches and offers her assistance.

"Are you alright, sir? Can you walk? There has been an unfortunate incident with the train, but all is good now. We will be changing onto buses soon. Do you need assistance?"

"I'm all right," winces Darryl.

"I don't think he is all right," I interject. "Some help would be great."

Although there appears to be no permanent damage, Darryl is obviously in great pain and having trouble walking; I have no idea how he is going to manage the steps off the train, and assistance would be appreciated.

With help from the guard and two other gentlemen, we eventually find ourselves aboard one of three buses brought to transport passengers the next leg of the journey. As Darryl focuses on reducing his pain, the following 90 minutes are spent travelling the inky-black Croatian terrain. Tracing the train's original itinerary, our route takes us down narrow winding country lanes, through poorly lit towns and past tiny, desolate stations where the only sign of life is the odd dog or stray cat. As we travel, it is again brought home to me what a shame it is that this journey has all been undertaken in darkness. It would have been amazing to have been able to see some of the passing landscape.

Somewhere later, again with assistance, we disembark the bus and board the carriage of a crowded, light rail train. Here, our helpers disappear and we are back on our own.

Eventually, hours after the time we were due to arrive, our light rail pulls into the well-lit Zagreb Glavni Kolodvor, Zagreb's central station. It's incredibly fortunate that the hotel we have booked here, the Hotel Central, is so short a distance away. In fact, I can see its glowing red neon sign from the train as we wait to disembark.

It takes a while, but using sheer grit, Darryl manages to hobble the 200 meters to the hotel while I follow alongside with our bags. The hotel foyer smells strongly of the cigarette smoke emitted by the greasy-haired gentleman handling the reception, and our room is far removed from its glory days. Still, it has a bed onto which Darryl collapses and remains.

The following morning, Darryl, still in pain, manages to make it to breakfast, a buffet that finally begins to resemble the breakfasts we are used to. Less cucumber, sliced meat and tomatoes. More bacon, cereal and toast.

As previously discussed, our onward train to Split is not due to depart until 3:30 pm this afternoon and, grateful that he need not move for the following six hours, Darryl, after eating, heads back to bed.

Zagreb, capital of Croatia, is one of Central Europe's oldest cities, dating back to 1094. It is divided into three parts: Upper Town with iconic churches, cobbled streets and gas lamps; Lower Town with shops, restaurants, theatres and parks; and New Zagreb, built post-World War Two and full of high-rise buildings.

Although I have only a few hours, I am keen to explore and after obtaining a map from reception, soon find myself walking through Zagreb Lower Town. As I stroll through Josipa Park, I notice dozens of small white stalls under construction that appear to extend right throughout the city centre. Also under construction is a large ice skating rink. These are the early stages of Zagreb's award-winning Christmas Market, and I regret that I will not see it completed.

Ahead, an impressive spire catches my attention, so I set off in its direction. It's Zagreb Cathedral or the Cathedral of Assumption of the Blessed Virgin Mary. Built in the 11th century, this magnificent Gothic cathedral is the tallest building in Croatia, and although I don't enter, it warrants a few photos. From here, the hours slip by as I visit an outdoor market crammed with stalls of colourful flowers and intricate Christmas wreaths, obtain some Croatian kuna from an ATM and enjoy a thick, aromatic coffee in a small kerbside café.

Walking back to our hotel, I remember something from a journal written by my late father. His account of that overland journey from

London to India by motor caravan made when I was 11 months old mentions a quick overnight stop, spent camped in the carpark of a petrol station here in Zagreb. This is not, apparently, my first visit to this interesting city.

Although located a short distance away, we have given ourselves plenty of time for Darryl to limp his way back to the station. Here, a small takeaway counter provides us with tonight's dinner to be eaten on the train – a large calzone (stuffed, baked pizza dough), and some energising black coffees to be enjoyed now. As we sit drinking these coffees, our attention is caught by a couple standing close by. For the 10 or so minutes we watch them, they wail and sob, then dramatically embrace, then tenderly converse, after which the cycle repeats itself. It's compelling viewing and it's disappointing when, after one final heart-breaking sob and embrace, the lady alights a train alone, and the show ends.

The six-hour train journey between Zagreb and Split that stretches to nearly eight hours and occurs mainly in pitch-dark with Darryl in pain, will be another unforgettable train trip. More like a tram or subway car, with huge windows and hard, uncomfortable seats, our light rail tackles the craggy Croatian terrain as fiercely as any amusement park rollercoaster. With nothing to see from the windows for most of the journey, it's our bodies telling us we are climbing steep hills, plummeting down others and banking steeply to both left and right. When we do eventually reach the Croatian coast, and the lights of coastal towns become visible from our window far, far below, our rollercoaster only gets more excited. We dip and weave, slow down, speed up, stop then start until eventually over an hour and a half late, we glide into Split train station.

Our hotel in Split, the Plaza Marche Old Town, is located an easy 15-minute walk from the train station, but it's a walk Darryl is just not up to. We have phoned the hotel and warned them of our late arrival.

"We have arrived and will be catching a taxi to you," I advise the hotel receptionist.

"That is fine," she replies. "But vehicles are unable to enter the Split Old Town. I will meet you at the entrance to the Old Town and help you."

Like in Budapest, the station is empty by the time Darryl and I exit and head towards the taxi stand. It's drizzling and dark with no discernible life, and it takes a good 20 minutes before a taxi arrives.

The taxi ride is ridiculously short but necessary, and patiently waiting for us in the rain with her umbrella is Josipa, the hotel receptionist. With her help, we manage to hobble the final few hundred metres to our accommodation.

Located right on the Adriatic Sea with the dramatic coastal mountains we have just roller coasted down as its backdrop, Split, after Zagreb, is Croatia's second-largest city, with a population of about 250,000. Originating around the 2nd or 3rd century, it was the retirement of the Roman Emperor Diocletian in 305 AD that really put Split on the map – or rather, it was the house he built to retire in. More a fortified, walled palace than a house, Diocletian spared no expense: beautiful limestone was sourced from local quarries, gorgeous marble was imported from Italy, ornate columns from Greece and 12 sphinxes from Egypt.

Today, Diocletian's Palace, now considered the largest and best-preserved example of Roman architecture in the world, forms Split Old Town and simply bursts with trendy shops, stylish bars and great restaurants. Abutting the Palace's southern wall and facing the Adriatic Sea is Riva, Split's palm tree-lined promenade, a perfect place to eat, drink, people-watch, exercise or just soak up the sun.

Located within the Old Town's walls and mere metres from most of the city's best sites, the Plaza Marche is a beautiful new hotel built within a 1,700-year-old facade. As we check-in, marvelling at the lovely limestone walls, Josipa gives us a bit of a run-down.

"We have only been open for a year. It took a lot of planning before permission was granted to turn this into a hotel. If you look through here, you can see the actual basement of the Diocletian Palace. It may look familiar to you if you are *Game of Thrones* fans. This is the cellar where Daenerys kept her dragons."

Beautiful and thrilling as it all is, there is one drawback. The lift to our rooftop room commences from the first floor, and to reach it we must climb a set of stairs.

"It's fine," Darryl insists. "I'll use them as my physiotherapy."

With Josipa carrying most of our luggage ("I gave up my gym membership when I started working here"), we arrive at our beautifully furnished room with a bigger than king-size bed. Here, with the time approaching midnight and shattered from our long day, we simply collapse into the bed's soft, welcoming embrace.

Waking, and from our roof-top window, I can see that the previous evening's rain has disappeared leaving a startlingly blue sky in its wake. Also visible is a creamy-white stone building with a Rapunzel-like turret and a cobbled marble market square. Surrounded by ancient limestone buildings with terracotta tiled roofs, it's a view straight out of *Game of Thrones*.

Making our way downstairs, a new friendly receptionist greets us.

"Dobro jutro. Good morning. You are looking for breakfast? Unfortunately, we do not have a restaurant but take this voucher and go to Zinfandels just down that laneway. They will give you breakfast."

While an off-site restaurant is unexpected and not the most convenient for Darryl, it does allow us to start exploring Split immediately. The following delicious à la carte meal is also a welcome relief from our recent run of buffets.

Full of my acai bowl and Darryl, his scrambled eggs, the morning is spent slowly exploring Split Old Town; we have decided to leave adventuring outside the city walls until Darryl's hip is feeling a little better. The Ethnographic Museum is located close by, and here we spend an hour or so viewing its collection of costumes, jewellery, pottery, knitting and other items that portray Split's old ways of life. It's easy to get a good view of everything as we find ourselves the museum's lone visitors. While the exhibits are slightly dull – there are only so many costumes one wants to look at – the views offered from the rooftop terrace are worth the visit.

Leaving the still-empty museum, we wind our way through Split's ancient, marble streets. Riva, the seaside promenade full of busy bars and restaurants, looks excellent and we look forward to returning for a drink or meal. There are even the beginnings of a Christmas Market. Still in the process of being erected, it promises more mulled wine.

The fish market or "ribarnica" repels us both with its strong smell of fish. We are not seafood lovers, but the Green Market – a fresh produce market full of seasonal fruit, glowing vegetables and vibrant flowers – looks great.

Our walk back to our room takes us through the very heart of Diocletian's Palace – the Peristyle, a stunning sunken marble rectangle surrounded on three sides by large limestone columns supporting marble and limestone arches. From here, it's possible to access the Palace cellar where, despite its scattering of little artisan stalls, it's possible to imagine dragons lurking.

Having noticed over breakfast that the Zinfandel restaurant is also a boutique wine bar offering a large variety of Croatian wines, it's an easy decision to return there for dinner. Talked into ordering their speciality, a three-tiered tower loaded with freshly cooked pasta, warm soya salad, cheeses, salamis and olives, the evening passes slowly and pleasantly in a wine and food fug.

Our bed truly is bigger than king-size and incredibly comfortable. Following a repeat of yesterday's breakfast, I find myself back on this bed and while Darryl catches up on laundry, I start to make changes to our upcoming itinerary. With Darryl's hip limiting our immediate movements, we have been forced to.

Our original intention, once we left Split, had been to spend two nights in Rome before making our way to the Amalfi Coast and Sorrento, where we have an apartment (with washing machine) booked for five nights. We had planned on visiting the little towns of Positano, Ravello and Amalfi, and a full day had been scheduled for visiting the buried city of Pompeii, a life-long dream of mine.

Unfortunately, the Amalfi Coast, with its steep mountainsides, difficult to negotiate terrain and vast crowds, is just not possible for Darryl now.

Although disappointed to be missing such a stunning stretch of Italian coastline, it is quite fun, with a map of Italy open on my laptop, to work out a new, less strenuous itinerary. With so much to choose from – should we revisit Lucca, a town we visited and loved back in 2017? Should we stay five extra nights in Rome? Should we revisit crowded Florence, or should we find an unknown little Italian village somewhere? – it's some time before a new itinerary emerges.

"How about this?" I call to Darryl. "We extend our time in Rome by an extra night, so it becomes three nights now. We then catch a train to Verona, Romeo and Juliet's city where we stay three nights. Then we re-join our original itinerary in Milan where we stay an extra night, so two nights there now instead of one."

"I'm sorry to be missing out on Sorrento," Darryl replies. "It's the only place we were staying for five nights, the longest stay anywhere on this trip. But what you're suggesting sounds good. I'm not sure about Romeo and Juliet, though."

"I love the idea of visiting the place where Romeo and Juliet was set," I reply. "Of visiting Juliet's balcony. I just have to book the trains and cancel the hotels."

"Is that easy enough to do?" Darryl questions.

"It should be. That's why I like using Booking.com. There won't be any accommodation cancellation charges providing we cancel within a day or two of arrival. We will lose a seat reservation fee on our train travel, but they will only be small seat fees rather than the full ticket charge."

By lunchtime, all train and accommodation cancellations have been made, new seat reservations secured and hotels booked or extended. The worry of future uncertainty eliminated.

Months ago, when booking this adventure, it had been hit and miss as to whether we would be able to obtain cabin tickets on the Jadrolinija ferry that would transport us from Croatia to Italy, the following country on our itinerary. Plenty of seats were available if you wanted to spend the night sitting upright in uncomfortable chairs, but cabins with beds were a little scarcer. Fortunately, we had managed to secure one, and with Darryl now capable of walking a little further, this afternoon we set off to locate the Split terminal. It is here that our ferry will depart in a few days.

Like yesterday, the morning's bluebell sky has sadly disappeared behind grey afternoon clouds. Walking further along the Riva promenade under this damp canopy, we enjoy the sight of a group of fishermen eagerly hauling in their catch. It's only on closer inspection do we see that they are fishing where a wastewater or maybe sewer pipe discharges into the sea.

"No wonder they are doing so well," we laugh.

We also explore further into the heart of Split. Here, beautiful limestone buildings dating back to the 6th century like St. Johns Baptistry, Diocletian's Mausoleum and the Cathedral of St. Domnius prove incredible viewing. Interestingly, again we are the sole visitors at many of the sites. A highlight of our afternoon is the sight of a group of men (a klapa group) singing in what is known as the Vestibul, a cavernous, domed, open-roofed stone structure. Here, we pause and enjoy the klapa's a cappella performance and marvel at the sound amplified by the building's crazy acoustics.

With sundown, the rain that has been threatening all afternoon finally triumphs. Few awnings cover the Split streets, and with the cobbled marble footpaths turning lethal, we are both loath to venture out into the wet, cold night. But hungry, and with the image of a cosy Italian restaurant noticed earlier etched in our minds, we brave the elements. In this little restaurant, the miserable conditions outside are soon forgotten as we feast on hearty lasagne, tender meatballs and crisp salad.

Later that evening, as the rain continues to splash against our window and as I work on a blog in our warm, beautiful bed, I quickly scan my emails.

"Brilliant," I cry.

"What?" replies Darryl.

"We have West Ham tickets."

"For Boxing Day? West Ham versus Crystal Palace?"

"Yep."

"Great. That's really great. Thank you."

Today, and the weather report is supposedly good for the entire day; no afternoon clouds followed by miserable rain. Which is fortunate, for tonight, the Split ice skating rink along with the city's second Christmas Market, will be opening and we are looking forward to enjoying a mulled wine while watching the locals skate.

Firstly, however, we plan to visit the Split Archaeological Museum. This museum, located a 20-minute stroll from the city centre, dates to 1820. It is the oldest museum in Croatia and also one of the oldest archaeological museums in Eastern Europe.

With the sun warm on our faces, the first time we have felt it so welcoming since we left Australia, we make our way along the harbourfront, past the well-stocked marina full of fat little yachts and through some sprawling green parklands, eventually arriving at an impressive creamy limestone building. For the following hour, we again enjoy being the sole visitors to a museum and poke happily amongst the ancient coins, jewellery and sarcophagi.

It's a Saturday today, a fact that becomes more apparent as we follow the waterfront back into the Old Town. Families are out in force, joggers are exercising, men are playing bocce and the Adriatic contains dozens of kids, each steering a tiny sailing boat. It must be their Saturday morning sport; their equivalent to our weekend football or netball. At some stage, we relax on a couple of conveniently provided wooden deckchairs. As we lazily recline, a massive bouquet of brightly coloured balloons in the shape of dogs, cars and other characters floats high overhead.

"Look," I laugh. "I think a stall holder has just lost their entire stock of balloons to the wind."

Located outside the Golden Gate, one of four Roman gates into Diocletian's Palace, is an 8.5-metre-tall statue of Gregory of Nin, a medieval bishop famous for helping introduce the Croatian language into Catholic services throughout Croatia. It is said that if you rub his big toe, your wish will be granted. That evening, as we make our way towards the newly opened ice skating rink, we rub Gregory's much-rubbed toe, make a wish, then grab ourselves some blitva, a savoury pie full of Swiss chard, and a cup of mulled wine. We enjoy these while watching exuberant kids and adults struggle to remain upright on the slippery ice, and nearby, a large 12-piece orchestra plays upon a rotunda.

Leaving here and keen to see Riva at night, we again traverse Split's rabbit-warren streets, eventually arriving at the waterfront promenade. It's currently crowded with Saturday night revellers and noisy with the music of a large rock band. At many of the Christmas stalls, patrons are feasting on kobasice (homemade pork sausages) and fritule (little balls of fried dough dusted with icing sugar) or swilling beer and mulled wine as they huddle over warming braziers. Above us, the moon competes to outshine myriad Christmas lights, and it's all a glorious fitting finale to our final night in Croatia.

Our overnight ferry to Italy departs at 8 pm and, fortunately, being a quiet Sunday, our accommodation has allowed us a late 6 pm check-out. Plenty of time for any last-minute sightseeing before showering, packing and boarding.

This morning, Marija, another of the Plaza Marche's lovely receptionists, tells us that Zinfandel is closed on Sundays and our breakfast will be provided by Plaza Marche's sister hotel. It's a good 15-minute walk through a dozing Split Old Town and along the waterfront to this new establishment, and I am quite relieved that it is not raining.

It's actually our sunniest Split day yet, and with the Riva cafés looking so inviting with their little canopy-covered waterfront tables, it's an easy decision to spend some of our remaining time in one of them. It will also be an excellent opportunity to spend the last of our Croatian kuna.

"We have enough kuna left for a drink each," Darryl says, pulling out his wallet.

"Nothing left after that?"

"Maybe just enough for one single drink."

"How about, seeing as your beer is more than twice the size of my wine, I get two wines?"

It's a good suggestion, and the day passes easily as we contentedly people-watch in the warm Croatian sun.

With our departure time drawing nearer and knowing we still must pack, we make a quick visit to the over-hyped and empty Game of Thrones Museum, rub Gregory's shiny toe one final time and farewell Daenerys' dragon lair. Packing is done methodically and quickly, seeing as the procedure is now very familiar. The only hiccup occurs when I discover ants have created a home in a block of chocolate in my backpack.

Looking forward to reaching Italy, it is nonetheless sad to be departing Split. Our accommodation here has been incredible, the nicest room yet with the loveliest staff. Our four-night stay has also enabled Darryl time to recover. He is still in pain and walking needs to be taken slowly, but this four-day extended rest has been precisely what he needed. Split has also been fantastic, with its beautiful limestone buildings, marble streets, great food, empty museums and friendly people; our stay here has been truly memorable.

It's completely dark when we farewell Josipa and wheel our bags through Split Old Town and out along the esplanade. Ahead, our ferry with its lights fully ablaze, looks awesome and very photo-worthy. Stopping to take a photo, I ask Darryl to stand slightly to one side so as he can be in the picture. To do so, Darryl lets go of his roll-on bag which immediately starts rolling towards the harbour's edge, gaining momentum as it does so. Paralysed with shock, we both watch in horror as it rolls closer and closer to the water. Certain that the bag will tip over the edge, probably never to be seen again, we are incredulous when a miracle occurs. A couple walking along behind us, unknowingly step between our wayward bag and the water at precisely the right moment. They simultaneously utter grunts of surprise when Darryl's bag careens into them, halting its momentum and preventing its watery demise. It truly is a miracle.

"What would you have missed most?" I ask once we have got over our shock and finished laughing.

"My new cashmere jumper," is his surprising reply.

While we know that there will be a restaurant onboard our ferry where we hope to purchase dinner, we have learnt not to ignore a supermarket while travelling. In the supermarket, conveniently located within the ferry terminal, we buy some replacement chocolate for me and a massive loaf of bread and cheese for Darryl.

From the supermarket, we head towards customs, where everything goes quickly and smoothly (no doubt because it's a quiet, winter Sunday night). After a cursory look at our passports and a stamp, we are free to board.

"Um. Can you see where we are meant to go?"

"No idea. And it doesn't look as if anyone else knows where to board either."

"You would think someone would be around to show people the way."

While there is plenty of help provided for the multitude of cars journeying with us to Italy, none has been provided to assist foot passengers. It takes time and is undoubtably dangerous, seeing as we end up just joining the queue of cars, but eventually, we board. Here, a lift deposits us at reception, a steward checks us in and we are handed our keys.

"Wow. It's small. And dirty. And green," I comment as we enter our cabin.

"At least it's got a toilet and shower," Darryl counters.

"I'll take the top bunk. There is no way you would be able to get up that ladder."

Dinner is a choice of buffet or à la carte, and we are the restaurant's first diners. The buffet wins our patronage seeing as it's available immediately, and we can see what we will be eating: enormous plates of meat stew accompanied by potatoes and a few vegetables. Despite the meal's oily appearance, it is tasty and is easily washed down with a local Croatian beer.

Keen to settle down for the night, it's not long before we return to our cabin, complete our ablutions in the small bathroom and tuck ourselves into our narrow bunks.

Constantly awoken by the loud clang of something against the ship's hull, the night is diesel-scented, disturbing and very, very long. The beds are rock-hard, small and narrow. Their only redeeming feature is that their size means there is little chance of tipping out with the ship's roll. While Darryl appears to enjoy a great night's slumber, I do not, and eventually, in the very early hours, give up on getting back to sleep. I just lie there in my little coffin-like bunk, in our small coffin-like cabin and pray for the long night to end, for the clanging and rolling to stop, to reach Italian soil.

CHAPTER 9

Italy

*I*T'S close to 7 am when our ferry pulls into the port of Ancona, and despite the lack of sleep, I am alert and keen to disembark. Making our way down a long, narrow flight of stairs (the lifts will not be available for at least another hour), it's with sighs of relief that we step out onto the bustling dock. Again, there's no real guidance on where to walk or where to exit the ferry terminal, and it's only through luck that we locate customs. Here, border control is even more cursory, and within minutes we find ourselves searching for a taxi under a cold, grey Italian sky.

"You don't require seat reservations if travelling on regional trains in Italy, our Eurail passes are enough," I mention as we wait. "But the first direct train to Rome from here leaves at 9 am. There isn't another until 3 pm."

"It's just on 8 am now," Darryl replies. "We should have plenty of time to reach the station and find the correct platform."

It's a good 20 minutes before a taxi does arrive, and by then, we are starting to feel slightly anxious; however, this anxiety proves needless. Italians are notorious for driving erratically and fast, and our taxi driver is no exception. Within moments of throwing our bags into the boot, we find ourselves catapulted out of the harbour, across long bridges and through Ancona city. It's not long before, with an uncomfortable jerk, we pull up in front of Ancona train station.

"That's probably the first time I didn't mind a fast taxi ride," I say as we wheel our bags into the station.

"At least it's given us time to get a coffee and find the platform," Darryl replies. "And I didn't get to eat any of my bread and cheese last night. I'll eat that now."

The correct platform is not difficult to locate, and while Darryl hunts out his bread and cheese, I search for a café.

"Due latte per favore," I say as I order and pay at the counter, then "grazie," as I collect our drinks.

Returning with our coffees, I can only laugh at Darryl. A loaf of unsliced bread is not the easiest to eat sitting on a station bench, and there are breadcrumbs scattered everywhere. Enjoying these morsels are a large flock of pushy pigeons eagerly surrounding Darryl and looking for more. My laughter on his behalf, however, is short-lived.

"What is this?" Darryl splutters, sipping his coffee.

"A latte," I reply.

"It tastes like milk."

"Oh," I frown. "Latte does mean milk in Italian. I think I was meant to say caffè latte. I've just bought two cups of hot milk."

It takes approximately four hours for our train to travel from Ancona to Rome, our east to west journey cutting through the belly button of Italy. Long flatlands with repeating orchards of olives and grapes and distant castles give way to mountainous terrain before closing in on the more industrial Italian capital. At 12:45 pm, we eventually pull into the vast Rome Termini station.

"Our hotel is near the Trevi Fountain. But it's too far to walk."

"How far is it?" Darryl questions.

"I'm not sure but probably a good 30 or 40 minutes. I think it would be best to get a taxi."

"I'd prefer to walk," Darryl argues, remembering past arrivals into cities where the walk to our room would be enjoyable and a good way of orienting ourselves.

"I'm not sure what the streets are going to be like. There are probably heaps of cobblestones here," I argue back.

"It doesn't matter; it's a great way to see the city. I want to walk."

Although not looking forward to the hike to our hotel, I surrender and almost instantly regret my decision. The following 30-minute journey spent struggling with rutted cobblestones, avoiding fast-flowing Roman traffic, dodging copious quantities of dog crap, all the while studiously ignoring each other, is one of the poorer memories of our global adventure.

Adding to the tension is the fact that we had forgotten that it is wiser to look for your accommodation by street address rather than name while in Italy.

Expecting a well-signed hotel, frustrations build as we search in vain for our abode and it's only when we concentrate on the address that we notice a tiny plaque alongside many others on a large residential building. The Domus Trevi, our accommodation for the following three nights is, surprisingly, not a hotel but rather a bed and breakfast located on the third floor of a housing block.

To enter the building, we need to announce ourselves by speakerphone, which we do and are shortly greeted by Giulia. Giulia is lovely and chatters incessantly as she shows us in.

"Welcome, welcome. This way, this way. We have a lift. It is very good, but it is very small," she says, as she notices Darryl's walking stick. To me she adds, "Maybe you can take the stairs?" And then to Darryl, "And you can go in the lift with the bags?"

Guiding us further into the building's dark, marble interior, a lot of our animosity evaporates when we come across the fascinating lift Giulia is so proudly espousing. This hundreds of years old, five-storey apartment block, originally built without a lift, encases a central, open-air courtyard. Here, years after the building's construction, a glass-walled tube was erected and inside sits a tiny movable platform. About the same size as a small refrigerator, it looks great, but there is no way we are both going to fit into it; it's a squeeze to get our bags in alongside Darryl.

Needless to say, Darryl is totally shattered when we eventually reach our tiny, worn room. Just big enough to hold a low-set double bed, its redeeming qualities are the newly renovated ensuite and large, shuttered windows, thick enough to drown out the sounds of humming Rome.

"I'm going to just rest," he tells me, exhausted.

"I think I'll go and have a look around," I reply.

Rome, one of the world's greatest ever civilisations, has a long and complex history. Spanning over two and a half thousand years from its humble beginnings as a small Latin village around 800 BC, to the centre of the vast Roman Empire (27 BC-476 AD), to today's capital of Italy, Rome's footprint on the world has undoubtedly been productive and fascinating. It was the Romans who brought us modern-day concrete, under-floor heating, social welfare, aqueducts, sewers, roads, bound books and carbonara. And it was the Roman Empire that aided the spread of Christianity around the globe. It goes without saying that a nation with such a history, a nation that has bought the world so much, must have a cityscape worthy of its heritage; we are looking forward to exploring it.

Making my way back down the flight of stairs, beautiful by their broad marble tread and heavy marble balustrades, I exit the building into a narrow cobblestone lane. This lane, no more than 70 metres long, terminates at a T-intersection. Stepping out from here, I come to an abrupt halt. Immediately in front of me is the Trevi Fountain, the incredibly gorgeous baroque masterpiece that 300 years ago replaced a fountain that had been sitting here since 19 BC. Carved from gleaming white calcium carbonate, the same material as the Colosseum, and looking like something from a movie set, this elaborate water feature is absolutely riveting, and I stand mesmerised along with hundreds of other staring tourists. It's nearly inconceivable that the elegant cloth-draped bodies, the smooth curved arches and the rounded columns of this fountain began their existence as large misshapen blocks of stone. It is some time before I can tear my gaze away and continue.

My walk takes me further along the cobbled path of Via Del Lavatore, a narrow street full of enticing cafés, pizza stalls and shops full of leather goods. It's hard not to get sidetracked by the gleaming displays of aromatic leather handbags, shoes and clutches, but I stroll on; the shops will still be here tomorrow. At the end of the street, I come upon a humming supermarket, handy for future supplies but, for now, only water. Hungry, as I make my back to our room, I stop and purchase a slice of pizza from one of the many little stalls displaying trays of the cheesy treat. For three euro or just under 5 Australian dollars, I get a massive slice of tasty pizza and eat it in front of the splashing waters of the Trevi Fountain.

Back in our cosy, shuttered little room, Darryl is happy to remain just where he is. His hip is sore, he is not hungry and the television, our first in a long while, is surprisingly therapeutic.

Refreshed after a good night's sleep, we both awaken eager to get out and explore. It's not the first time we have visited this city and we are looking forward to retracing our steps. In 1990 while working at a travel agency in London, it was my job to secure accommodation for large tour groups visiting here. In order to understand better the people and place I was working with every day, Darryl and I paid Rome a visit, appreciating the free accommodation we were given. Today, we are looking forward to creating new memories.

Before setting out, over flaky golden croissants, cereal, fruit and coffees, we chat with Giulia.

"We were thinking of using the Hop-On bus, but maybe we should just walk instead?"

"No need for the bus," Giulia replies. "This is a very good location. It is easy to walk everywhere. I will give you a map."

Handing us this map, Giulia also imparts the following titbits of information.

"Rome has more than 900 churches, and 280 fountains... The first-ever shopping mall was built in Rome around 107 AD... The Spanish Steps are not really Spanish."

Shortly after leaving Giulia still zealously imparting information to fellow guests, I have fun watching Darryl's reaction to the Trevi

Fountain.

"It's so close. We could probably hear the water splashing from our room," he marvels.

One of my lasting memories of our 1990 visit concerns the legend surrounding this Trevi Fountain. The tale went that if one threw a coin into the Fountain, they would return to Rome. For some reason, we never had a coin back then to throw, and over the years, I have wondered if that would prevent us from returning to Rome. Standing now, in front of this beautiful piece of art, I remind Darryl of this story.

"We still don't have a coin to throw in," he laughs.

Continuing our walk, it's not long before another observation from our previous visit to Rome comes back to me. I remember then being constantly surprised by the wealth of ancient buildings, the abundance of historical monuments, the medieval piazzas that appeared to present themselves around every corner. I remember continually uttering the refrain, "Wow, look at that." It's the same today as we leave the Trevi Fountain and make our way along Via del Corso stumbling first upon the Piazza di San Marcello, then the Piazza Venezia.

"Remember this?" Darryl asks, as we stop and gaze at the elaborate monument known by locals as the 'typewriter' situated in Piazza Venezia.

"We stopped and had lunch near here in 1990," I reply.

"Yes, and it costs us over $40 for a miserable sandwich and beer each. That would equate to nearly $80 today."

"It looks a bit dirtier than I remember, but it still looks pretty amazing."

A short time later, standing in front of the vast relic-strewn area known as the Roman Forum, I comment, "It looks like they have done a lot more excavation work here! I'm sure it didn't have this many temples nor look this impressive."

"It looks a lot bigger," Darryl agrees. "It might be good to have a look through once we have visited the Colosseum."

Lending weight to my observation there is something incredible to see around every corner in Rome, the Colosseum is within a stone's throw of the ancient ruins where we are currently standing.

Commencing in the year 72 AD and constructed over eight years, the limestone Colosseum, the largest amphitheatre ever built, is without doubt the main symbol of Rome. Able to hold up to 80,000 spectators, it was built to host spectacular gladiatorial contests, battle re-enactments, executions and dramatic performances. Today, despite being ravaged by vandalism, earthquakes and fire, it attracts nearly 6 million visitors per year.

Approaching the Colosseum without pre-booked tickets, it takes some minutes to orient ourselves. We know many European sites offer 'skip the queue' entry for the infirm like Darryl or the elderly; we just have to work out where to obtain this dispensation. Fortunately, a security guard notices our hesitation and points us in the right direction. Within a short time, we have managed to not only skip the line but have also obtained free entry, the only payment being for the portable audio guides we now consider mandatory.

Inside, it's immediately apparent that, like the Roman Forum, much renovation work has occurred here since our 1990 visit. Back then, there was very little of the amphitheatre's floor; today, a very recent landing seems to be either under construction in parts or entirely reconstructed in others. Surface walls also look significantly cleaner, and one extensive section has been wholly shored up by scaffolding. What is the same, however, are the large crowds. For the 90 or so minutes we spend exploring this great building, we do so fighting for space amongst the many other tourists, with the audio guides expounding in our ears.

"There were some female gladiators... Gladiators were generally slaves or prisoners of war... Up to 10,000 animals could be killed in one day during a gladiatorial event... After four centuries it fell into neglect... Used as little more than a quarry for a thousand years... All of its marble seats disappeared..."

We depart the Colosseum with the impression that despite the crowds, we have just witnessed something incredible, that it is so fortunate that ancient structures like this still exist.

Hoping to augment this sense, we head back to the Roman Forum where we find tickets are required to enter.

"Where do we buy them?" we query a nearby attendant.

"Back at the Colosseum," we are told. "But, if you still have your Colosseum tickets, you can use those to enter."

"You mean these?" I ask, pulling two tatty, scrunched up pieces of paper from the bottom of my bag.

"Yes, those."

"That was lucky," I say as we enter through the turnstiles. "I nearly threw those tickets away."

The Roman Forum, we soon learn, was ancient Rome's showpiece: its beating heart. Thanks to one of the world's earliest sewerage systems, in the 7th century BC the Romans turned a marshy burial ground into an extensive district of grand temples, imposing civic buildings and vibrant public places. This perfect showcase of Roman power is where Julius Caesar was cremated and where Marc Antony displayed the heads of his fallen enemies. Like the Colosseum, this area also fell into ruin with the collapse of the Roman Empire, and it is only through excavation works that commenced in the 18th century and continue today that we can wander amongst the remarkable ruins that exist here.

It is within one of these ruins that we shortly come across a sad scene. A man has collapsed onto the cold, dirty ground, and his wife is desperately calling for help. Too far away to offer assistance and with little in the way of Italian language skills, we can only watch as a crowd gathers, and a jacket is gently placed over the man. It's a good 40 minutes later, as we are exiting the Roman Forum, that an ambulance pulls up in front of us. No doubt here to help the unfortunate patient, we can only hope that all goes well.

The Pantheon, the best-preserved of Rome's ancient monuments, was the first building we came across during our 1990 visit and we both have a soft spot for it; although back then, it was not possible to enter its impressive doors. Unexpectedly stumbling across it now, it's a real buzz to discover that today not only is admission permissible, but it's also free.

Completed circa 127 AD, it's a bit of a mystery how the Pantheon, a building so ahead of its time, survived Rome's tumultuous past. With its giant domed ceiling, famous oculus (eye) and windowless walls, it remains the world's largest unsupported dome and a true testament to the genius of Roman architecture. Operating since 609 AD as a Catholic church, we eagerly follow the hoards into the building, where we are immediately hushed by our surroundings.

"The diameter of the dome is 43.3 metres," Darryl eventually reads as we stand staring at the impossibly large domed ceiling that cups us like a giant stone umbrella. "Which is the exact distance from the floor to the top of the dome."

"And they built it 2,000 years ago?" I marvel, shaking my head. "How did they do it and how is it still standing?"

Whatever the answer, the building is truly incredible, and we spend time not only gazing at the captivating stone ceiling but also at the original marble floor and surrounding stone tombs.

"Raphael, the artist, is buried here – I wonder why?" is my final, unanswered observation.

Departing the Pantheon, our route takes us through tiny, dark cobblestone alleys, past compelling ancient buildings and alongside 2,000-year-old Roman remnants. We pass sculptures by creative masters such as Michelangelo and fountains by Bernini. Constantly awed and surprised, we appreciate even further the ease with which one can see and experience so much in Rome.

At one stage, our path is hindered by the arrival of the S.S. Lazio football team, and we are forced to watch their antics as they parade down the street. Another time, I am captivated by an alley bursting with leather goods. With the lovely aroma of leather surrounding me, I browse a few of the shops but again leave the purchase of something until later. Eventually, we stumble upon Rome's iconic Spanish Steps.

The Spanish Steps are a set of broad, irregular stairs that climb a steep slope to connect the lower Piazza di Spagna (Spanish Square) with the upper Piazza Trinita Dei Monti on which sits the Trinita Dei Monti Church. Unique in design, these 138 steps constructed in 1723 have been a popular meeting place over the centuries, attracting tourists, artists and poets alike. John Keats, the English poet, lived and died in a house adjoining these steps which is now a popular museum.

Not wishing to make the arduous climb, we stand alongside the 17th century Fountain of the Ugly Boat that rests at the base and just observe.

"I read recently that a rule has just been passed forbidding anyone to sit on the Spanish Steps now," I muse.

"Why is that?" Darryl queries.

"People would sit here for too long. They would get in the way of those actually using them. The rule was only introduced in August this year. At the same time, a rule forbidding anyone from wading in the Trevi Fountain was also passed. And they are called the Spanish Steps, not because they are Spanish, but because the Spanish Consulate was once located here."

Making our way back to our room, I can only appreciate that we didn't bother with the Hop-On bus. Rome is quite a small city with a lot crowded into it, and today's exploits have proven that even someone with walking difficulties can traverse it easily enough.

Via del Lavatore, the popular tourist street minutes from our accommodation, is busy at night and touts are kept active as they attempt to lure customers into enticing little restaurants. Searching for dinner and one such tout is successful. Entering a dark, cavernous bistro strewn with red tablecloths, it's not long before huge plates of tender veal scaloppini and steaming beef bolognese appear in front of us. Costing around 60 Australian dollars – expensive compared to all our previous meals to date – the feast is nonetheless tasty and filling. A creamy Italian gelato purchased on our walk back to our room from one of the many ice-cream stalls makes a delicious dessert.

With Giulia's endless anecdotes again raining down on us over breakfast, we can only enjoy our buttery croissants and listen.

"There is no need to buy water in Rome, you can drink the water from the many fountains... Raphael was buried in the Pantheon because he asked to be... Rome is older than Italy. Rome only joined Italy when it was unified at the end of the 19th century... There is a secret passageway to the Vatican from the Castel Sant'Angelo."

Highly impressed by Giulia's fount of knowledge, we jump in when she pauses for breath and question her further on visiting Vatican City and its museum.

"We haven't pre-purchased tickets. What do you think the queues will be like at this time of year?" Darryl asks her.

"The queues are usually very long," she replies. "As you approach the museum, you will be approached by touts selling guided tours. They are very good. I would suggest you purchase one of their tours."

"Any idea how much it will cost?" I ask.

"Around 50 euro for the both of you."

"That sounds reasonable; we'll see how it goes."

Vatican City was established in 1929 as the answer to the pope's refusal to accept the 1861 unification of Italy. Loath to relinquish more than a thousand years of control over Rome, numerous popes took refuge in the Vatican, and it wasn't until the signing of the Lateran Treaty by Pope Pius XI that they were appeased. The Lateran Treaty paved the way for the establishment of the independent state of Vatican City and reaffirmed the status of Catholic Christianity within Italy. Today, Vatican City, the smallest country in the world, mints its own euros, prints its own stamps, issues its own passports and has its own flag. The only government function it lacks is taxation, instead relying on contributions, its accompanying museum and souvenir sales for revenue.

Like everything else so far in Rome, it's also located within an easy stroll from our room: a walk that will take us past countless ancient buildings and alongside the River Tiber. The water, we note when we reach it, is just as filthy and polluted as it was during our 1990 visit.

While it was as recently as 1929 that Vatican City was established as its own independent country, the actual buildings themselves commenced with the construction of the first basilica over the grave of St. Peter in the 4th century. Subsequent centuries saw the emergence of other notable structures such as the Sistine Chapel, the Apostolic Palace, the home of the pope should they choose to live there (Pope Francis doesn't, preferring a humbler abode) and the newer second St. Peter's Basilica. Not long after leaving the polluted Tiber, we eventually arrive at the currently gated, football pitch-sized area that borders the basilica: breathtaking St. Peter's Square.

"Look. It's gated and closed – it doesn't look as if we can enter," I say with dismay. "People are being turned away. Why?"

"I'm not sure but let's give it a go anyway," Darryl says, using his standard reply.

Approaching one of these gates, each with an X-ray scanner every bit as forbidding as those used at airports, the guards are at first hesitant to allow us in. Then spying Darryl's walking stick, they wave us through. Once inside, their presence (and reluctance) become apparent: Pope Francis has just begun Mass, and until he finishes, no one else will be entering. While we stop, take photos and listen for a good 20 minutes, the standing is uncomfortable for Darryl, so we decide instead to search for the Vatican Museum. We'll return and explore St. Peter's Square and the basilica later.

The Vatican Museum is located outside of St. Peter's Square. Trailing the imposing brick wall that will guide us to it, as Giulia predicted, a tout approaches. This tout, however, advises that 'skip the queue' tickets will cost 57 euro *each,* which is a bit more than we were expecting.

"That's twice what Giulia said, and more than I have researched," I comment. "I think we just brave it and queue."

"I agree."

It doesn't take much longer to reach the museum entrance, and here a welcome surprise awaits us.

"Look, there's no queue at all."

"And look at the entry fee," Darryl drily adds. "Only 17 euro per person."

Amassed within two palaces, three courtyards and 7 kilometres of halls and corridors, the Vatican Museum contains one of the world's greatest collections. With over 70,000 pieces of work ranging from Egyptian mummies, Etruscan bronzes and ancient busts, to old masters and modern paintings, this is the collection of treasures stockpiled by the various Popes over the centuries. Established during the 16th century, these days, the Museum receives over 6 million visitors annually, most here to see the Michelangelo's Sistine Chapel and the suite of rooms covered in frescoes by Raphael.

Entering with our de rigueur portable audio guides, it takes us two hours to explore the enormous, sprawling complex, and we depart, never having gazed upon anything like it. Better than the images conveyed by the most lavish movie or satisfying book, it's even more incredible than Putin's Kremlin, Mao's Forbidden City or Marie Antoinette's Versailles. Long corridors completely covered in complex, colourful frescoes. Imposing marble and bronze statues. Grandiose mosaic floors. Innumerous ancient relics. Egyptian mummies. Paintings by Titian, tapestries by Raphael and masterpieces by Leonardo da Vinci and Michelangelo. The list is endless. Someone once said that world poverty would be eliminated if all the treasures in the Vatican Museums were sold, and I can now understand how.

While the four rooms displaying the frescoes of Raphael and his workshop are undeniably impressive, they don't come close to Michelangelo's Sistine Chapel. Fortunately securing a seat in this serene sanctuary, we can only sit and gaze in wonder at the masterpieces enveloping us.

"Incredible that this is also the place where they select a new pope," a lady next to me sighs. "The eligible cardinals are locked in here until they reach a two-thirds majority on a new pope."

"And isn't the result of the vote indicated by smoke?"

"Yes. Twice a day a vote is taken. If there isn't a two-thirds majority winner, the votes are burnt with a dye or something that will produce black smoke. When a winner emerges, the votes are burnt with something that will make the smoke white, thus letting everyone waiting outside know that a new Pope has been chosen."

Dominating the Roman skyline, St. Peter's Basilica is the largest church in the world and the most famous piece of Renaissance architecture. It's also the final resting place of 91 of the 264 Popes who have died since St. Peter, the church's first leader. It impressed us hugely during our 1990 visit and it's the same today, although this time, eavesdropping on a guide lecturing to his group, we learn something new.

"St. Peter's is not actually the official seat of the Pope! That honour belongs to St. John Lateran, Rome's oldest church."

With our stay in Rome almost over, and as we make our way wearily back to our room, we can only both agree that this city has definitely been one of the best on our travels so far. Nowhere else has really been able to offer quite as much antiquity within such an easily navigable area, and combined with the legendary Italian food, it's little wonder it sits high on my 'favourite cities' list. And although, once again, we haven't thrown a coin into the Trevi Fountain, Rome is sure to entice us back.

This morning's train to Verona, situated in northern Italy, departs at 10:45 am, allowing us ample time to pack and enjoy one final continental breakfast. This time there's no argument about walking to the station; we are both quite happy for Giulia to order us a taxi.

Our train, red, sleek and gleaming, is nonetheless rowdy and crowded. Kids are crying; businessmen are talking incessantly into their phones, and girls out for a day's shopping are giggling noisily. Despite feeling the beginnings of a headache, I am too interested in the outside passing scenery to bother closing my eyes. I watch as we make our way up through the throat of Italy, where Rome becomes Florence which in turn becomes Bologna. High above me, a pale, watery sky peers down upon flat, far-reaching terrain of empty ploughed fields pending their next crops, while in the far distance, I spy twig-like trees awaiting their summer coats. Eventually, just as the noise of the carriage becomes unbearable, our train glides into Verona, and here our three-hour journey terminates.

With a history shrouded in mystery, so much so that it's not even known where the name Verona came from, around 89 BC the Romans arrived and prospered here. Today, the results of this Roman prosperity, along with that of other subsequent ruling powers like the 13th-century Scalinger family, make Verona one of the richest cities of ancient remains in northern Italy. The third-largest surviving Roman amphitheatre is here (although we do not know this beforehand) and is still used today for pageants and performances, while other ancient buildings and churches are abundant. While it is unknown whether William Shakespeare ever visited Verona, it is his play Romeo and Juliet that ensures Verona's enduring place on the world tourism map.

Only partially aware of Verona's history, as we had not expected to be visiting here, it is nonetheless perplexing when we exit Verona station to find ourselves in a nondescript commercial area. Across from us is a modern bus shelter and close to that, a busy petrol station; of ancient ruins, fabulous churches, beautiful buildings, there is nothing to be seen. It requires a quick reassuring look at Google Maps to realise that Verona Station is located outside of the city itself, and we shortly find ourselves tagging behind the majority of our fellow passengers. The 15 minutes walking it takes to reach Verona City takes us alongside wide-open roads, over a swiftly flowing stream and past the first of Verona's ancient gates.

A few hundred metres shy of the city's second city gate, the impressive stone Portoni della Bra, is our accommodation, La Casetta di Lina. Like our B&B in Rome, it's also not a hotel but rather a suite in a residential building whose rooms have been turned into B&B accommodation. Again, it's challenging to locate.

"You would think when booking," I say in exasperation, "that you would be told that the building will be hard to find. That you shouldn't bother looking for a big sign but rather a miniscule nameplate or plaque."

"How come all our rooms in Italy seem to be B&Bs anyway?" Darryl asks.

"I have no idea. Probably because when I applied a price filter, all the hotels were too expensive and didn't show up in my search. Now that I think about it, in 2017, we only ever stayed in B&Bs while in Italy."

"Look," Darryl interrupts me. "La Casetta di Lina."

Fortunately, Darryl has located our accommodation, and shortly after pressing the intercom, Federico, a suspiciously friendly gentleman, welcomes us into his establishment. Consisting of an office, small breakfast room and three bedrooms, each with its own external bathroom, La Casetta is worn but spacious. Federico delights in pointing out our large, detached bathroom and fellow guests.

"This is your bathroom. No one else will use it," he tells us proudly. "I have staying some English people in that room, some Italians in that room and you, the Australians. I have the United Nations staying," he laughs.

Reaching our room, Federico hands over a set of keys and a map which he explains in great depth.

"Verona has a lot to see, and it is very easy to get around. You must get a Verona city pass from the tourist office here," he tells us as he circles a location on the map. "You can buy a one- or two-day pass which will allow you to visit all the attractions. It is very good value."

With Federico then proceeding to name and circle every attraction on this map *and* mention all the local restaurants nearby, it's sometime later when, with relief, we close the door on him.

"Mmm," Darryl says. "He is friendly enough, but there is something about him I don't quite trust."

"I agree," I reply. "He's just a bit *too* friendly."

Deciding to forgo any actual exploration of Verona until the following morning, the afternoon is spent catching up on our washing, some blogs and just relaxing. After our exertions in Rome, Darryl's pain has flared up, so it's good just to rest.

For dinner, we take Federico's advice and head to one of the neighbouring restaurants he has suggested. With the night somewhat damper and colder now that we are further north, it's with relief that we come across the cosy-looking little restaurant just a short stroll from our room. Inside, it's warm and comfortable, and a cheerful waiter approaches to explain the menu.

"We have lots to choose from, but maybe you would like to choose one of our specialities?" he asks.

"And what are they?" we reply.

"Verona is very famous for its honkey," he tells us.

"Honkey? What's honkey?"

"You know. Honkey. Hee-haw, hee-haw."

"Donkey! You mean donkey?" I say incredulously.

"Yes, honkey. It's a very special dish here. Honkey bolognese or honkey lasagne."

"There's no way I'm eating donkey," I say to Darryl.

"It may not be all that bad."

"Then how about wabbit? You know bunnies?" our waiter asks as he puts his hands to his head and makes some rabbit ears.

"No. Not bunny either," I laugh. "I'll just have the ordinary lasagne."

"And I'll have the mushroom risotto," says Darryl.

We're still laughing sometime later when we leave the restaurant and make our way back to our room. A speciality it may be here, but I'm not ready for 'honkey' just yet.

Tucked firmly within the confines of a large residential complex, our room is well shielded from outside noise, meaning we awaken refreshed from an undisturbed sleep. Although it's after 7 am, outside, it's still pitch-black, and with breakfast not served until 8:30 am, we must wait patiently until the sun rises and breakfast appears. This breakfast, set up within the little breakfast room, consists of various breakfast condiments such as juice, yoghurts, cereals, pastries and coffee. The idea is you load what you would like to eat onto trays and eat within the confines of your room. It's as we begin to fill our trays that the true Federico starts to emerge.

"Put your tray here. Not there," he says bossily as he hovers near Darryl.

"Don't leave the juice there. It goes over here."

It's a relief to escape back to our room, although this relief is short-lived.

"Where are your trays" he demands, as later, we prepare to leave and start our exploration of Verona.

"Sorry, they are in our rooms. We thought maybe the housekeeper collects them."

"No. They go in the kitchen."

"Sorry," we apologise, grabbing our trays. "We didn't even realise there was a kitchen."

"We were right, weren't we?" I say to Darryl as we leave the building. "He was too friendly to be true when we first arrived."

Continuing along the road that yesterday brought us closer to the Verona city centre, we shortly find ourselves passing beneath the ancient double-arched city gate, the Portoni della Bra. Here, our wanderings are bought to an abrupt halt. In front of us is the most unexpected sight. It's the Verona amphitheatre, a beautiful, near-perfect, pink and white stone, two-tiered Roman arena built in the 1st century AD.

"That's what's great about not knowing anything about a place before you visit," I state happily. "I had no idea that something like this existed in Verona."

"It's not as big as the Colosseum," Darryl replies. "But it looks in much better condition."

Keen to explore what later turns out to be one of the best-preserved ancient structures of its time, we search for and locate the local tourist office mentioned by Federico where we buy Verona's two-day city pass.

"Federico may be a bit strange," Darryl comments, "but his recommendations so far have been pretty good."

The city pass does appear to be good value. For 25 euro each, this pass will allow us entry into Verona's main tourist sites, skip the line convenience wherever applicable and unlimited travel on public transport.

Ten minutes later and it easily allows us entry into that impressive amphitheatre whose interior, while not as imposing, is still noteworthy. With no handy portable audio guide available, like we did at St. Peter's Basilica – we covertly eavesdrop on a group following their own personal and vocal tour guide.

"The amphitheatre was almost completely destroyed by an earthquake in 1117... It originally had three tiers, but only two have survived... It could hold up to 20,000 people... The most popular events were the blood sports," this guide enthuses, "and 'arena' refers to the sand which covered the floor and was used to absorb the blood spilled."

Leaving the amphitheatre both impressed with what we have seen and happy to have had a guide to explain it to us, we make our way deeper into the centre of Verona. Coming across a crowd, I am keen to avoid it, but Darryl pauses.

"What are they all looking at?" he questions.

"Oh my god," I exclaim. "It's Juliet's balcony. I nearly missed it."

Many theories flourish as to the degree of truth in William Shakespeare's famous tragedy about two young teenagers, Romeo and Juliet, whose deaths reconciled two conflicting families. What is accepted is that his play borrows heavily from alternative sources, is based on a local legend about two warring families and is the most famous love story ever written. Truth or not, the city of Verona, where most of the action in Romeo and Juliet takes place, has over the centuries truly capitalised on Shakespeare's brilliant piece of fiction. Proof in point is the courtyard we are now standing in. This courtyard, currently swarming with tourists, is the forecourt to Juliet's alleged house, and the balcony the court looks towards is Juliet's famous balcony. Despite being added 600 years after Juliet's death, 'Juliet's balcony' has become the ultimate Verona tourist attraction with thousands having their photo taken here each day. 'Juliet's house' is now a museum.

Despite knowing that this originated from fiction, it's incredible how much you want it to be real and how much you pretend that it is. I am quite happy to stand and gaze up at the tiny stone balcony and pretend that Juliet once called to Romeo from here. I am even happier to use my city pass to enter the dark, timber-built museum, find the balcony and wave down to Darryl waiting amidst the throng below. Nearby Juliet's balcony there is a stone wall covered in scribbles from people asking for guidance in love. It's apparent that I am not the only one overlooking truth in favour of fantasy.

Aware that Verona will have other titbits of Shakespearian fantasy to offer us, like Romeo's House and Juliet's Tomb, we turn to depart the crowded courtyard but are stopped by a puzzling sight. A line of tourists, waiting to have their photo taken alongside a gleaming brass statue of Juliet, stretches far ahead.

"Why are they all grabbing hold of Juliet's breast?" Darryl questions. "Everyone having their photo taken grabs hold of her right breast."

"And look how shiny the breast is," I reply. "It's obviously been happening for a long time."

It turns out that it is considered lucky to have your photo taken alongside this statue of Juliet while clutching her right breast. Happy as I was earlier, to stand and pretend upon Juliet's balcony, I draw the line at this.

"I'm definitely not getting a photo of that. How did the tradition even start?" I voice as we walk away.

According to our guide, the Piazza delle Erbe, one of Verona's oldest town squares, is not that far away, and as it's nearing lunch time, we head in its direction. Our progress is frequently delayed by well-preserved Roman ruins, touristy little gift shops and even a fascinating, still-operating 5th century church built underneath a newer 11th century one. The Piazza delle Erbe, we are pleased to discover, not only has a thriving retail market currently in progress but also Verona's largest Christmas Market. Indulging in huge arancini balls (crispy fried risotto balls stuffed with cheese and mince) washed down with Veronian mulled wine, I later browse this market while Darryl rests in front of the bubbling Madonna Fountain.

"I knew I should have bought a leather handbag in Rome," I complain shortly after. "There isn't nearly as much choice here, plus they are more expensive."

"Maybe you'll find one in Milan," Darryl replies. "Isn't it meant to be the shopping capital of the world?"

While our city passes allow entry to many more places, we are content just to wander the streets, to work off our earlier lunch. Passing a little stand selling postcards, Darryl suggests we purchase some to send back home.

"But we haven't got stamps," I point out.

"Well, it shouldn't be hard to buy some," he replies.

A statement that we soon discover is slightly misguided. Stamps can be purchased but only from a post office and only at a price.

"How much for four stamps to Australia?" Darryl asks when we eventually locate a post office.

"Let's see. Four stamps, that's 15 euro."

"Fifteen euro for four stamps!" Darryl exclaims.

"That's $25," I utter unhelpfully.

"That's a lot of money," Darryl says to the post-master.

"It's a long journey," is his pragmatic reply.

That evening we return to the cosy little restaurant we had so enjoyed last night. This time Darryl decides to be adventurous and orders the 'honkey bolognese.'

"It tastes fine," is his verdict. "But I know it's donkey which makes me feel a little ill just thinking about it. I wouldn't order it again."

I have ordered a pre-dinner drink, an Aperol Spritz, and when it arrives, it comes accompanied by some bowls of olives and crisps.

"Sorry," I say to the waiter, "but I didn't order this."

"No, it's all good," he replies. "It is aperitivo. If you order a drink, then you will get a snack."

Aperitivo, as we have just discovered and continue to come across on our travels throughout Italy, is the Italian happy hour. Usually set between the hours of 7 pm and 9 pm, it's when tourists and locals can just order a drink and it arrives with a variety of snacks such as olives, chips and even sandwiches. Designed to take the edge off your hunger before a later dinner, I find it an excellent substitute for an actual meal.

"I don't need to order anything," I say happily as I tuck into my olives and chips. "This is great."

Not ready to return to our room and keen to view Verona by night, we eventually find ourselves in the sizeable piazza that abuts the currently well-illuminated amphitheatre. This popular square, known as Piazza Bra, is Verona's largest piazza and is lined with buzzing cafés and elegant restaurants. At this time of year, it's also full of large, brightly lit carnival vans selling an assortment of Christmas food, most of it confectionary. It's easy to stand drooling in front of the vast, colourful arrays of fudge, sugar-coated nuts, doughnuts, nougat and more.

"What is that?" I eventually ask one of the van assistants, pointing towards a tube-shaped piece of fried pastry.

"Cannoli," she replies. "It is filled with ricotta, and you can have different flavours like chocolate or pistachio."

"I'll have a pistachio cannoli," Darryl pipes.

"And I'll have a chocolate one. Also, some of that chocolate salami and a bag of those sugar nuts."

Deep within the murky depths of the Museum of Frescos, a former convent, inside a dark vaulted room lies an open sarcophagus made from red Veronian marble. It is, our city guide tells us the following morning, the final resting place of Juliet: the place her limp bloodied body, after her suicide, was laid to rest. There's no body, the room is dirty, dark and cold, and it's inconceivable that the world's most tragic heroine would end up here.

"Are you kidding?" I exclaim, on entering the dismal place. "This is meant to be Juliet's final resting place. There is no way she ever would have been buried here. It's horrible."

"They could have found a better place," Darryl agrees with me.

"What an awful place to be laid to rest," I continue. "Even if it is make-believe. Poor Juliet."

With its source high above in the Swiss Alps, the Adige River is a broad, swift-flowing body of water that slices through Verona. On each embankment, great walking tracks exist, allowing one to follow the turgid torrent while admiring the beautiful scenery. Joining one of these pathways, still muttering indignantly about Julies conditions, the morning's chill slowly disappears, and overhead, feathery alabaster clouds generated by high altitude winds create a stunning contrast against the perfect blue sky. To complement the photogenic scene, an incredibly picturesque vision comes into view on the river's far banks. It's the Castel San Pietro, a medieval fortress built atop the ruins of a viscount's castle. While the castle no longer exists and the fort is closed to the public, the vision of this hilltop building with its mantle of green cypress trees, standing stark against the azure sky, is truly striking. It's easy to understand how this vista features heavily in Verona's tourism campaigns.

By mid-afternoon, having gazed upon the dank crypt where Romeo and Juliet supposedly married, traipsed through innumerable gorgeous churches, lingered in a virtually pristine Roman Theatre and crossed the ancient Ponte Pietra bridge, we are heartily sick of antiquity, Roman or otherwise. We only want to sit down and unwind.

"How about we return to the Piazza Bra, find a café and write our postcards," Darryl suggests tiredly.

"That sounds like the best idea of the day," I reply, equally tired.

Returning to the popular, sunny piazza currently filled with Saturday afternoon diners, the hours slip past and afternoon becomes early evening as we write our postcards, enjoy our drinks and share a pizza.

"Verona has been great," Darryl eventually observes. "Lots to see and do. But you only need to visit once."

"I agree. It's been a good place to rest, and I love the fact that I now know where Romeo and Juliet was set, but I wouldn't want to return. Although I have enjoyed this afternoon's sunshine. Milan tomorrow, then Switzerland. It might be sometime before we get to enjoy the sun again."

A statement which, when we awaken the following morning, proves very prophetic.

Yesterday's blue sky and warm sun have disappeared, and fog has settled low on the Veronian streets as we depart La Casetta di Lina and make our back to the train station. It's miserable and cold, and it's with relief that we settle into the train's warm carriage. Today's journey to Milan is a short one and riddled with underground tunnels. With little to see, I pull out my book and shortly after, its entrance marked by industry, the city appears, and we glide into her central station.

We are really looking forward to spending the next two days exploring Milan, Italy's leading financial centre and a global capital of fashion and design. Having lost most of its architectural treasures to World War Two bombing raids, we are not expecting sights like those visited in Rome, but we do know that Leonardo da Vinci's "Last Supper" is here along with the Gothic Duomo, high-end restaurants and plenty of shops.

We are also aware that due to its latitude, Milan is infamous for its summer humidity and heavy 'pea-souper' fogs. Although not a pea-souper today, there are the lingering remnants of an early morning sour-scented mist as we alight the train and search for a taxi in a large, ageing station. It's a frustrating search, only rectified by asking two intimidating carabinieri (police officers) where the taxi stand is. It is a relief, sometime later, to arrive at the Milano Brera Relais, our B&B for the following two nights.

It's still early, only a little after 11 am and with our room not yet ready, we drop our baggage and head back out into the Milanese gloom. Here, I take stock of our rather residential-looking surroundings.

"It looks a bit more suburban than I was expecting. I'm not sure why I booked accommodation here. I usually find somewhere closer to facilities. This looks to be in the middle of nowhere."

"It doesn't look like much," Darryl agrees. "But there's a park over there. Let's have a look."

"I want to find the 'Last Supper,'" I respond. "It will be closed tomorrow. Today will be our only opportunity to visit."

Painted onto the drywall of the dining room of the former Convent of Santa Maria Delle Grazie, Leonardo da Vinci's 15th-century mural of the 'Last Supper' between Jesus and his disciples, the supper where Jesus reveals that he is aware that he has been betrayed, is one of the worlds most recognised paintings. Unfortunately, a combination of factors such as the drywall, Leonardo's inexperience at the time with large projects and frescoes as well as environmental conditions have contributed to the deterioration of this famous mural. Over the years, it's had to undergo numerous restorations, the most recent in 1999. Today, as we set off searching for it, I sceptically wonder just how much of the painting is original and how much is new.

With Google Maps indicating that the Convent of Santa Maria Delle Grazie is a 30-minute walk, we choose to traverse the park Darryl has just noticed rather than one of Milan's busy streets. This park, with its long grass, plethora of dog walkers and overall neglected appearance, in turn, leads to a busy Sunday market currently crammed with weekend browsers. Although we join the fray, it's just too busy to get close to any of the little stalls, and it's a relief to escape its clutches and find ourselves at our destination.

"Tickets sold out for two weeks. No cancellations," I mournfully read from the large sign attached to the ticket box entrance.

"Two weeks," Darryl exclaims. "We didn't even know two weeks ago that we were coming to Milan."

"I just thought it would be as easy as in Rome," I reply.

Hoping that there may still be some online tickets available somewhere, I search but to no avail. "They only allow groups of 25 people in at a time, every 15 minutes," I read. "No wonder there are no tickets left anywhere. If we had tried buying them online a few days ago, we probably could have bought some, but it's too late now."

Although extremely disappointed to be so close yet so far from one of the world's most significant art pieces, there is nothing we can do; it can be a lesson for next time. Google Maps shows that the Duomo is not far away, and so with new plans, we head in search of it.

The Duomo is the incredible Gothic cathedral that appears on calendars and postcards the world over. Covered in a pinkish-hued white marble, its exterior spiky with countless pinnacles and spires, this stunningly beautiful, extravagantly detailed building is covered with more statues and gargoyles than any other in the world. It is also considered the largest Gothic church in the world.

We are looking forward to viewing it in person, and our anticipation is well rewarded a short stroll later, when, like with Moses, the crowd parts and we capture our first glimpse of its pearly-white façade currently glowing in the weak midday sun.

"Oh wow," is about all I manage to say.

"How old did you say this building was?" Darryl asks.

"Building started in 1386. It's taken 600 years and it's not yet complete."

"Look at all the statues on top of the spires," Darryl points out.

"How detailed they are."

"It's absolutely stunning, isn't it" I reply. "It's just a shame about the crowds."

Maybe because it's lunchtime on a Sunday, or perhaps this is normal, but the shoving crowds that surround us as we stand in front of the Duomo are horrendous. We are pushed and shouldered, our vision repeatedly obscured and the queue to enter the building looks enormous.

"Does it cost to enter?"

"What does that sign say? No, it says its free, but you do need an entrance ticket. That's what the queue must be about."

While we would have loved to have entered and viewed this incredible building's interior, we realise that it's going to take a good hour of queuing. Maybe we'll try again tomorrow.

Adjacent to the Duomo is the Galleria Vittorio Emanuele II, an ornate 19th-century shopping arcade bursting with luxury emporiums, international chain stores and gourmet eateries. Of course, I want to have a look – my sought-after handbag may conceivably be within – but Darryl is reluctant.

"Look at the crowds inside. They are probably the worst we have seen."

"Let's just have one walkthrough, then find somewhere to eat," I cajole.

Capitulating, Darryl follows as I push my way through the magnificent arched entrance and into the crowded interior. Unfortunately, once inside, the sheer volume of bodies means that the intricate mosaic floors, the awesome glass ceiling and the exciting shops are impossible to appreciate. It takes a lot more pushing and shoving before we exit, battle-worn, at the rear of the arcade.

"I'm sorry. That was worse than the tube at rush hour," I apologise as we leave the centre behind us. "I don't know how anyone could enjoy shopping with crowds like that. Let's find somewhere to eat."

It takes a frustrating hour of searching before we eventually find a place that will allow us to purchase some lunch. Every other eating establishment we have passed has been filled to overflowing with Sunday diners. Tired and cranky, we are beyond grateful when a kindly maître d' takes pity on us and allows us to perch atop two stools while he plonks a fried pastry in front of us. Unsure as to what we are eating, I ask an American university student in the same predicament who informs me that it is panzerotti. Similar to the calzone we ate while travelling to Split, this panzerotti is a fried pizza turnover rather than a baked calzone. It's greasy, warm and tasty and gives us the energy to start the slow journey back to the Milano Brera Relais B&B. Although most of the shops we pass are closed because of siesta or because it's a Sunday, a conveniently open supermarket allows us to purchase some salads and yoghurt for tonight's dinner.

Back at our B&B and an elderly dumpling greets us with no English. She mutely hands us a set of keys and guides us along a long, empty corridor before throwing open the door to a room at its very end. It's one of the strangest rooms we have encountered on our travels to date, more like the cabin of a ship with two narrow single beds and walls covered in wooden panelling. In the early hours of the morning, after an evening spent reading and browsing our phones, I am woken by an eerie clopping noise. It sounds a bit like a one-legged pirate, reaffirming the room's nautical theme, and a little while later, it is accompanied by some strangled mutterings. Although slightly disturbing, I soon settle back to sleep and awaken refreshed and ready for breakfast.

This morning our silent lady from yesterday has been replaced by the lovely and chic Emmanuel, who, although probably around my age, is undoubtedly better preserved and groomed. Over our breakfast of coffee and croissants, I mention to her that I would like to explore some shops, to experience the 'fashion capital of the world.'

"We've had enough of churches and museums for the time being. And I need some clothes to supplement my wardrobe. I'm currently living in two pairs of jeans and some t-shirts. I would also like to find a nice, cheap Italian leather handbag. Can you suggest anywhere?"

Emmanuel helpfully provides a few suggestions, and once breakfast is over and our jackets, scarves, and gloves are donned, we step out into another foggy Milan morning.

Since his accident, Darryl has lost all sense of direction (although he is the last to admit this), and as we stand on the street trying to make sense of Emmanuel's directions, a mild argument ensues as Darryl insists it's one way, and I, another. Eventually, I pull out my phone to settle the debate, which has us walking shortly in the direction I have argued for, Darryl with a slightly disgruntled look on his face.

Reaching the first of Emmanuel's suggestions, this disgruntled look has disappeared from Darryl's face only to appear on mine.

"I'm not sure what Emmanuel thought I was after but it's definitely not these exclusive little boutiques," I complain. "Where are the nice big department stores?"

It takes a lot more walking before I eventually conclude that the shops in Milan are not for me. "They're all too expensive, too cliquey, too posh," I sigh.

Resigned now to looking, not shopping, the following few hours are easily spent enjoying very thick hot chocolates in a trendy bakery, browsing a street market full of busy little stalls and braving the inner city crowds to return to the Duomo. Here, the snaking line is every bit as awful as yesterday, which means that for this visit at least, the interior of Milan's most beautiful building will have to remain a mystery to us.

That afternoon, as we rest in our little cabin, social media is full of some terrible news from New Zealand. A volcano has erupted on White Island, a small island within the Bay of Plenty. Apparently, there were a large number of tourists visiting the island at the time of its eruption, and many of them are still missing, presumed dead, while others are seriously injured. With many of these tourists originating from a cruise ship and knowing we will be visiting this Bay region shortly, also by cruise ship, the horror of the situation is even more imaginable. It's in a sombre mood that we later brave the dark, cold night and head out in search of dinner.

It's a search that yields a welcome surprise. Less than five minutes' walk along a previously unnoticed route, we pop out into a sizeable, cheerful square full of cafés, bars and a supermarket.

"I knew I chose this location for a reason," I exclaim. "It just didn't make sense compared to all our other locations."

A little bar, warmly glowing with Christmas lights and playing soft music, entices us to enter and over our aperitivo of pasta and quiche, we voice our opinion of Milan.

"It's too crowded," is Darryl's verdict. "If I were born here, I would move."

"I am so disappointed," I sigh. "I had really high expectations of Milan, but it's missing the quaintness of other European cities. It's too modern, commercial and crowded. And the shopping is non-existent in my price range."

After a night again interrupted by pirate Pete and his unexplained thumps, clumps and bangs, we awaken eager and ready for today's northerly journey to Lucerne, Switzerland. Emmanuel, ever elegant, friendly and helpful, organises a taxi for us and bids us farewell as we await this cab on a damp Milan footpath. When, 20 minutes later, cold and increasingly concerned by the taxi's no-show, we approach Emmanuel for help, she instantly and commandingly steps out amongst the busy morning traffic and forces a cab to stop and collect us. It's an impressive example of the power a modern, self-assured Italian woman can command.

CHAPTER 10

Switzerland

*T*ODAY'S almost four-hour journey takes us from northern Italy's dozing, naked vineyards to the Switzerland conjured by my childhood *Heidi* and *Chalet School* books. Soaring mountainous peaks crowned by crisp white snow. Deep green valleys dotted with tiny wooden chalets. Sparkling lakes mirror-like and icy. Fluffy fat sheep. Doe-eyed cows ready to contribute milk for the world's best chocolate.

Like our earlier journey to Milan, the first hour is full of long dark tunnels, and of the great and famous Lake Como, I spy but a sliver, so frequently do we travel below ground.

It's easy to tell when we cross the Swiss border as my iPhone immediately lights up with messages advising of such. A guard approaches but, distracted by his ringing phone, simply nods, smiles and walks on by. One of our easiest border crossings to date.

From an early age, the beauty and allure of Switzerland, so appealingly described by authors Johanna Spyri and Elinor M. Brent-Dyer, totally enthralled me and studying modern history in high school only inflamed this. It intrigued me how such a tiny but densely populated nation, surrounded by warring powers, could remain neutral in the face of two world wars; how, despite its liberal reputation, women only got the vote in 1971; how every citizen has access to a fallout shelter either in their yard or close by.

Switzerland is another of these European countries that fared well under Roman influence. For 500 years, commencing in the 1st century BC, Switzerland, under Roman rule, thrived economically; her people became highly civilised, and trade flourished with the establishment of strategic military roads. Jump forward to the 19th century, and by 1850, Switzerland had become the second-most industrialised country in the world after Great Britain. Today, Switzerland, home to cheese, chocolate, yodelling. Inventors of Velcro, cellophane, the potato peeler. A country without its own language, continues to fascinate me. I say without its own language because the Swiss have four official languages – German, French, Italian and Romansh – each spoken in different regions.

At Lugano, we change trains, and here an American mother and daughter sit in the seats across from us. The daughter, nose running, eyes streaming and barking like a seal, is obviously sick and we watch in sympathy as she tries to rest. Our sympathy is compounded by her mother's actions, who doesn't stop blathering for the entire journey and continuously disrupts her daughter's sleep with her gestures and prattle.

"Look at the quaint little houses," she coos. "And gosh, look at the snow on that big mountain. It's just all so beautiful. Switzerland is wonderful although I could murder a McDonald's coffee!"

Annoying as she is, the American mother does have a point. Outside, the scenery is becoming increasingly more beautiful, a picture book of how we expected Switzerland to look.

Despite the ever-improving scenery, it's a relief when Lucerne appears and we can disembark, escaping the Americans.

"She was starting to drive me crazy with all her talking," Darryl complains. "We are in Switzerland. Who wants to hear about her McDonald's coffee?"

"I just hope we don't catch the daughter's cold," I reply.

Our accommodation, The Hotel Central, is thankfully just that – a very central hotel. Within 10 minutes of alighting, we have checked into our cosy well-heated room, noted the two doonas on the queen-sized bed (we discovered on our last trip that this was common to these mountainous central European countries) and found that we do not have a power adaptor suitable for Switzerland.

"We have four adaptors," I mutter as I go to charge my phone. "And one is supposedly an 'international' adaptor, but none of them work here."

"Maybe reception has one we could borrow," Darryl suggests.

"That would work for tonight, but we are in Switzerland for eight days," I answer.

Nestled among the foothills of the Swiss Alps and positioned on a stunning lake, Lucerne, with its medieval architecture, fresco-painted houses, cobbled streets and the Museggmauer, an incredibly well-preserved city wall, is one of the most popular travel destinations in the world. Its inhabitants speak German. Poets have immortalised its beauty, and Switzerland's oldest bridge spans the River Reuss which divides the city.

To explore what we can of this striking place, we obtain a handy map from our hotel's receptionist, who, unasked, kindly marks the location of the city's two Christmas Markets.

"They are both good, but this one offers better food."

"We'll definitely find the Christmas Markets," I reply. "But is there anything else you suggest we see? We are only here for the afternoon."

"Make your way down to the river," she suggests. "It's only a five-minute walk. From there you can cross into Lucerne Old Town using the 600-year-old Chapel Bridge. It's the world's oldest supported wooden bridge. You might also want to have a look at the Lion Monument or the original city walls which are nearly 800 years old."

Although only 200 metres long, it takes some time to negotiate Chapel Bridge, distracted by the magazine cover scenery we find ourselves in. Paintings depicting Lucerne's history decorate the covered bridge awning above us. Elegant swans glide beneath us. An ancient octagonal stone water-tower-cum-torture-chamber stands alongside us. Traffic-free cobbled streets flanked by medieval guildhalls stretch in front of us. This could very easily be, and most probably is, the picture on a jigsaw puzzle somewhere.

For most of the afternoon, we continue to be captivated as we traipse Lucerne's meandering streets. The ancient city walls spruiked by our receptionist are indeed fascinating with their nine stone towers, and it's fun to use the city's 500-year-old clock to check the time. The Lion Monument, unfortunately, alludes us, but a power adaptor is thankfully located within a well-stocked little shop. Eventually, in need of sustenance, we stop at a small, bustling bakery. Here, over crumbly cheesy tarts and large lattes, we sit and people-watch.

"These are expensive coffees," eventually comments Darryl, and at nearly 8 Australian dollars each, they are.

"I think the Swiss have the most expensive coffee in the world," I reply.

"And I'm surprised by the number of tourists from Asia," he continues. "Have you noticed?"

"Apart from the Americans on the train, they have all been Asian."

"And they're not just tour groups," he puzzles. "There's families travelling with young kids and loads of couples. I had no idea Switzerland was so popular with travellers from Asia. It will be interesting to see if it's the same elsewhere in the country."

With night approaching and a cold afternoon turning even frostier, warming lights guide us as we make our way towards the first of the two Christmas Markets marked on our map. Full of tiny wooden stalls selling Christmas goodies like wooden toys, handmade crafts and nativity scenes, it looks like something from Brothers Grimm, but it's jam-packed with shoppers. Searching for the alternative Christmas Market, we find this one situated right on the banks of Lake Lucerne. It's less touristy, more local than its counterpart and offers a large variety of market fare such as Bratwurst sausage, crepes and gingerbread. It also has the mandatory mulled wine stalls where we purchase two steaming mugs and drink them on one of the benches that overlook the dark, glassy lake.

Warmed from our mulled wine, a shortcut through Lucerne train station full of weary commuters returns us to the vicinity of our hotel.

Here, a cheerful restaurant entices us to enter, but a glance through the menu compels us to leave. Fifty Australian dollars for a single hamburger is more than we are willing to pay. Instead, we make do with the McDonald's located next door. Switzerland, as forewarned, is proving an expensive destination, and this McDonald's provides a convenient, cheap dinner option.

Reinforcing our view that Switzerland is popular with Asian travellers, we find ourselves the following morning enjoying our typically Swiss breakfast of bread, cheese, meat and muesli in the company of scores of Chinese, Japanese and Korean tourists. We are, in fact, the lone westerners, and it's interesting observing the different nationalities breakfast behaviours. One couple have us especially entertained as they first flatten then attempt to squash whole croissants into the hotel's toasters.

Switzerland are world leaders in rail travel, and with the world's most dense rail network, they have capitalised on this commodity. Creating 'must-travel' train routes with fancy names and even fancier prices, they are popular with tourists and must earn Switzerland a fortune. Today, we will be adding to the Swiss coffers by travelling the 'Golden Pass Line' between Lucerne and Interlaken. This route travels alongside Sarnersee and Lungernsee lakes before scaling the 1,008-metre Brunig Pass then plummeting back to the valley floor. To scale these heights then safely descend, the trains use what is known as a 'rack' or 'cog' railway, a toothed rail designed to mesh with cogwheels fitted to the undercarriage of a train.

Returning to Lucerne train station, there is some concern when the train number on our ticket, purchased before leaving Australia, does not match the train number on the station departure board. Failing to find anyone to clarify this problem, we tentatively board. Fortunately, tucked in amongst others holding a good sample of the world's nationalities, two seats remain vacant. A name plaque indicates they are ours and we settle in, ready to experience the first leg of the acclaimed Golden Pass Line. A journey that will take us up and into the Swiss Alps and see us ticking off another Bucket List item.

It's a leg that takes a mere 90 minutes, and there is little in the train's appearance to differentiate it from any other train, but it's an unforgettable journey; in hindsight, the most visually spectacular 90 minutes of our entire adventure. From comfortable, padded seats and through bloated panoramic windows, we watch as we travel alongside dazzling blue lakes, through lush, fertile valleys, over plunging chasms and to the base of soaring peaks cloaked in mantles of rose-hued snow.

Here, the cogs come into play, and after slowly hauling ourselves up these mountainous alps, we enter a winter wonderland where snowflakes swirl then fall thickly to the ground, and the dense, snow-laden forest envelops us. At their summit and with the outside temperature below freezing, the spectacular views are gulped appreciatively before we begin our plummeting descent to the alluvial valleys below. In one such valley, nestled between Lakes Thun and Brienz, lies Interlaken, our home for the following three nights.

More of an overgrown Swiss village than anything else, Interlaken is a base town for those wishing to partake of the numerous hiking and skiing trails, boating and thrill-seeking activities that abound here. Presided over by three mighty mountains, Eiger, Monch and Jungfrau, it has been attracting a conglomerate of tourists since the 1800s. Equally popular with summer and winter crowds, it is not the most attractive of towns but with its excellent location and plethora of facilities, it is convenient. With no idea of what to expect, we have arrived hoping to use it as a base to rest for a few days, to catch up on our laundry and to find some good fondue.

The Hotel Weisses Kreuz is located on the main road that bisects Interlaken and connects its two polarised railway stations, Interlaken Ost and Interlaken West. Alighting at Interlaken Ost, it takes 15 minutes of trundling our bags along this long straight artery, noting the glut of watch shops, the gourmet chocolate shops, the daredevil paragliders swooping overhead before we reach our cute traditional Swiss-style accommodation and check in. While our first room with its in-bath shower is not suitable for Darryl, the upgraded suite we are offered instead is happily accepted.

Keen to explore, it's not long before we have dropped our bags and returned to the meandering streets. Here, we frown at an ugly concrete hotel that dominates the town's centre but enjoy the traditional pastel chalets with their iconic gabled roofs. We admire the beautiful 1130 AD former Augustinian monastery and gaze appreciatively at the wide-sweeping river that runs parallel to the main street. But what really grabs our attention, what we register more than anything else, are the sheer number of predominately Asian tourists squeezed into every chemist, watch and chocolate shop we pass. Served by bilingual staff, this is obviously a well-established lucrative market, and we watch in fascination as they crowd the watch shops trying on timepieces, spend fortunes in the luscious chocolate shops and, in the case of the women, exit the chemists clutching huge bags of expensive cosmetics.

While Darryl is looking for a new watch, he has no desire to compete with such a well-heeled market and refuses to enter the fray, but with regards to the chocolate, nothing is going to deter us. Produced in pillow-sized slabs that are then broken down into smaller chunks, it comes in endless flavours and is often made directly in front of you. Salivating from both the chocolatey aroma and from the sheer choice in front of us, it takes ages to decide, but eventually, we exit a shop, both tightly clutching chocolate-filled paper bags.

Interlaken lies nestled in a valley dwarfed by towering mountain peaks to which sport-loving tourists flock for their fix of skiing and snowboarding in winter and hiking or canyoning in summer. Paragliding, as those currently soaring high above us attest, occurs all year round. Making our way back to our room and prompted by the sight of these adrenaline junkies, I remind Darryl of a tragedy that occurred here over 20 years ago.

"Do you remember that terrible canyoning accident that occurred here in the 90s?" I ask him. "Where a heap of Australians and some other nationalities were swept away by a wall of water as they were canyoning through one of the gorges near here?"

"I do remember something," Darryl replies. "But not the specifics."

With my memory also vague, I pull out my phone and retrieve some of the details.

"In 1999, 45 young people from two Contiki groups and three guides were canyoning in the Saxetbach Gorge here, around 6 pm, when a natural blockage burst causing a flash flood which killed 21 of them, 14 of which were Australian," I summarise from my readings.

"That's terrible," Darryl utters. "And it was near here?"

"Yes, some of the bodies were washed down into Lake Brienz. It *was* terrible. The company responsible ended up going out of business, and six of their directors were charged with manslaughter. I've never forgotten it. It's something that could have happened to us when we were younger or to any of our friends who travelled."

While there exist recipes for cheese fondue dating back to the 17th century, it was during the 1930s that the communal dish really became popular. In an effort to bolster cheese consumption, the Swiss Cheese Union successfully spruiked the humble fondue as the Swiss 'national' dish, and the gooey creation has never looked back.

I love a good fondue. I discovered them during my university years, and I am looking forward to enjoying one in their place of birth. Approaching reception later that evening, we are recommended the restaurant of the sister hotel of our current accommodation. Here, in a heavily panelled room strung with old wooden skis, beneath photographs of pink-tinged mountains and surrounded by cowbells and cuckoo clocks, we order our fondue and enjoy a carafe of mulled wine as we wait.

At some stage, a young Chinese couple enters the restaurant, and we watch in interest as the man, unsure of what to do with his jacket, dumps it over the electric heater located near their table. With deepening interest, we watch as the jacket slowly starts to steam and a burning aroma begins to fill the room. Just as I am about to say something, a disbelieving waitress appears and hands the man back his now smouldering jacket.

The fondue, when it arrives, comes in a deep pot atop a brightly burning flame. There are a good two litres of it, and it's accompanied by baskets of bread, bowls of pickled cucumbers and a massive mound of small firm potatoes, all of which we slowly ingest.

Reaching the bottom of our fondue pot, I weakly lean back in my chair and clutch my stomach.

"That tasted incredible, but I feel awful now. I'm too full, and I have no idea how my body is going to digest all that fat."

"It feels like I have a ball of cheese lodged in my stomach," Darryl agrees.

"Yes – a basketball of cheese."

While it was delicious – and having a fondue in Switzerland could nearly warrant its own Bucket List entry – the after-effects may not make it worth it. It takes three days before my stomach starts to feel normal again and begins to lose its bloated appearance. It is defiantly the only fondue I want to eat on our Swiss travels.

For some reason, along with the main heating, our room has four wall-mounted oil heaters, all of which are handily utilised the following morning to drape our freshly hand-washed laundry. From chores, we turn to breakfast, where the creamy Swiss yoghurts complement our brimming bowls of cereal, our croissants, cheese and cake. Over lingering coffees, we chat with our waitress.

"We were going to visit Jungfraujoch," I mention to her (at 3,466 metres above sea level, Jungfraujoch, a saddle between two mountains, is known as the 'Top of Europe'). "But it's going to take all day to get there and back, and we are already doing a lot more train travel over more Swiss mountains, so we have decided against it. Can you suggest an alternative?"

"At the very least, you should see one of the higher ski resorts while you are here," she replies. "I would suggest Grindelwald. It's not far."

Heeding her advice, we continue our talk where we glean a little more knowledge of Interlaken.

"That horrible tall brick tower in the centre of the town, the Metropole Hotel, was approved by a money-hungry mayor who ended up losing his job over it... We used to get a lot more American tourists, but these days it's Chinese, Koreans and more recently Indians... Indians love it here, that's why there are so many Indian restaurants... Yes, we have a Christmas Market, but it will not open until next week."

To reach Grindelwald, a postcard-perfect ski resort that sits at the base of the famous Eiger, we return to Interlaken Ost. Here, jostled by locals lugging flashy skis and tourists clutching streamlined snowboards, we purchase discounted tickets using our Eurail pass and board our train. This train, again efficiently utilising its cogs for much of the journey, pulls us higher and higher into the Swiss Alps. Interlaken's green valley disappears to be replaced by icy cliff faces, patches of deep, undisturbed snow and drifts of snow-draped trees.

Arriving at snow-drenched Grindelwald and, beneath a crystal-blue sky, the fearsome Eiger, a monstrous mountain which has claimed over 60 lives, immediately impresses as it towers over us. Unsure of exactly what we want to do here, we depart the station and head towards the cluster of picturesque wooden chalets that demark Grindelwald's main street. It takes only a few metres of walking upon slippery, icy pathways to realise that visiting here may not be such a good idea.

"It's incredibly slippery," I caution Darryl.

"It is," he agrees.

"And it's quite steep," I continue, "with nothing to hold onto."

"Yes, I'm aware."

"It would be terrible if you slipped over and hurt your hip again."

"Yep. Aware of that also."

With my unease growing, we carefully continue onwards where my concerns skyrocket when first one man, then a second soon after, slips over directly in front of us.

"That's it. This is an accident waiting to happen. I want to go home."

While we do manage to spend a little more time skulking along the safer paths, stopping often to gaze awed at the incredible mountains that surround us, I've worried enough about Darryl's hip recently and am more than relieved, after a warming coffee in a small touristy café, to head back down the mountain to Interlaken. To hibernate in our room and to eat our bag of chocolates for dinner.

In a fitting tribute to today's date, Friday 13 December, I awaken this morning to the beginnings of a sore throat and runny nose – most likely caught from the American girl in our train carriage a few days ago. I marvel at the tenacity of germs. Surrendering to my burgeoning cold, I spend a few extra hours in bed, happy to have some English-speaking television to watch. The news channels are full of the British general elections where Boris Johnson has just been elected Britain's newest Prime Minister.

Mid-morning, and with the view from our window showing a glacial blue sky laced with tendrils of grey cloud, we make enquiries at reception regarding steamboat rides on one of Interlaken's icy lakes. Knowing that both Lake Thun and Lake Brienz offer numerous cruises to eager tourists, we have visions of spending the day catching a steamboat to the various towns that dot the lake's shores, poking about their streets before returning this afternoon. Unfortunately, our receptionist has bad news for us: steamboats and most of the other cruising vessels only operate during the summer months. There is one boat ride available, but it's a one-way journey to the town of Thun, and it departs later this afternoon. If we use it, we will be required to catch a train back to Interlaken sometime this evening.

"It's definitely Friday the 13th," I mutter as we thank our receptionist and walk away.

"How about we just explore outside the town a bit further?" Darryl suggests. "Maybe walk along the riverbank between the two lakes."

Liking the suggestion and again well-padded, we navigate our way through Interlaken, this time leaving the main street and heading towards an older part of town along which the swiftly flowing river gushes. While we discover, during our subsequent walk along the banks of this Aar River, that there is no navigable connection between the two lakes, we do find some lovely architecture, some exciting locks and weirs, and most impressive of all, stairs for fish.

"It's a salmon ladder," Darryl reads from a sign posted in front of series of ascending small pools. "It enables the salmon, which are quite plentiful here, to swim upstream. They leap through the rushing water, then rest in the next pool before repeating the process until they reach the top of the ladder."

Although keen to continue our walk and explore a little further, the fast-changing weather has other things in mind. Overhead, plummeting paragliders have disappeared to be replaced by thick, angry clouds and just as we navigate a lovely old covered wooden bridge, the heavens open. I have bought my small travel umbrella with me, but it's as useful as a cocktail ornament in the fierce winds and driving rain. With flurries of snow also entering the fray, we head back towards the town centre as fast as Darryl's gait will allow. Here, drenched, we come across a vast cafeteria, Migros, full of equally saturated people either sheltering or eating. It's a great discovery, and with our dripping jackets hanging from conveniently provided hangers and our jeans steaming, we gratefully feast on cheap, chunky vegetable soup and cheesy bread rolls. To prolong our drying time, we sip large milky coffees before grabbing our jackets and heading upstairs to a huge supermarket.

As previously mentioned, I enjoy exploring supermarkets, and this is one of the best yet. More like a vast K-mart combined with an immense Woolworths, we spend ages just browsing. The chocolate aisle is stunning and enormous and warrants its own Instagram video while the cheese section comes a close second. Eventually, with the weather improving and weighed down with toiletries, cheeses, yoghurts and salad – tonight's dinner – we head back to our room. Here, we again make use of the convenient wall heaters to dry our damp clothes before spending the remainder of the evening eating, reading and staying warm.

Our stay in Interlaken is over, and I awaken this final morning feeling even worse than yesterday. It's been a terrible night's sleep, having been woken at 4 am by someone exercising loudly and protractedly in the room above us, only stopping when a little after 5 am, I thump the ceiling using Darryl's walking stick. And my cold has really taken hold. I am looking forward to reaching today's destination, Montreux. I'm also aware that until we get to Paris in six days, there will be no further extended stays anywhere. It will be a different town, a different bed each night now.

Today's journey is the second stage of the Golden Pass Line travelling from Interlaken to Montreux via Zweissman. After departing lower altitude Interlaken, it doesn't take long to find ourselves back in Santa's winter playground, which, while again beautiful, is not quite as breathtaking as the first leg. Adjacent to us sit a group of locals, and so loudly and continuously do they talk that we are careful when changing trains in Zweissman to choose a different carriage to them. In Switzerland, unlike most other European countries, you do not book seats; you just buy a train ticket and sit wherever.

For this sector, Zweissman to Montreux, some special carriages have been tacked onto a regular train. Provided for those travelling the Golden Pass Line, these carriages, with their plump, upholstered green armchairs, heavily panelled wooden ceilings and antique wire hat racks evoke a sense of having stepped back to those golden years of train travel – Agatha Christie's Orient Express times. A feeling only compounded by the many tourists currently waving around glasses of champagne.

"It all looks good and fine," complains Darryl. "But where are we supposed to put our luggage?"

He has a point. For travellers like us, encumbered by suitcases, there is nowhere in the carriage to store them; instead, we must make do with them blocking the aisle next to us.

In all, it takes four hours to journey to Montreux and the final hour is the most memorable as the train weaves its way downward from the higher alpine peaks to reach the town that sits well-shielded on the shores of Lake Geneva. From our window, we spy plentiful surprising vineyards made possible by the microclimate that exists here, and the glittering lake appears to grow the lower we descend.

Although settlement has occurred here for centuries, it was its discovery by British and Russian nobility in the 19th century as an excellent place to winter that really put Montreux on the tourism map. Today with its comfortable temperature, flower-lined streets, beautiful statues, belle epoque buildings and offshore medieval island castle, it's every bit as popular with tourists. It's also not surprising to discover that this is where Queen created some of their best-selling albums, Prince declared his love of the place, David Bowie frequented and Charlie Chaplin spent 25 years of his life.

It's a little after midday when we disembark and find ourselves in the centre of a town that appears to cling to a steep bluff running from ridge to water by way of a series of hillside terraces. It's impossible to see the terraces themselves as they are so covered with buildings and roads, but it is possible to discern the town's steeply stepped appearance. To reach our accommodation, the Hotel Parc and Lac, situated on the bottommost terrace nearest lake level, we can use either the steep stairways, handy escalators or convenient elevators that span the numerous terrace levels.

Situated above a little Italian restaurant currently emitting the most mouth-watering odours, our room – reached by another of those tiny jolting European lifts – is aged, dark and dingy but redeemed by a tiny balcony. This balcony, little bigger than a bath towel, not only offers incredible views of glassy Lake Geneva with shining snow-capped mountains in the background but of the popular three-kilometre-long promenade that hugs the lake. Currently host to Montreux's Christmas Market and thronged with people shopping, eating and drinking at its many stalls, it's the first place we decide to head to.

A quick refresh and it's not long before we find ourselves browsing the market's Christmassy stands, mingling with the crowds and appreciating exactly where we are.

Loud Russian music (this year's theme apparently) pumped from huge throbbing speakers provides a different but rousing vibe further enhanced by energetic Russian dancers. Feeling slightly fragile with my worsening cold, we forgo the mulled wine this time but make do instead with sharing a giant, sugary doughnut. One of the most memorable moments is when we come across the Freddie Mercury statue. Situated right on the lake's foreshore and in the centre of the Christmas Market, this 1996 bronze statue of Freddie Mercury in a trademark pose was donated by friends, family and his former band to commemorate the life of this unforgettable musician. Today, as always, it is strewn with fresh flowers.

Following a few hours perched upon our tiny balcony watching the sun sink, clouds gather and rain fall, we head out in search of dinner. The Italian restaurant beneath our hotel is still erupting with delicious aromas, and that, along with its convenient location and the wet night, is enough to sway us. Entering, we manage to secure the last unreserved table and feast on massive plates of spaghetti puttanesca and warming local merlot while watching rain-damp diners get turned away. It's a memorable night.

Today's travel to Zermatt will have us once again scaling some high-altitude Swiss peaks using cog or rack rails. Travelling alongside Lake Geneva for the first part of our journey, our watery landscape eventually dissolves to be replaced by creamy rocky hills covered with countless grapevines. Not aware that Switzerland had such a prolific wine-producing region, we can only gaze in curiosity as we pass vineyard after vineyard. They stretch from the rails of the track right up and onto the snow-covered ridgeline and are a true testament to the microclimate that exists in this region of Switzerland.

Eventually, when the vineyards disappear, the weather starts to cool, and the incline steepens, the trains cogs come into play, soon hoisting us back into a snowy wonderland. We cross narrow bridges at dizzying heights, cling to mountainsides with vertiginous views and crawl closer and closer to the sharp peaks above us. Finally, at 1,600 metres above sea level, we pull into the snow-carpeted, car-free resort town of Zermatt.

Surrounded by a range of incredible mountains and in the shadow of the most famous mountain of all, the Matterhorn, quaint Zermatt has attracted tourists since the mid-19th century. Once an agricultural community, the scaling of the Matterhorn in 1865 (only three out of the seven climbers survived the climb), paved the way for tourism development. In this day and age, despite a population that can reach more than 20,000 during peak times, it's surprising to come across a town with just five or six streets and whose only methods of transportation are the odd electric taxi or horse-drawn sleigh.

Google Maps indicates that our hotel here, La Petite Charme-Inn, is a good 15 minutes' stroll and keen to stretch our legs, we soon find ourselves walking a slippery, cobbled slope. On either side of our icy path, copious boutiques, trendy restaurants and chic cafés abound. Behind these establishments, the populated terrain weaves and dips sharply with a fast-flowing river charging through the town's lowest depression.

While the cobbles are currently well-cleared, they are still treacherous, and it is a relief to reach our funny cheese-wedge shaped hotel. Tucked right up amidst the rafters, our recently renovated room is smoking warm with more jigsaw puzzle views of soaring peaks, their bases covered in alpine trees, and brown wooden houses with thick snow-covered rooftops. It's an incredible 'old worldly' view with a notable absence of a common commodity.

"Why are there no cars here?"

"It's to prevent pollutants from blocking the view of the Matterhorn. How fantastic is that?"

In these times where contaminants have obscured the views of the Himalayas, the Pyramids, the Great Wall and plenty of other noteworthy sights, it is indeed fantastic that a town has chosen nature over pollution.

With only one afternoon in Zermatt, we soon return to reception where a receptionist is happy to provide us with a town map and offer a suggestion.

"If I had only the afternoon here," she says, "then I would spend it having a drink and snack on the terrace of the Schonegg Chalet Hotel. Their terrace offers probably the town's best view of the Matterhorn."

Very much liking her suggestion and noting the hotel's location on our map, we spend the following hour slowly ambling our way towards it. With see-sawing icy roads and deep, snow-laden parks to negotiate, the journey is precarious, especially for Darryl, but incredibly picturesque. At the town's lowest point, we stop beside the Matter Vispa, the narrow quick-flowing channel whose waters sparkle a cold grey-blue and crane our necks to look at the breathtaking Matterhorn that completely dwarfs the town. It's a view unlike anything we have seen.

Reaching the Schonegg Chalet Hotel, we find that its entrance is through a long bat cave-like tunnel blasted through heavy rock. A convenient elevator buried deep within the dark, rocky mountain is provided to haul guests the eight storeys it takes to reach the hotel's restaurant and terrace. Feeling like adventurers as we step out onto this terrace, it's entirely understandable why our receptionist made a point of mentioning the place. Roofless, the long, wide balcony scattered with comfortable chairs and tables alongside warming braziers faces directly towards the pyramid-shaped Matterhorn colossus. It commands all attention and continues to do so for the time it takes us to nibble a tasting plate of cheese, cold meats and olives and to consume our drinks. With a crystal-blue sky as its backdrop, the sharp edges of the compelling mountain stand out distinctly, and from where we sit, the wind with its mantle of snow becomes fascinatingly visible. It's beyond incredible, and we sit here mesmerised until eventually, the sun sinks behind the Matterhorn's shoulders, and dusk starts to fall.

Knowing that this afternoon – with its blend of comfort, decadence, awe and beauty – could likely be the highlight of our entire trip, it's difficult to tear ourselves away but eventually, we return to street level again using the buried elevator. Although the sun has disappeared, there is still ample light to guide us back to our room, and this time our route takes us via Zermatt's Old Town, a fascinating collection of dark, wooden barns, stables and houses from the 16th-18th century, and past a small supermarket. Entering, we find the supplies meagre, the fresh produce anything but, and the prices outrageous, but we do leave with our dinner: bircher muesli for me and cup noodles for Darryl.

Today's eight-hour journey on board the iconic Glacier Express travelling between Zermatt and St. Moritz has been one of the most anticipated train journeys of our entire adventure. Our itinerary required a major readjustment to accommodate it, and tickets were hard to come by. Unfortunately, with a night's sleep interrupted continuously by my worsening cold, I have awoken feeling awful. Panadol, pancakes and coffee do go some way towards reviving me, but I still feel dreadful as we pack our bags, descend the elevator and farewell reception. A massive dumping of overnight snow has made the slippery roads even more lethal, so a taxi is called to transport us back to the station. More an electric golf buggy, this taxi soon has us standing amongst a hoard of other tourists waiting to board the large-windowed, modern, sleek, silver tube that is the Glacier Express.

Opening in 1926, the one-of-a-kind Glacier Express cuts through the centre of the Swiss Alps, scaling dizzying heights of up to 2,033 metres before plummeting down to lows of 585 metres. Known as the 'slowest express train in the world,' it is only named 'express' because it is a direct route between Zermatt and St. Moritz. Again, it uses the unique cog rail system to haul itself up these mountainous peaks, and by the end of our journey, we will have traversed 291 bridges and entered 91 tunnels. One of these tunnels, the 115-year-old crumbling Abula Tunnel, currently in the throes of being redeveloped, passes under a lake whose leaking waters have contributed to the tunnel's decline. This tunnel, I am not looking forward to traversing.

As expected, the train is packed but its wide elegant carriages with substantial panoramic windows easily accommodate the crowds. Eager to enjoy every moment, I spend most of the morning ignoring my cold and staring out at the changing scenery. Always the view outside is of alabaster snow, but our altitude or trajectory determines its depth. At lunchtime, I order a chicken salad and glass of red wine and consume these as we make the steep climb to the journeys highest peak – the 2,033-metre Oberalp Pass. Outside, it's a blizzard of white. While the cog rails work well on the steep inclines, they work equally well on the heart-stopping declines where, out of the panoramic windows, deep ravines with rushing rivers of foaming water and steep cliffs dotted with sparse trees greet us.

Mid-afternoon and with my head throbbing, we reach the extraordinary, much-photographed Landwasser viaduct. Built in 1902, this architecturally stunning bridge with its six arches is one of the most picturesque and famous in the world. Everyone crowds the right-hand side of the carriage to take the best photo as the train enters the bridge's sweeping bend, myself included. Unfortunately, try as I might, my pictures fail to do the viaduct justice.

While it's a relief to exit the dripping Abula Tunnel, a tunnel I had been dreading for months, it's even more of a relief when at 5 pm, eight hours after commencing our arduous journey, we pull into St. Moritz station under the cloak of darkness. It's been a long memorable day, but repetitive scenes of snowy valleys and even snowier peaks combined with a terrible head cold have taken their toll.

"Are you up to walking?" Darryl asks as we grab our bags and push our way through the crowds of other disembarking tourists.

"I don't think so," I reply. "I feel really bad."

"Let's grab a taxi then."

Playground of the rich and famous, birthplace of winter tourism (ski runs were introduced here in 1864), St. Moritz is undoubtedly Switzerland's most famous alpine resort town. With an abundance of thermal springs, St. Moritz has been attracting visitors for over 3,000 years and is known today as a skiing, sledding and snowboarding paradise. Each year its local population of 5,200 swells by another 500,000 as visitors flock to be here or be seen here.

Feeling shattered and with my nose now running faster than Usain Bolt, the glitzy shops, affluent hotels and swanky restaurants are wasted on me as our taxi whisks us up and along the St. Moritz high street before leaving us at the Hotel Arte. In an upgraded suite, by far our best room yet, I find myself not 20 minutes after disembarking, showered and comatose in a huge, fluffy bed.

After my best sleep in days, I awaken ready for today's five-hour journey to Basel. Breakfast is typically Swiss with lots of cheese, meat and bread, and it's not long before we are back in a taxi heading for the train station. It's still dark outside, which means that we have failed to see St. Moritz during the light of day and our taxi driver is extra chatty.

"You did the Trans-Siberian," he says in excitement. "I have always wanted to make that journey."

"Maybe you will one day," I reply.

"No. I'm too old now. And you have come all the way from Australia?"

"Yes, we've been travelling for nearly eight weeks."

"And is this it? Home now?"

"No," we laugh. "We have another 10 weeks to go. We'll be catching a ship home from England after Christmas."

The short journey passes extra quickly as he presses us for more details on our journey and provides us with some further insight into Switzerland's history.

"Switzerland prospered on its chemical, powdered milk and chocolate industries… Swiss banks are full of Nazi-looted gold… Taxi driving is a competitive business."

All too soon, we find ourselves back on a train, and today it's all downhill with a route that takes us past a snow-covered golf course, rapid-flowing streams and large wooden barns. At the sight of the first of these big brown alpine sheds, my curiosity is aroused. Where are all the famous Swiss cows and sheep? We haven't seen any for a while.

"Cattle, sheep and goats are moved up to the alpine pastures only in summer," I read from my phone. "They stay up here for about 100 days before being brought back down for winter."

With the altitude dropping and our ears popping, snowy fields start to make way for fresh green pastures, barren trees begin to sprout life and those elusive sheep and cattle begin to reappear.

At Landquart, we change to a high-speed train, and the outside scenery goes into overdrive as it discards the last of its snowy mantle. Long green flatlands appear on which we rocket along, sometimes disappearing into lengthy dark tunnels, sometimes travelling alongside glassy lakes.

At Zurich, a guy enters our carriage and proceeds to play a noisy game on his phone. After the tranquil start to the morning, the game's constant beeping and buzzing not only drives us crazy but brings us back to reality. We are not in the calm Swiss Alps anymore. But despite the loss of tranquillity, it does feel good to be out of the mountains – quite liberating. I had not been aware of quite how claustrophobic the elevated peaks could be until we had escaped them.

At some stage, we pass a caravan park – always a surprising sight in these cold countries. I more often equate camping with warm sunny climates than cold, snowy ones.

Requiring the toilet, I return to my seat and point out something that has been bothering me for most of our train journeys throughout Switzerland.

"For such an immaculate, forward-thinking country – I am surprised that all the Swiss trains empty their sewerage directly onto the tracks."

It's mid-afternoon when we reach Basel, and once again, I am feeling exhausted and snotty. Our hotel, the Hotel Metropole, is an easy five minutes' walk from the station and here I again collapse into bed, awakening a few hours later refreshed and ready for dinner.

Headquarters of pharmaceutical giant Roche, Basel is an underrated cosmopolitan city lying alongside the mighty Rhine. Its civilised origins begin in Roman times, and its city centre boasts a medieval old town whose world-famous Christmas Market we have been looking forward to visiting.

Now that we are here, however, and despite feeling much better, I find myself not up to locating the market nor tackling its crowds. All I want to do is find a nice little restaurant somewhere and eat some good Swiss food – but not fondue.

Our receptionist recommends a traditional Swiss restaurant located less than a block away, and here, in this warm pub-like room with its Swiss horns and cowbells, we relish our last Swiss meal. My pork schnitzel smothered in pot-gravy is delicious, while Darryl equally enjoys his sausages, leeks and potato. Our journey back to our room includes a stop at a supermarket where we stock up on food for tomorrow's onward trip to Paris. With a plethora of exciting food choices, including creamy chocolate bars, flaky pastries and gourmet sandwiches, I eventually settle on a few tubs of rice pudding. Darryl reverts to his staple bread and cheese.

Back in our warm room and for the first time in nearly a week, we turn on the television. Multiple news channels are reporting on rising upheaval in France. Large industries, the transport industry included, have begun striking in retaliation to the Macron government's proposal to increase the pension age. Paris, in particular, looks to be heavily affected by these striking industries. Turning off the television, we settle into bed with some degree of unease. Will our onward travel be affected by these strikes?

CHAPTER 11

France

*A*WARE that we may have some travel turmoil ahead of us, it's an early start to the day as we farewell our still-slumbering hotel and head back to the well-lit train station, stopping only to collect some fresh croissants and hot coffees. Overhead, the early morning sky is a menacing grey: hopefully not a portent for today's journey.

By 7:30 am, Basel's train station is swarming with travellers, and alarmingly the departure boards are listing rows of train cancellations – ours is one of them.

"Now what?" Darryl questions.

"No idea," I reply. "Let's ask what our options are at the service desk."

Here, a harried but helpful service agent with excellent English advises us to just get on the next regional train heading in the direction of Paris.

"While still travelling in Switzerland you will not need a seat reservation on a regional train, and there are no seats left on any of the direct trains to Paris," he tells us. "The next regional service terminates in Strasbourg where your initial train also terminated. You will miss your original connecting train, but you should be able to purchase tickets for another one heading from Strasbourg to Paris once you get to Strasbourg."

It's a long, cold wait on a long and windy platform where our previously purchased coffee and croissants are fully appreciated, but eventually a regional train arrives, and fortunately, there are seats available. It's another of those convenient European high-speed vessels, and within what feels like minutes, my phone indicates that we have left Switzerland and entered France. There are no border checks. However, sometime later, two young, attractive conductors approach, asking for tickets. Two American ladies sitting in the seats directly in front of us appear agitated and willingly hand theirs over to the conductors.

"We think we have missed our stop," one of them says in a troubled voice. "We wanted to get off at Colmar."

"You have missed your stop," the younger of the conductors replies. "You will have to travel through to Strasbourg now and catch a train back. Although, with the strikes, the next train back will not be until 3:20 pm this afternoon."

"But it's only 10 am now," the ladies cry in dismay. "What are we going to do in Strasbourg all day?"

"Strasbourg has a very good Christmas Market and is very pretty," the second conductor helpfully suggests.

It's a conversation that plays out in my mind when, a short time later, we pull into Strasbourg, step from the train and find ourselves enveloped in a serious mass of mayhem and confusion. Last night's news bulletins haven't nearly prepared us for the gravity of the strikes, and this is a rude introduction. Every arrival and departure board are a score of cancellations, most of the station's cafés and shops are closed, people flounder about everywhere and a huge queue flows from the sole information counter.

"I hope those American ladies manage to get a train out of here," I utter in dismay to Darryl.

"I hope we do as well," he grimly replies. "Ours is long gone and the ticket counters are closed. The information counter is the only thing open. We are going to have to join that long queue."

It's a depressing, slow-moving line with little success at its end. Rather than purchase onward tickets, ("Non. We have no tickets to sell,") we are instead advised to simply jump on the next train to Paris using our defunct tickets.

"It should be ok," are their parting and troubling words.

Like battery chickens, the platform is crammed with jostling bodies when a train heading to Paris finally pulls in and no one is allowed to board without first presenting a ticket. Although ours are useless and the scanner beeps forebodingly, we are allowed through and into the packed carriages.

"They must be trying to move all the foreigners on," I say in relief.

Travel on any high-speed train in France requires not only a ticket but also a seat reservation, something we had on our original train but not on this one. No seat reservation means no seat, and for the two hours it takes to travel from Strasbourg to Paris, I spend most of it either standing upright or, like many others in the same situation, huddled on the dirty floor. It doesn't worry me – I'm just relieved to be heading towards our next destination. Darryl has fared better. An incredibly kind passenger has surrendered his seat, allowing Darryl to spend the journey sitting, observing the passing flat, winter landscape, the grey overcast sky and the chaotic, crowded stations.

It's closing on 3 pm by the time we pull into Paris East. Our three-hour journey has stretched to nearly eight, and if Strasbourg was a grenade of confusion, then Paris is the nuclear bomb. With no metro running and very limited public buses, the streets are an absolute quagmire of taxis, cars, scooters and pushbikes. Always a noisy city, today, with the air rent by shrill whistles, piercing sirens and stationary traffic roar, it's deafening and depressing. Not the happy, exciting arrival into 'Gay Paree' that we were expecting.

While the history of Paris dates to approximately 259 BC when the Parisii, a Celtic tribe, settled on the banks of the Seine, it did not gain the name Paris until the 4th century. It only started showing serious signs of prosperity during the 11th century thanks to a lucrative trade in silver and its location as a strategic pilgrimage and trading route. Fast-forward hundreds of years, throw in the 1328 bubonic plague which killed thousands, the 14th-century tumultuous hundred-year war, Joan of Arc's defeat of the British, frivolous and extravagant monarchies, the increasing poverty of the masses and you come to the 1789 French "off with their heads" Revolution. A revolution that ultimately led to the abolition of the monarchy and the establishment of Napoleon Bonaparte as First Consul. Now skip to the 19th century. Here, a complete urban restructure results in a new, contemporary Paris with beautiful boulevards, well-lit cobbled streets, plentiful green parks, a modern sewerage system and clean drinking water. None of which matters when Paris shortly finds itself embroiled in two devastating world wars and a host of subsequent riots or terrorist attacks. The most recent being the memorable 2015 attack which left over 400 injured and over 130 dead.

It's fair to say that Paris, today the single-most visited city in the world, has undoubtedly had a turbulent, albeit exciting history.

After giving up on trying to find an Uber driver willing to come to us, it takes a good 40 minutes of queue jumping and queue arguing before we sink gratefully into the back of a cab. Our driver is conversant in English and happy to talk about today's strikes and yesterday's history.

"The strikes have been going on for nearly three weeks now… Business is down everywhere as tourists are staying away… Rail, transport, air, ground crews, ambulance, hospitals and many more are striking… It's all to do with Emmanuel Macron making changes to the pension scheme."

"What changes is he making?" we ask.

"Currently, there are around 42 different types of pension plans. The best belongs to the public servants who can retire before the legal retirement age of 62 with very good pensions. Macron is trying to streamline the 42 plans into one."

"Retirement age is 67 in Australia," we reply, "so 62 sounds good to us."

"The French do not like to give up anything without a fight. It's in our history, our blood."

"I have been doing some reading on your history," I reply. "I'm fascinated by your French Revolution, and Haussmann's restructure of Paris."

"If you visit the Palace of Versailles," our driver replies, "then you would understand why the French revolted. And although many thousands of buildings were destroyed in the 20 years it took Haussmann to restructure Paris, and thousands more lost their homes, we wouldn't have the beautiful city we have today without this upheaval."

Our initial itinerary had us spending two nights in Paris, but some last-minute changes resulting from the Switzerland reshuffle have us now staying for three. It means that tonight we will be staying at the Hotel de L'université before tomorrow moving on to the Villa Du Louvre.

Paris is divided into 20 administrative districts referred to as arrondissements. The Hotel de L'université is in the Saint-Germain-des-Prés district of Paris (or 6th arrondissement) and within walking distance of many major attractions.

Entering, we find the attractive stone building to be elegant and comfortable with friendly staff, although our initial optimism wanes somewhat when we are shown a noisy street-level room.

"It's very noisy," I say to the hotel receptionist. "Is there a reason you have given us this room?"

"Your booking mentioned your husband has problems with stairs. We thought you would prefer this ground floor room," is the reply.

"Is there an alternative room available?" Darryl asks.

"And you have a lift, don't you?" I question.

"Yes, we have a lift, and I would be happy to show you an alternative room," he replies before shortly changing us to an upgraded suite.

"We are doing well with the upgrades on this trip, aren't we?" Darryl mentions cheerfully sometime later as he reclines on our cloudy bed and looks out of our generous window.

That evening, keen to return to a restaurant discovered on our previous

2017 visit to Paris, we navigate the thin threads of dirty pavement heading towards the river Seine. Our passage is made difficult by the narrow footpaths, the copious garbage cans and flower barrels that block our way and the mass of fellow pedestrians. Although the thread does widen once we reach and follow the Seine, the number of other walkers – most of whom appear to be strike-affected commuters – makes progress slow. This slowness, however, does give us time to peruse our surroundings: to observe the little green boxes of the bouquinistes or booksellers alongside us, to note the Bateaux Mouches or riverboats gliding silently upon the Seine metres below, to admire the beautiful nearly full moon shining brightly overhead. It's a memorable walk and takes us from the 6th arrondissement into the 5th, better known as the Latin Quarter.

In 2017, we spent five nights in this quarter staying at the Hotel Levant on the Rue de la Harpe. Immediately across from the Levant, we enjoyed a three-course menu du jour at a nameless tiny French bistro which tonight, we are hoping to replicate. Heading deeper into the Latin Quarter, we are surprised to find the normally bustling cafés and restaurants empty, touts miserably trying to entice the few tourists that do mill. Over our meal of cheese-crusted French onion soup, beef bourguignon and crème caramel, our waiter sheds a little more light on the current situation.

"It's the strikes," he says mournfully. "All the tourists have gone. It's been like this for three weeks, and today they say that they are going to continue."

"It's Christmas next week," I mention. "Will it be any better then?"

"Non. It will be a very bad Christmas for us."

Maybe it's best not to try and replicate a great memory, or perhaps it's a result of the downturn in trade, but our meal doesn't live up to our expectations, and it's with disappointment that we exit the Latin

Quarter and slowly negotiate our way back to our hotel. This time, as we follow the winding banks of the Seine, we notice the lights of the Louvre twinkling at us from the river's far banks. At the same time, in the distance, the beautiful Eiffel Tower glows and pulsates like the most outrageous Christmas tree – and all lingering feelings of disappointment disappear entirely.

The following morning over a typical continental breakfast where I happily rediscover that the croissants in France far exceed those found anywhere else in the world, we make our plans for the day.

"The Villa du Louvre, tonight's accommodation, is only a 10-minute walk from here. We just need to cross the Seine and make our way through the Louvre precinct. It's immediately behind."

"Why don't we check out of here now," Darryl suggests. "Find the villa and either check-in or leave our bags if the room is not ready."

"Hopefully it's ready," I reply. "It's a tiny apartment, and it has a washing machine. We can get some washing done. I booked it about eight months ago, and it was a fantastic deal. A tiny free-standing fully furnished apartment across the street from the Louvre. It was less than $140 a night."

"We are there for two nights, aren't we?" Darryl asks.

"Yes," I reply. "Then it's the Eurostar to England. Although, with these strikes, I am getting worried that our train may be cancelled."

I have reason to be worried. After reaching France and realising the extent of the upheaval here, I have been keeping an eye on our future Eurostar train booking. Each day, the Eurostar site displays a list of cancelled trains for the upcoming days. We should know this evening or early tomorrow as to whether our train has been cancelled or not. If it has been cancelled, then we truly have a problem. Replacement tickets, if we are lucky enough to secure some, are going to cost in the vicinity of 1,000 Australian dollars each – a considerable increase from the 50 Australian dollars we paid for our current seat reservations.

By 9:30 am, we are once again negotiating the narrow Parisian footpaths, this time with our bags trundling behind. The traffic-heavy streets are at a noisy standstill, and it's a relief to leave the mayhem and fumes as we navigate the Pont des Arts and enter the 1st arrondissement Louvre courtyard. Here we rest on handy stone bollards, happy to take in the iconic glass pyramid, the immense cobbled Napoleon courtyard and the beautiful creamy stone French renaissance Palace Museum that surrounds us. A light shower of rain moves us on, and, as promised when booking, the address for our accommodation is found a few short minutes later. Situated on the Rue de Rivoli, one of Paris's most famous and commercial streets, our tiny apartment is hidden behind a massive wooden gate which is itself tucked discretely amongst copious bustling shops. As organised, we approach one of these gift emporiums where we are directed to leave our bags and to return later this afternoon when our room will be ready.

The Tuileries Gardens is a stone's throw away and, seeking to escape the traffic madness, we soon find ourselves wandering this convenient 23-hectare parkland that runs alongside the Seine and joins the Louvre to another of Paris's central public squares – the Place de la Concorde. Our stroll takes us past a sterile-looking Christmas Market which we forgo for the time being, and amongst a plethora of statues by artists such as Maillol, Giacometti and Rodin. Located in the garden's western corner, we come to the Musée de l'Orangerie where a few hours are lost forever as we stand mesmerised in front of immense compositions of Claude Monet's "Water Lilies."

"Look at this," I say to Darryl after taking some photos of the enormous oil landscapes. "The paintings are so large that they look a little blurry as you stare at them with the naked eye. But look at my phone. The paintings look crisp and clear."

Continuing on, this time hugging the Seine's banks, we eventually leave the Tuileries Gardens and enter the 7th arrondissement whose star attraction is the Eiffel Tower. Known as the Grand Iron Lady, the Eiffel Tower – built in 1889 as a temporary entrant in that year's World Fair – is these days a global cultural icon and the world's most-visited monument. The ongoing strikes have resulted in the Tower's closure today, but this doesn't concern us. Having visited here previously, all we want to do now is wander her base and gawk up her iron skirts which again impress us but also slightly shock us.

"Look at how rusty she is," Darryl observes.

"I noticed that as well," I reply. "She didn't look this bad back in 2017."

Hungry from the morning's exertions, we find a typical French bistro with tiny tables covered in vibrant red cloths and chalkboards that announce today's 'plat du jour.' Here, I settle on the soupe a l'oignon while Darryl remains content with a beer. Outside our bistro, our attention focuses on the activities of a 'scooter stand.' A handful of scooters sit lonely and neglected until released from their binds by phone-tapping tourists.

"I didn't realise so many people hired these scooters," I muse. "That's the fourth person who has come along, unlocked the scooter with their phone and taken off while we have been sitting here."

"It's probably the easiest way to get around at the moment with the strikes going on."

"I think you would have to be pretty mad or desperate to try and negotiate this chaotic traffic on a scooter!"

Our tiny apartment, once we have collected our bags and been entrusted with the secret code that opens the heavy wooden gates that lead to a hidden inner courtyard, is every bit as good as we had been hoping. With its previous existence, presumably a garage or stable, this bohemian-style ground-level flat, hidden behind high walls and dominated by apartment blocks, is a welcoming oasis in a jungle of high development. Although small – the sofa morphs into a bed that dominates the lounge/dining area, and a chandelier fills most of the minuscule bathroom – we are not complaining. It's the first time in weeks that we have seen a stove or microwave and how many other tourists have a washing machine in lavish, overpriced Paris?

With dinner sourced from a nearby supermarket – fresh broccoli soup for me, cheese and bread for Darryl – the evening is spent sitting eating upon our bed while our washing spins merrily in the machine. Four hours later, having finished eating, cleaned up, read a book and watched a movie, our washing is still spinning happily away.

"What setting did you use on the machine?" Darryl eventually asks.

"I have no idea," I reply. "It's all in French. I just took a guess."

"Well, I think it was the wrong guess."

Before settling down for the night, my final chore is to check the Eurorail site where, with indescribable relief, we find that our train to England is still running.

"The train before ours has been cancelled and four others," I read. "But thank goodness ours is still operating. It would have been an absolute nightmare trying to rebook."

"You can go to sleep feeling a bit easier now," Darryl replies. "That's if the washing machine ever stops."

Yesterday's supermarket haul also included rice pudding, muesli and fruit, suitable for this morning's breakfast. Loath as I am to say it, it feels great pottering around a kitchen again preparing this simple feast. Today, with the metro down, buses non-existent and taxis mired in traffic, we are reliant on walking to get anywhere. We decide to use the Tuileries Gardens as our thoroughfare once again, although this time our destination is the Champs Élysées which will deposit us at the Arc de Triomphe.

With a history spanning back to 1640, the 1.9-kilometre Champs Élysées, with its massive sidewalks, leafy plane trees and luxury shops hiding behind elegant facades is, often described as the 'world's most beautiful avenue.' This is a nomenclature I find hard to reconcile with the garbage-strewn boardwalk, traffic-clogged road and shuttered shops I find myself walking alongside this morning. Obviously, the Champs Élysées doesn't fare well under a city on strike.

Despite this, it's interesting to navigate the bustling Place de la Concorde, location of Marie Antoinette's beheading, inspiring to pass the beautiful Grand Palace Museum and fun to see so many high-end stores – Gucci, Dior and Valentino, to name a few.

In Gap, I purchase a mustard cashmere jumper for 60 Australian dollars while Darryl looks in bemusement at a naked protester sitting on a bench outside the store. At McDonald's, in need of a rest and toilet break, we refuel on Big Macs and thick shakes.

Finally, our journey halted by the huge 12 lane roundabout known as Place Charles de Gaulle; we stop, and stare at the junction's centrepiece, the Arc de Triomphe. As famous as its neighbour, the Eiffel Tower, this 50-meter high Roman-inspired stone arch took 30 years to build (commissioned in 1806, it was eventually inaugurated in 1836). Honouring those who fought and died for France in the French Revolution and Napoleonic Wars, it also stands as a symbol of French fortitude.

"It looks much more impressive now that we are closer," I say as we gaze upon the etched limestone monument. "And it's hard to believe someone flew a plane through that arch."

"I would like to see someone try these days." Darryl replies. "Can we get any closer?"

A flight of stairs leading down to a dirty tunnel allows us to navigate the chaotic intersection safely, and we resurface directly beneath the Arc and alongside the wreath strewn Tomb of the Unknown Soldier. With the eternal flame burning (it is rekindled at 6:30 pm every evening), the famous arch above us and ringed by crazy traffic, it undoubtedly feels like we are in Paris.

Tucked amongst the arched stone arcades that line the Rue de Rivoli where our accommodation is located are numerous souvenir shops and fragrant bakeries. We get further proof that we are in Paris a short time later when, after purchasing a croque monsieur (a hot sandwich made with cheese and ham) from one of these bakeries, we cross the street and eat it directly in front of the Louvre's glass pyramid.

Situated on the Ile de la Cité, the Gothic Notre-Dame Cathedral, another of Paris's iconic attractions, took 200 years to build and has been an unmissable feature of the Parisian landscape for over 850 years. Home to Christs' 'holy crown of thorns,' as well as a chunk and a nail of the Cross, it is incredible that these three treasures, along with Quasimodo's Bells and the famous stained glass 'rose window,' managed to survive the April 2019 fire that ravaged the building. In 2017, with our hotel close by, the majestic mesmerising Notre-Dame was a compulsory stopping point on our daily jaunts, and we are anxious to see her post-fire. Using the Seine's handy walking trail, in the late afternoon we make our way to the 4th arrondissement. Today, she looks nothing like our happy memories of her. Instead, we find her a sad and sorry sight with her cloak of scaffolding, towering cranes and missing spire.

Returning to our room, we stop off at the bustling souvenir shop where only yesterday we stored our bags, and settle up our account. As a 'thank you for booking' gift, I am given a kitsch snow globe filled with a tacky Eiffel tower, fake snow and gaudy macaroon cookies. It's made from plastic, hideous and will be a nuisance to carry, but I adore it. It will be another of my favourite 'travel treasures.'

Although after 7 am, it's still completely dark when we farewell our little accommodation gem and step out into a frigid, wet morning. As we wait for our Uber, the only traffic is a thunderous garbage truck, and the ordinarily bustling shops are still sleeping behind their heavy metal shutters.

"I'm going to remember this," Darryl says as he gazes at the empty, foggy streets. "This is normally one of the busiest areas in Paris. Now, look at it."

"It's probably the only benefit of having to wake up so early," I reply. "Most people probably never get to see the Louvre looking so quiet and empty."

The Eurostar to England departs from the Gare du Nord, and with an Uber our most reliable means of reaching the station, we give ourselves ample travel time. It doesn't take long to traverse the dark, slick Paris streets, the rain a steady shower, and we arrive at the station with a little under three hours to spare. Usually, passengers are not allowed to traverse customs nor enter the waiting rooms until two hours before departure, but we are waved through, and here, finally, my anxiety over travel disruptions begins to dissipate.

Sometime later, full of chocolate croissant and hot coffee, any remaining angst disappears as I sit and listen to some fellow Australians: Kate and Akubra-wearing Gary. They are also waiting for the Eurostar.

"We only arrived in Paris two days ago," Kate tells us. "Yesterday, we went for a walk along the Seine when we both felt something splatter down on us. It looked a bit like bird poo. Luckily, two young Caucasian girls nearby came running up and helped wipe the poo off. They even had wet wipes which helped. They seemed nice and so helpful. That evening Gary and I went out to a restaurant for dinner. When we went to pay, we found that our credit cards were missing from Gary's wallet. The cash was still there, but the cards were gone. As I had left my wallet back in our room, we had no way of paying for our dinner and so were in a really bad situation."

"So, what do you think happened?" I ask.

"The only thing that could have happened," Kate replies, "is that the girls first sprayed us with something and then pickpocketed us as they were patting us down. It's incredible how professional they were and how slick the whole scam was. Not only did they manage to pickpocket Gary and take his cards, but they also managed to return the wallet without him noticing. They even left the cash so as we wouldn't notice the cards missing straight away."

"And did you end up paying for dinner?" Darryl questions.

"We had to," Gary replies. "The restaurant wouldn't let us leave until the bill had been paid. We knew we had a spare card in our room so we phoned our hotel and asked if they would go to our room and get it. The hotel refused saying they couldn't do that but thank goodness, the receptionist said he would settle our account, and we could pay him back once we returned."

"So, he paid our restaurant bill," Kate again takes up the story. "We then had to return to the hotel, grab the spare card, find an ATM, get some cash and pay back the receptionist."

"And then I had to spend the rest of the night cancelling our cards," Gary interjects bitterly.

"They had already racked up thousands of euro's worth of purchases."

It's an awful tale, one I wouldn't have thought possible and one all visitors to Paris should be aware of.

It takes around 90 minutes for our Eurostar missile to propel itself through the bleak, flat French countryside and to land in grey, misty England, where we rewind our watches another hour. Like last time, I hate the 20 minutes spent 70 metres under the English Channel and spend the entire time with my head buried in a book. The relief when we exit the tunnel, of not only having survived the underwater chamber but of escaping poor mixed-up France, is palpable. I have always had a soft spot for France; this is actually my third visit. But this stopover, seeing a country brought to its knees by the strikes, so many Christmas plans go to ruin and being always on edge about our own onward journey, has changed my perception of this country. Any soft feelings have disappeared, and I am more than ready to arrive in familiar, dishevelled London.

CHAPTER 12

England

*T*ODAY, London is one of the largest and most important cities in the entire world, but it has endured much turmoil and many hardships to achieve this status. Founded as a trading port by those industrious Romans back in 43 AD, it grew quickly, only to be completely razed to the ground 17 years later by Celtic Queen Boudicca and her marauding army. Undeterred, the Romans rebuilt the city and continued here until the beginning of the 5th century, when the collapse of the Roman Empire saw them flee back to Rome. Over the following 500 years, successive invaders saw London inhabited by the Angles, Saxons, Jutes and Normans when William the Conqueror took control. Under William, London gained the Tower of London, and a wooden London Bridge was turned to stone.

When the Black Death struck in 1348, at least a third of London's 50,000 strong population were killed, but due to a growing textile industry and a centralised European trading location, the city recovered and prospered. By 1665, when the Great Plague struck, its population was around 500,000. The 1666 Great Fire of London, which resulted in over 80,000 people becoming homeless, did pave the way for a 10-year reconstruction period and eventuated in a more appealing city with St. Paul's Cathedral as its centrepiece.

With a population nearing 2 million, in 1832 severe overcrowding saw London combat a cholera outbreak, and in 1858 a people's revolt, 'the Great Stink,' over the stench emanating from the sewage-filled Thames River that flows through the heart of the city.

Cue Queen Victoria's reign (1837-1901), and here we get most of modern London, including a new sewer system, Big Ben and the

London Underground.

It's at St. Pancras International, also known as Kings Cross St. Pancras Underground Station, that we alight two hours and 20 minutes after departing Paris, in a London that now numbers over seven and a half million.

England is the country of my birth, and it is difficult to contain my elation as we leave the platform and head in the direction of the King's Cross ticket information office. After constantly being on edge in Paris, it feels great to have arrived in London. And after having had to communicate and negotiate in so many foreign languages over the past eight weeks, it also feels so good to now be able to correspond effortlessly.

We are on our way to the ticket office to purchase a couple of Oyster Cards. These cards, purchased for 35 pounds each, will entitle us to travel throughout various London zones utilising the bus and train networks. Public transport is costly in the United Kingdom, so an Oyster Card does go some way towards alleviating the financial pain.

With our Oyster Cards easily secured and our bags once again mooching along behind, we negotiate the Saturday crowds and take the circle line to Notting Hill. London is a large cosmopolitan city and knowing we were going to be here for eight days, it wasn't easy determining which suburb to book accommodation, but Notting Hill eventually prevailed with its easy access to large parks, convenient location and numerous pubs where we are keen to enjoy some typical British grub.

Again, it's confusing finding our accommodation, the 202 Apartments; there's no signage, just a door with a security code tucked between a pub and an office block. We have prearranged the code for the building and find a key hidden for us on the third floor. Entering what's to be our home for Christmas this year, we see a relatively spacious kitchen and bathroom alongside a small lounge-cum-bedroom. There's a narrow balcony that faces other similar buildings and a small hallway. It's aged, stark and minimalist, but it's home for now; thus, it's perfect. Although we soon glumly discover, it is missing one thing.

"There's no washing machine," I cry in disbelief. "I was sure it had one. I can't believe I have again booked an apartment without a washing machine. I must have been distracted by the location and price."

"We are not having much luck with our washing this trip," says Darryl drily. "Apart from Paris that is – a machine which I didn't use. I was going to do all my washing here."

"We'll just have to find a laundrette somewhere," I reply. "I gave up on the Paris machine after it took so long to do that first load."

Notting Hill is a funky little area of London full of expensive pastel-coloured houses and trendy cafés. It was the setting for the 1999 Julia Roberts smash-hit movie of the same name and is home to London's best market – Portobello Road antique market. That afternoon, I book a leg wax (handy when you're travelling) for tomorrow at a nearby beautician, and we choose Sainsbury's of the three supermarkets that thrive here to stock our fridge and pantry. Not willing to fall back into cooking for ourselves just yet, a dinner of sausages and mash is eaten at the Old Swan, a traditional English pub next door to our accommodation.

"It's good to be able to understand a menu again," Darryl mentions, as we settle ourselves on stools in the pub's warm, dark interior.

"Isn't it," I reply. "And it's so much easier when the dishes are familiar. I hadn't realised until now how exhausting it can be trying to choose a meal from a menu where you have no idea what the dishes are."

"It's fun to experiment with food as you travel," Darryl muses. "But it's also great to get back to something familiar."

Hyde Park and Kensington Gardens, home to not only a large handful of royals but also to London's most expensive real estate, is a five-minute walk from our room, and the following morning, we take great delight strolling its greenery. As we slip alongside Kensington Palace, official residence of William and Kate, I can't believe how easy it is to get so close to such British nobility. From Kensington Gardens, we follow High Street, full of upmarket shops, to eventuate at Holland

Park, full of cute squirrels.

Citymapper, a handy app on my phone, advises a number 148 bus will deliver us from our current location to a large Westfield in Shepherd's Bush, so we jump on one, gleefully flashing our Oyster Cards.

There's an alternative agenda to sightseeing in London, and that is to secure clothing suitable for our cruise back to Australia. Our modest suitcases currently contain mainly winter gear with a few items of necessary evening wear. We are both in need of casual summer t-shirts, shorts and evening shoes while Darryl also requires a dinner jacket. Westfield, whose humid tropical climate is at odds with its heavily clad shoppers, does successfully deliver, on this occasion, a set of small heels and men's dress shoes. But with its Christmas crowds and uncomfortable temperature, we don't linger for long; instead, we catch another bus back to Notting Hill. Here, back in our apartment, we find a 'thank you for booking with us' gift of chocolates and prosecco from the apartment owners, both of which go well with our simple steamed vegetable dinner.

This morning it's another leisurely start to the day with toast and coffee in bed. It's surprising how much you appreciate doing something so simple as preparing toast and brewing your own coffee after not doing so for so long. With our dirty washing accumulating, a visit to a nearby laundromat is a necessity, and here, as our clothes regain their shape and lose their 'eau de travel odour,' we sit amongst our fellow washers. They are an eclectic bunch, a young mum doodling on a notepad (maybe a future J.K. Rowling), a grey-haired hobo who appears to require three machines and a languid youth clutching what seems to be a cherished skateboard.

Energised by a hearty lunch at the Old Swan, back in our boots and jackets and keen to see some of London's world-famous Christmas lights later this evening, a tube soon deposits us at Marble Arch station. Starting point for one of London's major shopping thoroughfares: Oxford Street.

Emerging above ground, it doesn't take us long to realise that visiting one of the world's most famous and popular streets only two days before Christmas is probably not such a good idea. It's currently heaving with tourists and shoppers, and it becomes a struggle to see anything or even stay together as they drag us along Oxford Street in the direction of Oxford Circus. While we do manage to browse through Selfridges and to use the toilets in Debenhams, it's an easy decision when, battle-worn, we arrive at Oxford Circus, to use another tube to escape the clawing crowds and shortly resurface at nearby Pimlico.

Pimlico, an upmarket residential area, is thankfully crowd-free, and it's with interest we happily stroll its quiet streets, noting the stately 19th-century houses and green parks, before converging with, and walking alongside, the sombre Thames. This walk along London's famous embankment has us passing the Tate Museum, Houses of Parliament, Westminster Abbey and Big Ben.

"This embankment alongside the Thames," I mention at some stage. "Was built in about the 1800s to carry the sewer lines out of the city. Previously, all the sewage just got dumped into the Thames."

"So, this is all reclaimed land? And how do you know this?"

"I read about it last night," I answer. "And yes. They managed to reclaim about 22 acres in all and not only cleaned up the river but gave London this great walkway."

Although not long after 4 pm, as in Europe, early darkness is descending and aware that the Christmas lights will shortly be ablaze, a quick consult of Citymapper directs us to a nearby bus stop located on Trafalgar Square. Arriving at the large, paved area with its commanding Nelson's Column, crouching lions and plethora of pigeons, Darryl reminds me of something.

"Remember back in February 1990? Accidentally visiting here on the day Nelson Mandela was released."

"Yes," I answer. "How incredible it was. The huge crowds. Everyone happy and singing and disbelieving that he was finally being released after 27 years."

London's Christmas lights have been a part of the December city landscape since 1954, when local retailers along Regent Street arranged for a warming winter light display. The idea spread and these days, many of London's major shopping arteries sparkle and glow during this period, and 'switching on' the show is a celebrity-attended event.

While considered a nightmare mode of transport to most Londoners but quintessential to tourists, it's not long before one of London's ambling red double-decker buses pulls up in front of us. A stop or two later, and we manage to secure top deck, front row seats. These are perfect for viewing not only the festive illuminations but for gazing loftily upon the hordes of Christmas shoppers and end-of-day commuters that, if possible, now throng even more thickly on London's streets. Some Indian tourists sitting alongside us have us smiling as one of them gives an excitable running commentary to his wife.

"This is definitely the place to be," he cries in his lovely, accented English. "Look at all those people trying to get somewhere. And we are just sitting here looking at them all trying to go somewhere. I told you Amma. This big red bus is definitely the place to be."

Christmas Eve and it's another decadent start to the day as we laze around drinking coffees, munching toast and contentedly watching television. Although loath to return to the steamy gymnasium-like shopping centre, we need to purchase an additional roll-on suitcase and other travel items. With its crush of frenzied last-minute Christmas shoppers, the centre is even steamier and more horrendous than our last visit, but we depart happy with our purchases. Back in Notting Hill, nothing looks more enticing than spending the remainder of Christmas Eve in the festive Old Swan. Here, alongside fellow tourists and well-planted locals, we savour our drinks, munch our nachos, follow the Premier League on TV and discuss how one celebrates Christmas.

"They're completely different, our Australian Christmases and the continental Christmases, aren't they?" I muse. "Mulled wine, early nightfall made bright and cosy by Christmas lights, stodgy but warming Christmas fare versus bushfires, raging temperatures and cold salads."

"I agree they are different," Darryl replies. "And mulled wine, Christmas pudding and Christmas lights do make a great Christmas, but I wouldn't swap them for ours. Don't forget we have icy-cold beers, quick dips in a cooling ocean and pavlova."

Christmas Day, and we awaken to our first child-free Christmas in 24 years. While Pierce and Paige have already celebrated an Australian Christmas hours ago, our day has only just begun. Each Christmas, the supermarkets in England offer a wide selection of premade Christmas fare such as custardy trifles, glazed gammon joints and pork wreaths topped with pigs in blankets. Lying in bed this morning, free of any parenting responsibilities, I feel no guilt whatsoever as I consume my specially bought breakfast cream trifle and think about today's Christmas lunch. English pubs are famous for their Christmas menus, and their popularity means a reservation is required. Knowing this, some weeks earlier, while holed up in Split, we had emailed numerous pubs. Today, we are off to the Duke of Wellington on Portobello Road to enjoy a three-course feast.

It's a 15-minute walk along an eerily empty Portobello Road to reach the pub, and it's surreal to traverse what is usually a heaving, tourist-choked thoroughfare.

"It's strange, isn't it? Seeing Portobello Road like this."

"It must be the only day of the year it looks like this," Darryl replies. "No market stalls or cars or people."

The Duke of Wellington is expecting us, and we are the first to be seated in a private dining room set for about two dozen customers. Our waiter is exceptionally skinny, wears a vacuous expression and has trouble pouring our complimentary champagne.

"He reminds me of Hugh Grant's flatmate in the Notting Hill movie," I whisper to Darryl.

"Spike," he whispers back.

As we are served our first course – creamy asparagus soup for Darryl, goose-liver pâté for me – a father and daughter accompanied by two small bouncy dogs are seated alongside us. With the six of us the dining room's lone occupants, it feels rude not to wish them a merry Christmas.

"Merry Christmas," they reply. "We are late, so it's surprising that no one else is here."

"We thought it would be much busier," I answer.

"It usually is," says the daughter. "We come here every year, and this is the first time it's been this quiet."

For the following few hours it takes to enjoy our roast beef, Yorkshire pud and roast vegetables followed by Christmas pudding and custard, the four of us, along with the bouncy dogs, remain the restaurant's lone diners. We learn that he is a retired antique dealer.

"I had a shop on Portobello Road for 40 years… Antiques are not what they use to be… Too much fake stuff coming from China these days."

And the daughter, a commercial estate agent: "It's incredible how much I sell to the Chinese."

Eventually, after having experienced one of the loneliest Christmas lunches of our lives, we farewell our dining companions and depart the dining room, where, in the pub's main bar, we discover a hoard of well-lubricated Christmas Day revellers.

"So, this is where everyone is," Darryl says.

"So weird," I reply. "The four of us and dogs, had that large room to ourselves while this area is packed. Although, by the look and sound of it, these people have had more of a liquid lunch than a roast."

Boxing Day and today, those Premier League tickets that we were so thankful to secure are to be put to use – we are off to Selhurst Stadium to watch West Ham play Crystal Palace. Most of Britain's public transport shuts down over the Christmas period, and it's taken a lot of research to work out just how we will get to today's game. A tube from Notting Hill takes us to Victoria station, and here we purchase tickets on Southern Rail, a line not covered by our Oyster Cards. An hour after our departure, we find ourselves in the surprisingly grotty Crystal Palace main street rapidly filling with football fans. With our intention to have a drink and maybe a meal before entering the stadium, we head towards a nearby pub: Pub 3. It's packed and reserved for Crystal Palace supporters only, but Darryl, with his walking stick and myself, are waved in. Inside, it's just too crowded even to approach the bar, so we leave and eventually settle on coffee and a toasted sandwich at a nearby Costas.

Approaching Selhurst Stadium a short time later and a steady drizzle makes me grateful that I have bought along my small travel umbrella. Darryl, excited to finally be watching his football team play, doesn't even notice the rain.

Inside the stark concrete structure, cheerful security guards direct us to busy counters selling beverages and greasy 'game' food. Slightly damp, we join the other fans.

"This is great. Next time, if there ever is a next time, we'll just get something to eat and drink at the stadium," Darryl happily mumbles into his beer.

With game time approaching, we locate our blue plastic seats, thankfully completely undercover, and look towards the immaculate pitch where players are currently warming up. The stands encircling us are rapidly filling, team flags are flying and a deep pulsating drum reverberates around the stadium, its throbbing heartbeat.

Truth be told, I hadn't really been looking forward to attending today's game, especially with the miserable weather, but sitting here now, caught up in the swelling excitement, the noise, the mayhem and listening to that constant throbbing beat, my feelings completely change. This is fantastic; little wonder football supporters turn out in droves every weekend.

Unfortunately, West Ham goes down 2-1 and sitting as we are in a Crystal Palace supporter section (we had to become Crystal Palace supporters to secure tickets), it's difficult to remain impartial. Darryl, when West Ham does score their lone goal, completely outs himself by being the only person in our area who jumps up and cheers; the sour looks quickly forcing him to sit and not repeat the performance.

Despite the loss, the warmth and euphoria created by the whole experience remain with us as, in the dark night with constant drizzle, we join the crowds scrambling for seats on the few public holiday curtailed trains and slowly journey back to Notting Hill.

Our final day in London is spent packing our bags – our new suitcase very much appreciated – and catching up on sundry business. I spend time chatting with my sister Michelle, wishing her a happy 50th birthday, and learn that Australia is currently 10 hours in front of us and still in the grips of some severe bushfires.

With our week in London over, we are now heading to Caversham, near Reading, to spend the next six days with my Aunt Charlotte and her partner, Derek. We house-sat their place in 2017 and are looking forward to catching up with them, although this time, it will be at their new home, their old place having been sold.

With England transport still in holiday mode, Citymapper is again indispensable as it maps out how we should journey from Notting Hill to Reading, although the barely manageable four-minute change time at Waterloo is not altogether appreciated. Appreciated or not, it does get us onto a high-speed, direct train which means that 32 minutes after leaving London, we pull into familiar Reading Station.

The following six days are full of good company, good conversation and, more importantly, Charlotte's incredibly good cooking. One afternoon, Charlotte's daughters (my cousins) Fiona and Rosamunde and their families join us as we feast on a traditional English roast with all its accoutrements before wrapping up warmly to spend time at a nearby park. Another afternoon I have all my hair cut off at Charlotte's hairdresser.

"It will be much easier to manage on the boat," I say to Darryl as he looks for my missing locks.

Yet another day is spent in nearby Wallingford, a quintessential English market town situated on the River Thames. Full of antique shops exploding with ancient treasures and op shops full of modern ones, it's easy to while away the hours hunting for that lucrative must-have item. Lunch is eaten at the refurbished Wallingford post office, which, a plaque on the wall tells us, Agatha Christie used to frequent.

After hearing about our numerous escapades with mulled wine, New Year's Eve is spent hovering over the stove while Charlotte shows us an old family recipe for mulled wine, the results of which are happily consumed that evening as, together with a neighbour, we eat delicious food, watch the fireworks on television and welcome in the New Year.

With our cruise departure date drawing near, we head back to Reading where we purchase last-minute items such as toiletries from Boots, t-shirts from H&M and a dinner jacket for Darryl from one of the many op shops.

A local barber has Darryl fuming, when, asked what he wants done to his hair, does not understand his reply of "just cut 10 weeks of growth off."

"How is anyone meant to understand what that means?" I argue with Darryl.

"Melissa (his normal hairdresser) understands what it means," he replies.

"Well, you've completely wasted 15 pounds," I continue. "It doesn't look like they have cut anything off at all."

On our final full day, Charlotte introduces us to the delights of porridge served with whisky and cream for breakfast and spoils us with a traditional home-cooked Christmas pudding for dessert that night.

"Finally. I've been waiting all week for this. She wouldn't serve any pudding on Christmas Day instead saying we had to wait until you were here," grumbles Derek.

"Well, we appreciate the wait," I reply, laughing.

It's been an incredible week spent with two incredible people, and it's sad on the morning of Friday 3 January to bid Charlotte and Derek farewell. The Arcadia, the cruise ship which over the following seven weeks will transport us back to Australia, awaits us in Southampton. England once again has proven to be an exciting, memorable stopover on our travels, and I know I will once again miss her beautiful countryside, her abundance of opportunity, her trains.

Still wary of the Christmas transport timetable, we allow ourselves plenty of travel time and arrive at the Southampton Mayflower terminal an hour early of our allotted 3 pm embarkation time. The well-packed departure lounge indicates that we are not the only ones who have arrived early, and it takes another two hours before, customs cleared, we step once more onto the decks of the Arcadia. It feels great to be back on the road, to be continuing our adventure, and it feels even better to be doing so on such a familiar vessel, a ship which, in 2017, we spent five weeks travelling from Singapore to Southampton. Like last time, we are back on A or Australia deck; in fact, we are in the cabin next door. We like this location and this deck. It's immediately below the Belvedere buffet restaurant and the Aquarius outdoor bar, meaning we never have to walk far for food or beverages.

Within minutes of locating our room, an emergency drill is announced over the loudspeaker. As we make our way to our evacuation area, it becomes evident that the Arcadia has had an overhaul since we were last on board. Now 15 years old, she's looking a little smarter, her carpet and furniture a little newer than on our previous cruise.

The emergency drill, tedious but necessary, soon passes. The only thing we learn is that all the people currently sitting at the table with us at this drill are full around-the-world passengers.

"Yes," says one couple. "This will be our third world cruise."

"We are doing the full cruise as well," says another. "It will be our first world cruise although we have done the Sydney to Southampton leg before."

"Last time we were on this ship," I mention. "Less than a quarter of the guests were doing the full world cruise. It looks like there are a lot more of you this time."

"There are," someone replies. "There are nearly 900 of us."

With current passenger numbers totalling around 1800, it means that nearly half of them will be on for the entire duration. As I mention to Darryl back in our room sometime later, "I had forgotten how many Brits take this cruise. It surprises me every time how many of them do the full world cruise and not just once. They do it every year."

"I don't know how they can afford it," he replies.

After living out of our suitcases for the past 10 weeks, it feels great to unpack fully, to find homes for our toiletries, our clothes, our shoes. Making use of a voucher that allows us to purchase bottles of alcohol at duty free prices, we buy some single malt Glenfiddich and a bottle of Aperol and find homes for these as well.

Dinner is eaten in the Meridian restaurant where we meet recently retired Swede, Kersten. She's memorable not only because of her purple hair but because of her admission: "Oh, no. I didn't want to speak to anyone tonight. I have come to the wrong restaurant." Her honesty makes all at our table laugh.

At 11 pm, as the Arcadia, under a dark but mercifully rain-free sky, gently revs her engines and sounds her horns, we open our cabin door and step out onto our balcony. The streamer-waving departures of old have been modernised, and tonight, from our balcony, we watched enthralled as a fantastic vibrant firework display lights up the slowly disappearing terminal. Goodbye for now, England.

CHAPTER 13

Madeira

I*T's* still dark when around 7 am I roll out of bed and conduct my stretching yoga routine, the first time I have done so in weeks. The see-sawing motion of the ship doesn't seem to affect my cobra pose nor my downward dogs; it probably helps them. Afterwards, with night's mantle lifting to reveal a brisk fresh day, we make our way back to the Meridian for a full à la carte breakfast. My preference would have been a buffet breakfast in the Belvedere, but Darryl likes the Meridian's fluffy golden omelettes. Seated at a table for six, the conversation is all about Donald Trump and America.

"America has just launched an airstrike on Iran," one gentleman tells us. "Trump's killed Iran's most powerful commander, General Soleimani."

"Iran is not happy," someone else chips in. "They are calling for harsh retaliation."

"Well, I'm glad we are here at the beginning of a world cruise and not back in England worrying about World War Three," an elderly lady contributes. "I'm going to just ignore world politics for the next four months."

It will take four days to reach Madeira, our first port of call, and three of these will be spent at sea. Familiar with 'sea days,' we soon slip back into old routines, a favourite being attending guest lectures. Today's guest lecturer is Ben McBean, a former Royal Marine who, after a gruelling 32-week training course, was posted to Afghanistan, where he shortly after stepped on a Taliban IED. Minus two legs and an arm, it's genuinely inspirational to hear Ben's story and watch as, with his artificial legs, he quickly learns to accommodate the roll of the ship. Knowing that our food intake is about to increase substantially, this first day onboard, I devise a walking routine which I hope I will continue for the remainder of our cruise. It involves copious laps around the promenade deck where, apparently, three laps equal one mile.

"If I can do six or nine laps a day," I say more to myself than to Darryl. "That will be about 2 or 3 miles, nearly 5 kilometres."

"Good luck," Darryl replies.

Lunch is eaten in the Belvedere, where, over soup and salad, we hear deaf Derek from South Africa's story.

"I'm 91, and I'm originally from England but have lived in South Africa for the past 40 years... My wife died seven years ago... this is my third world cruise."

Initially prepared to be polite and listen, Derek's sincere tales, told in such a funny, forthright manner, soon have us grinning.

"I started packing about 10 weeks ago," he tells us earnestly. "I folded my shirts and put each one into a separate plastic bag."

"Why?"

"Because it keeps them flat. And I always bring some buttons and needles and thread with me."

"Why?"

"Because what happens if a button comes off my shirt and rolls away and I can't find it? My wife's not here to find it for me."

Returning to our cabin later that evening, along with the usual chocolate, we find an envelope lying on our bed.

"It's an invite to a party tomorrow night with the ship's captain," Darryl reads. "And guess who the captain is?"

"Not Captain Cook," I say.

"It is Captain Cook," Darryl replies.

Captain Ashley Cook is the ship's captain who, in 2017, not only commanded the cruise that shipped us to England but also commanded another voyage we undertook that same year around Ireland.

"Three times. Big coincidence," I say. "And I presume the party will be black tie?"

"It is," Darryl replies gloomily.

This morning it's my alarm going off at 8 am that wakes me. It's unusual for us to have slept in this late, although the fact that it is still dark outside may have something to do with it. Before going to bed last night, ideas were tossed around on how best to spend our days on this cruise.

"I would like to depart the ship having learnt something," I mention. "I remember last time being disappointed that I didn't pay more attention to the courses offered onboard."

"What's available on this cruise?"

"Well, currently they are offering Spanish and ukulele lessons, and there is also bridge for beginners."

After a lengthy conversation, it was agreed that while I would probably be useless at bridge, it would be good for Darryl, who enjoys cards. Not being very musical also ruled out ukulele lessons. "I'm going to learn how to play shuffleboard and deck quoits," I finally state.

Today, as the Arcadia travels further alongside the west coast of France towards the notorious Bay of Biscay, I take myself off to my first deck quoits competition. At the same time, Darryl becomes a foursome with Alan, Denise and Jacquie at bridge for beginners. "I'm not very sure about bridge," is his lunchtime assessment. "There is so much more to it than I was expecting. Cards usually mean some fun and a few beers, but I can't see that happening with bridge."

"Keep persevering," I reply. "It may get better and at least you are learning something. Deck quoits is fun, but I'm not very good at it. Hopefully, I'll do better with shuffleboard this afternoon."

Surprisingly, that afternoon, I do manage to do a lot better at shuffleboard. Teamed up with Bryn, another complete beginner, somehow, we manage to win the entire competition, although this is the only time I ever do so.

"I have no idea how we did that," Bryn laughs. "Complete beginner's luck."

There's little that Darryl finds more annoying than having to get dressed up. He managed to avoid having to do so last time we cruised on the Arcadia only by not having enough room in his suitcase to pack suitable clothes. Determined that this cruise we will attend the black tie events means that this evening, while Darryl unhappily pulls on his jacket and tie, I scramble into my evening gown and new heels. Decked out in our finery, we make our way to the mid-ship Neptune Bar where tonight's party with Captain Cook is to be held. We find it heaving with bodies squeezed vice-tight against the ship's swimming pool, and securing a drink is akin to winning the lotto. While Captain Cook does give a rousing "we are about to sail around the entire world" speech, in all, it's an anti-climactic, disappointing introduction to black tie affairs; something I'm not all that keen to repeat.

"Maybe we will avoid the whole ballgown thing," I say to a much-relieved Darryl. "But we can still dress up enough to be able to go out on black tie nights."

Today, my deck quoits partner is Kevin. Kevin is very good at quoits and pretty competitive. Kevin is definitely not very happy with my quoits performance which results in us being thrown out in the first round.

"I think I'm going to have to practice," I sigh to Darryl over lunch. "The quoits crowd is so much grumpier and more competitive than the shuffleboard crowd."

"You should try bridge," Darryl sighs back. "There is so much to it, and it's so confusing. Alan thinks we should download a bridge app to help us keep up."

To forget about my lack of sporting prowess, that afternoon, I take myself off to a hairstyling class while Darryl rests. Watching outrageous hairdresser Isham perform miracles on nodding grey heads is cheering, and at dinnertime, I am further buoyed by the Welsh couple we sit with. While having heard about the 'sing-song' accent of Welsh speakers, it's the first time I have come across such a blatant example, and I sit there in open-mouthed disbelief, trying to work out if they are joking with us.

Peeking through the cracks of our cabin curtain are the inquisitive rays of the most vibrant fire-red sunrise. Which, I note, as I push the curtains further apart, perfectly illuminates the little white houses with their red terracotta roofs that scale the escalating hills before me. We have arrived in Funchal (the name Funchal derives from the fennel plant which once grew in abundance here), capital of Madeira.

Lying west of Morocco and north of the Canary Islands, the Madeiran peninsula, an autonomous region of Portugal, is an archipelago of four islands, of which only two are inhabited. We have arrived at the largest of these islands, characterised by its rugged green hills, high volcanic cliffs and stony beaches. Discovered in 1419 by Portuguese explores, the resulting colonisation saw the island become a leader in the sugar-producing trade by 1490 and by the 17th century, experts in wine production, the most notable of which is the acclaimed Madeira wine.

Not sure of what exactly we want to do here, we have decided to search out this world-famous wine, maybe try a piece of 'Madeira' cake and perhaps partake of the famous Madeira 'toboggan' ride.

Before we do all this, however, we catch up on the world news, which briefly mentions a new virus currently causing concern in the Chinese city of Wuhan.

"Wuhan?" I cry. "Isn't that where the family we met on our Terracotta Army tour came from?"

"It is," Darryl replies. "He makes screens for phones there."

And my phone lights up, indicating that we have unexpected internet, which proves useful as we catch up on emails and quickly FaceTime the kids.

"I'm not taking the graduate nursing position at Mater Hospital," Paige tells us. "I've been accepted to do social work at the Queensland University of Technology."

"I can't believe how messy the house gets," says Pierce. "I'm always having to clean up."

"That was an unexpected catch-up," I say as I turn off my phone. "I wasn't expecting this sim card to work once we left England. If I had realised just how global it was, I would have purchased some extra credit. Or bought a second one."

Funchal, we discover sometime later, is a vibrant, easy-to-navigate and modern city, packed with English speakers, cafés, restaurants, museums and historical sites. Its most famous resident is football superstar Ronaldo who owns a museum near the port here. The harbour is located centrally, meaning we are within easy reach of this museum and many other attractions. Having obtained further information regarding Madeira's toboggan ride from Arcadia's port guide, we intend to ride first, eat, drink and explore later.

Dating back to 1850 as the primary method of downhill public transportation, the Madeira toboggan or sled ride is these days the most popular of all Madeira's activities. The 2 kilometre journey commences from the elevated suburb of Monte, reaches speeds of up to 50 kilometres per hour and occurs in a large wicker and eucalyptus wood basket. Two drivers, clad in white uniforms, power the basket, gliding on its greased-up wooden slats. Their special rubber-soled shoes are the only things standing between you and a high impact disaster.

To reach the ride's starting point situated high above the city, we have three options – walk, taxi or cable car. We choose the popular cable car, and unlike our recent rural cable car experience in China, this one is an endless uphill suburban journey; shakily raising us over large asphalt highways, deep water-ravaged gorges and an abundance of those terracotta tiled houses. When we finally reach our destination, the view of Funchal and the sweeping blue Atlantic Ocean is gorgeous, as are the beautiful botanic gardens that abut our viewing platform.

It costs 25 Australian dollars each to sit in our wicker nest; to listen to the laboured breath of our drivers as they act as breaks or push us over the flatter areas; to shut my eyes when we veer too close to a stone wall or a water-filled gutter and to clutch tightly as we roughly navigate sharp corners. This also includes a stop for a photo opportunity but not the photo, and it doesn't get us all the way back down the long steep hill.

"You walk from here," we are told about a 20-minute walk shy of the town centre.

"Don't you go any further?"

"Not anymore. Too many cars. Too many accidents."

Despite this additional long downhill walk that tomorrow will have our calf muscles screaming, the entire experience has been great, one we would definitely repeat.

It's mid-afternoon when we eventually arrive back in downtown Funchal and hungrily search for our Madeira cake. Madeira cake is a favourite morning tea at home, and we are keen to compare the supermarket-brought product with the real thing. Surprisingly and with some disappointment, we discover that Madeira cake here isn't at all the same as that in Australia. Madeira cake in Australia is a delicious, buttery, golden ingot, while here it's a rich, honey-flavoured disc topped with almonds.

Our disappointment doesn't stop us, however, from digging into huge slices of the moist round cake and downing large lattes, all purchased for less than 10 Australian dollars.

Some fellow Arcadian passengers have recommended we visit the Mercado dos Lavradores, Madeira's workers market. Here, in this open-topped area, we linger over stalls full of items made from Portuguese cork, produced from the Quercus rubber tree (Portugal's most predominant tree – the country is responsible for more than half of the world's cork output). While I love the cork handbags, they are costly and so, disappointed, walk on to the stalls groaning with meat, cheese, colourful flowers and delicious fruit. Pausing at one stall selling *monstera deliciosa*, a tropical plant, laughter erupts when we hear the stall owner spruik his product to a nearby tourist.

"Is pineapple. Taste very good – you buy?"

Giving up on sampling some sticky Madeira wine, we instead head to a local modern-looking supermarket intent on buying some water for our cabin and some mixers to have with our duty free alcohol. Finding the soft drink aisle stripped bare, we can only surmise that many of our fellow passengers have had the same idea but have been a little quicker off the mark.

"Cruise ship passengers are a bit like swarming locusts," Darryl comments.

Back on board, while Darryl searches optimistically for an empty washing machine in one of the highly popular laundries, I use the remaining data on our sim to get off a blog. I time it perfectly, with the data expiring shortly after I post the article.

At around 5:30 pm, with night falling, the Arcadia lets go of her lines, clears the Funchal breakwater and turns in a south-westerly direction. The Atlantic Ocean lies like a big challenge in front of us; there will be no stops now until we have traversed it and arrived in Barbados, our next port of call.

CHAPTER 14

Barbados

A NEW day and it's an interesting start to the morning. After waking and putting our watches back yet another hour – we are now 11 hours behind Australia – we turn on the television to hear the news that in retaliation to Trump's earlier barrage, which resulted in the death of Iranian General Soleimani, Iran has launched their own missile attack. They have targeted American bases in Iraq, and the world is watching on with deep unease. While it flits across my mind how far from world events we are out here, I decide it may be more prudent to do like that little old lady at dinner, to leave the news channels alone, to ignore global politics for a while.

My uniform for the past two months has been jeans and jumpers, and it's a welcome surprise this morning when I make my way to shuffleboard, to find that these clothes are too heavy for our current climate. Somehow overnight, the temperature has risen significantly, evident by the number of bodies lazing on sunbeds, and it's with jubilation that I quickly return to our cabin and exchange my jeans for shorts. While shuffleboard doesn't yield great results, I do somehow make it to the semi-final of quoits. Darryl meantime, continues to struggle with bridge for beginners.

The afternoon passes easily and pleasantly as we sit on our balcony and watch the vast Atlantic Ocean slip by. With absolutely nothing but the beautiful blue water to look at, we sit here with our books and our sudoku until the sun sinks and the chilly night forces us to return inside. Continuing with our uncomplicated day, we forgo fine dining and instead, dinner is a feast of lasagne and ravioli from the Belvedere's Italian buffet.

Another morning, more time adjustments (Australia is now 12 hours ahead), and this time we take our breakfast trays and eat on the Arcadia's back deck where the sun is shining hotly and the pool is splashing happily. Someone has mentioned that pineapple is good for your digestion. It helps your body process the preservatives used in the ship's food that can wreak havoc on your stomach, so my toast is layered with thick chunks of the sweet sticky fruit. It tastes delicious, and time will prove the advice correct.

We get two great guest speakers today: Ardella Jones, an author, who presents us with 21 tips on how to write a bestseller and Sally Kettle. Sally, in particular, is very entertaining. She studied theatre at university and thus knows all the tricks on keeping an audience enthralled, which she does as she tells us how she rowed the entire Atlantic Ocean, not once but twice.

"The first time I rowed, it was meant to be a fundraiser with my boyfriend. Unfortunately, he had to pull out three days into the race due to an asthma attack, so I got on the satellite phone and called my mum. 'Mum, come and help me,' which she did. She flew out from England, and together we 'rowed south until the butter melted then turned right' until we reached Barbados. We became the first mother and daughter team ever to row the Atlantic Ocean."

Sally also talks about her second Atlantic crossing, this time as part of a group of four girls. As she talks about resilience, facing fears and those 'rolling Atlantic breakers' – long, undulating swells that we are becoming familiar with – I picture her in her tiny rowing boat on this vast ruthless ocean and wonder how on earth she did it. It would be terrifying.

Friday 10 January, our one-week anniversary on board the Arcadia, and today we pass over the Mid Atlantic Ridge. This ridge, separating the Eurasian from the North American continental plates, is part of the most extensive mountain range in the world and sees the water level decreasing from 5,000 to 1,000 metres. The day also marks another time change, with Australia now 13 hours ahead of us.

"All this having to change our watches makes time seem so irrelevant."

"I agree," Darryl replies. "When you're travelling this way, you don't notice the change in time. You get up and go to sleep each day. There's no jet lag or side effects. Nothing feels like it changes, the sun rises then falls, but in Australia, it's doing that 13 hours ahead of us now."

"And in a few days, Australia will be even further ahead of us," I continue. "I wonder how we catch up. I guess we'll find out eventually."

Today we spoil ourselves and head to the Meridian restaurant for one of their decadent afternoon teas. Over buttery scones, finger sandwiches and moist tea cakes, we meet Margaret and Bill from Redcliff, Brisbane, the first Australians we have met onboard, and we welcome the easy camaraderie that instantly flares between fellow Australian travellers. Like us, they are amazed by the number of Poms undertaking their third or fourth world cruise, and like Kate and Gary in Paris, they also have an interesting story to tell.

"We booked this cruise through an Australian agency," Margaret tells us. "It's part of a package deal which also included New Year's Eve in Paris, a few days in London and all accommodation and transfers were meant to be included. However, when we flew into Paris, there was no one at the airport to pick us up.

"Someone was meant to be there," Bill chirps. "We had paid for all our transfers."

"Due to the strikes," Margaret continues, "it took hours to get a taxi, but eventually we arrived at our hotel – too late to have the special New Year's Eve dinner and celebration we had planned. And as it was New Year's Eve, it was impossible to get a hold of our travel agent to find out what had happened, but we did phone the local transport company who were meant to collect us."

"We had their details on our reservation," adds Bill.

"They advised that all of our Paris transfers had been cancelled," says Margaret again picking up the story. "Which meant we also had to find and pay for the transfer back to the airport. But that wasn't the worst of it. We had also paid for a transfer from Heathrow to Southampton."

"And that didn't turn up either?"

"That's right," continues Margaret. "That transfer had cost quite a bit of money. Everything is currently closed in Australia due to the New Year period, but once they reopen and if I can find some internet, then we'll be chasing this up. It's cost us a fortune in additional transfer fees, and it nearly wrecked our New Year."

Taking this as confirmation that it's not always good to rely on any single agency or person for all your travel plans, and happy in our decision to usually go it alone, we leave Margaret and Bill, knowing we will probably never find out what actually happened.

That afternoon and we discover a waterfall cascading from the ceiling outside our cabin door. It's a little disconcerting floating on a ship somewhere in the vast Atlantic Ocean with water gushing down the corridor walls and the carpet inches deep in water. While maintenance men eventually reduce the flow to a trickle, it takes another week before I can safely enter our cabin without my shoes getting wet.

Saturday 11 January, and we are now 14 hours behind Australia. This morning's news mentions more about that virus circulating in China. Identified as a 'coronavirus,' it's apparently becoming a little more serious, with reports suggesting that it originated in one of Chinas fish or 'wet markets.' Familiar with wet markets from time spent in Asia, with their stalls of raw meat and filthy, sticky floors, I am not surprised. Although knowing that many of Asia's wet markets were closed following the 2012 MERS outbreak, I am surprised that China still allows them. I also briefly wonder whether Darryl's cold, caught after meeting that family from Wuhan, could have had something to do with this virus. On a lighter note, the news also mentions how Prince Harry and Meghan are resigning their positions as senior royals.

Sometime during the day, Captain Cook or "Captaaain Cook," as he calls himself, advises that the Arcadia is travelling just north of the Inter-Tropical Convergence Zone (ITCZ). Known as the doldrums, the ITCZ is a belt around the Earth that extends approximately 5 degrees north and south of the equator, where the trade winds of the northern hemisphere collide with the trade winds of the southern hemisphere. This collision causes air in this zone to circulate in an upward direction resulting in little surface wind. Reason enough for sailors of yore to fall into the 'doldrums.'

Our fifth straight day at sea and edging closer to the Caribbean, every day is now hat, shorts and singlet weather. Tomorrow, we arrive in Barbados but today it's all about keeping busy on board. I'm persevering with my daily laps; in fact, I'm enjoying pounding the promenade. The only thing that annoys me as I power walk the decks are the unhurried couples who stroll the narrow boardwalk hand in hand. They make it difficult to pass, and I can't understand why so many couples need to get their daily exercise while clutching their partner's hand.

Overboard, the ordinarily rolling blue ocean is becoming increasingly streaked with tendrils of brown. Called sargassum, this floating plant life starts its journey in the Gulf of Mexico before prevailing currents push it out into the Atlantic. Here, these floating 'seaweed rafts' are not only becoming more noticeable, but they are also serving as vital feeding grounds for the local marine life.

Mealtimes today are entertaining. At lunch, we meet elderly British couple June and Peter. While June is sitting at the table we all share, the only sign of Peter is his rapidly cooling meal.

"I don't know what's happened to him," June says in consternation. "He's been gone for about 20 minutes. Could you look after our meals while I go and look for him?"

Returning a short time later, Peter in tow, June thanks us while Peter fills in the blanks.

"Needed to use the toilet," he says matter of factly. "But I got a bit lost. Ended up on F deck."

F deck is seven decks below us which shows just how off-track Peter was.

Chatting further, we discover that this is June and Peter's 10th world cruise, but it may be their last.

"Why is that?" Darryl asks.

"We've had some trouble on this trip," says June. "Peter normally uses an electric scooter. We organised for a company to collect this scooter from our home and deliver it to the Arcadia, but the company never showed up."

"So, a neighbour helped out," Peter continues. "He collected the scooter and bought it to Southampton wharf, but he didn't tell anyone."

"He just left it on the dock," says June.

"So where is it now?" I ask.

"It's onboard," says Peter. "But the key isn't."

And at dinner, we meet Australians John and Cheryl.

"We booked this cruise through an Australian agency," Cheryl tells us. "It included New Year's Eve in Paris and some days in London."

"But we had some trouble," says John.

"Don't tell us," I interject. "Your transfers never turned up."

"How the hell did you know that" John exclaims.

"There is another Australian couple on here who had the same problem. They like the afternoon teas in the Meridian restaurant. You might find them in there one day if you need to compare notes."

Seven thousand, three hundred kilometres after leaving Southampton, five days after departing Madeira and now 15 hours behind Australia, we awaken in Bridgetown, capital of Barbados, a small island in the sparkling Caribbean Sea. Incredibly, we have crossed the Atlantic Ocean.

"It wasn't that difficult," considers Darryl. "Not much to see but the conditions were pretty good. It'll be interesting to see what the Pacific Ocean is like in comparison."

"I don't mind the days," I reply. "But it's a little daunting being so far from land when I wake up and can't get back to sleep during the night. And surely the Pacific will have more to see. I can't believe we didn't see any land, nor birds nor a single boat for the entire crossing."

While recent archaeological discoveries suggest Barbados has an ancient history that dates to 1623 BC, when Amerindians in dugout canoes arrived from Venezuela, its modern history starts in 1625 when a British ship landed and claimed the island for England. This claim was held until 1966, when Barbados attained independence. Because of this long association with Britain, its culture, government, schools and religion bear a striking British influence; however, its West African heritage (built by descendants of slaves bought to the island) also prevails. Today it's a melting pot of Barbadians or 'Bajans,' the name given to these descendants, and others – Europeans, Caucasians and Middle Eastern people.

Although aware of Barbados – an awareness no doubt bought about by its inclusion in the Commonwealth, its association with the West Indies cricket team and its competitive Olympians – we never expected to visit here and thus were not sure how to plan our visit. Fellow Arcadians have advised that they will be sipping cocktails under sun umbrellas on one of the many pristine beaches or attempting to snorkel with turtles. Not interested in chasing the sun ourselves, we eventually put our names down for an afternoon local rum tour, but first, we'll head into Bridgetown to do a bit of exploring.

"I need to find some cooler clothes and hopefully some thongs," I say to Darryl. "It's too hot playing shuffleboard in my Skechers and I can wear them on our tour."

"I'm not sure about the rum tour," Darryl replies. "I hate rum."
"Rum was invented here," I remind him. "It should be good."

The Arcadia has berthed at the island's main terminal, a 20-minute walk from the town centre. Stepping ashore, we find ourselves in a large building filled with bustling souvenir stalls, persistent touts and a colourful, pumping bar. Another cruise ship, the P&O Ventura, a vessel capable of holding 2,800 passengers, is moored alongside, which means the place is heaving. It's a relief to find a shuttle bus and escape the hustle.

With its Caribbean location, it's hot enough that when we arrive at Bridgetown's centre, we must peel ourselves from the shuttle's plastic seats and the footpaths have slightly melted. Looking around us, the town's British heritage becomes abundantly apparent: Georgian houses, neo-Gothic public buildings, English signage, a square complete with a statue of Lord Nelson, not to mention the large Kensington 'cricket' oval passed on the way here. For the following few hours that we explore Bridgetown, passing countless jewellery and watch shops while we search in vain for my clothes (made from nylon and the wrong size) and thongs (non-existent), we are continuously kept surprised by this 'Britishness;' unfortunately, it appears to be a neglected legacy. Although plentiful and colourful, the shops are tired, the former grand historical buildings dilapidated and the bitumen streets narrow and potholed.

"It doesn't look like they have done any maintenance on the place since they became independent," I comment to Darryl.

The one place that has managed to avoid the decline is the Careenage, an area whose boardwalk, marina and Chamberlain Bridge make it a pleasant place to stroll.

With the departure time of our rum tour nearing, we shun a shuttle bus and instead walk back to the Arcadia. Our walk takes us alongside the calm, azure Caribbean waters of the island's west coast – its east coast fronts the Atlantic where the waters are much more powerful – and through flowering gardens punctuated by eclectic market stalls.

At one booth, we purchase a colourful 'Barbados' inscribed nip pourer to add to our 'travel treasure' collection.

While these days tourism, finance and offshore reserves of oil and natural gas contribute significantly to the Barbados coffers, sugar was once its presiding export. Its legacy lives on today in the form of its rum trade. Rum – made from molasses, a by-product of sugar – originated here, is revered here and its name was coined here. Our tour today will visit the 1720 AD Foursquare Rum distillery and one of the world's oldest distilleries, the 1637 AD Mount Gay distillery.

The success of a tour usually depends on the attributes of your tour guide. As we leave the confines of Bridgetown and make our way alongside the Barbados coastline, heavily populated by large hotels hogging views of golden beaches, it appears as if we have scored well with 'Andy,' short for Anderson, today's driver and guide. Andy, for any fans of *Death in Paradise* – a TV series filmed on the nearby island of Guadeloupe – is a dead ringer for Dwayne. Very friendly, slightly shifty and easily manages to keep up a constant informative chatter as he negotiates the narrow, winding roads that soon have us traversing fields of sugarcane and villages of small, wooden pastel-hued homes.

"Wa gine on?" he asks, before going on to explain. "'Wa gine on' is Bajan for 'what's going on?' Bajan is our unofficial language. It began when slaves were bought here and were forced to speak English. Although English is the official language, most of us talk Bajan."

Andy continues: "Queen Elizabeth is our head of state, and our schooling is based on the British system… Our main religion is Christianity, but we also have many other faiths… We have over 300 churches in Barbados." A fact substantiated by the many colourful wooden or brick churches viewed from our coach windows.

"Our rum is the best in the world, and you will get to sample a good amount here – but don't overdo it," he calls, as he drops us at Foursquare Rum, the first of our distilleries.

Alongside us on this tour is one of my shuffleboard mates Daphne, who, unlike us, is a great fan of rum. Daphne and her husband come in very handy when after an extensive tour of the facilities and a thorough rundown on how rum is produced, we are plied with copious samples of the rich, golden liquid. While better than the Bundaberg rum we remember from home, the glasses are too numerous and too generous, and we are happy to pass them on to an increasingly perky Daphne and partner.

Making our way to Mount Gay, the second of our distilleries, Andy takes pains to point out some machinery working hard amidst the sugarcane.

"Those are oil mules," he tells us. "Barbados has a small reserve of oil under her, and those mules pump enough for us to be self-sufficient."

Unlike the Foursquare distillery, which was situated amongst lush sugarcane fields and produced its rum onsite, Mount Gay is more a retail outlet, and its tastings are even more liberal. Thankfully, Daphne and partner again willingly help us out.

It's early evening when eventually, we arrive back at Bridgetown. Before reboarding, we join many of the Arcadia passengers who are making use of the terminal's free wi-fi. Emails are caught up on, Facebook is perused and the kids are messaged.

"What date are you home?" questions Pierce. "I think I had better look for a cleaner."

At 9:30 pm, under a surprisingly wet night while we are happily ensconced in our warm comfortable bed, the Arcadia thrusts off her berth, swings her bow to port at 90 degrees and slowly heads out to sea, destination Curaçao: our next port of call.

CHAPTER 15

Curaçao and Panama

*L*YING just off the northern coast of South America, Curaçao, like Barbados, is another of those small quirky islands that dot the brilliant sapphire Caribbean Sea. From Barbados, it takes a full day sailing and two nights to reach Willemstad, Curaçao's capital. The day is spent reading, lounging on our balcony and observing the passing scenery. Unlike the Atlantic Ocean we have just traversed, the Caribbean is full of heavily laden cargo ships heading to or from the nearby Panama Canal, and tiny palm-frond islands are littered here and there. Overhead, the sky is the most profound crystal blue, meaning every photo I take is magazine-worthy.

On the morning of 15 January, around 8 am, whilst we eat breakfast in the Belvedere Restaurant, the Arcadia lazily dances around the Willemstad harbour before the captain secures her to a wharf half her size. It's another great example of skippering, a skill that continues to fascinate us. From our elevated perch, it becomes apparent that Curaçao is pancake-flat and exploring should be easy.

First visited by Europeans in 1499, it was the arrival of the Dutch in 1634 that had the most influence over this small Caribbean enclave. It was they who turned the island into a major centre of trade with the Dutch West India Company, and it was they who turned what was once a fair slave trade into a thriving industry. Fast-forward a few hundred years, and while the slave trade has been abolished and the population become more cosmopolitan, Curaçao is still in Dutch hands, only gaining independence (although remaining within the Kingdom of the Netherlands) in 2010. Today, ownership of some of the western hemisphere's largest oil refineries combined with a booming tourism industry mean Curaçao is a prosperous little nation.

It's also a nation that lies outside the hurricane belt that so detrimentally affects neighbouring islands, offers near-perfect weather (the average temperature is 27 degrees), and whose turquoise waters gently lap crystalline sand.

With such stunning beaches, it's little wonder that most of the excursions on offer involve a water activity of some sort, most of which are readily available to Australians and we are unwilling to repeat. For these reasons, we have decided to forgo them all and instead head into Willemstad. Willemstad, we have been told, could have been plucked straight out of Europe.

It doesn't take long to disembark, and as we leave the port and stroll towards the nearby small city, the island's Dutch heritage becomes apparent. Large public buildings scream European and neat rows of gabled, tiled houses abound. The only glaring difference between these buildings and those found on the continent are their bright pastel colours.

"Rumour has it that the reason all the buildings here are so colourful," I read from our port guide, "is because a former governor claimed that the glaring white gave him a migraine. He made everyone paint their houses in any colour but white. It was only on his death that it was discovered that he owned the largest paint factory in Curaçao."

Willemstad is divided into two districts: Otrabanda, which contains the cruise ship terminal, and Punda, location of not only many of Willemstad's most popular sites, such as the city's main square and floating market, but many orderly shopping streets full of un-air-conditioned funky shops. Dividing the two is St. Anna Bay, a wide stretch of aquamarine waters crossed by a floating bridge. Known as the Swinging Old Lady, this pontoon bridge (whose actual name is the Queen Emma Bridge), floats atop the water, and powered by a diesel engine, will swings open multiple times throughout the day to allow ships into the harbour. It's a unique experience to cross this bobbing wooden bridge to reach solid land just as a siren sounds. And it's exciting to watch those still on the bridge pause and wait as the engine fires up, the bridge swings open and a small fishing vessel sashays through.

While it's fascinating to see so much aged European architecture here, such as the 18th-century Fort Amsterdam and the 1742 Fort Church, it's the funky little shops we are more interested in probing. The contents of a city's stores will give you an instant insight into the heart of a place, and it's in these that the cosmopolitan nature of Willemstad is revealed. Outlets full of expensive Swiss watches and Italian designer handbags sit alongside others full of colourful Rastafarian clothing and African souvenirs. At the same time, an Afro-Curaçaoan shoe shiner conducts a roaring trade outside an upmarket American hotel.

What is also on offer, and in plentiful supply, is the famous blue Curaçao liqueur. Made from the dried peel of the bitter orange laraha, a citrus fruit brought to the island by Spanish explorers, this liqueur more than anything has put Curaçao on the world map. We determine to stop at one of the many bars selling the blue liquid at a later stage.

First, we must continue our exploration, to further pound the wide pedestrian-friendly footpaths, to walk amidst the colourful buildings. In one sizeable dusty store, I gratefully find a pair of fake Birkenstocks suitable for shuffleboard, while in another, we both find light cotton t-shirts emblazoned with the name Curaçao, ideal as a memento. Coming across a small barbershop, Darryl hesitates.

"Do you think I should get a haircut?"

Although he only had his last haircut in Caversham a few short weeks ago, the experience was a debacle, so I instantly nod my head.

"Definitely. But this time tell them how much you want cut off."

Despite the barber speaking only Spanish and Darryl having to mime his wishes, the haircut is a success. It even includes a quick eyebrow shave, something Darryl is unfamiliar with and has him jumping in startled surprise. Paying with some American dollars, Darryl departs the store happy while the barber looks after him in bemusement.

Continuing on, we find the floating market unfortunately closed, but a table with panoramic views of St. Anna Bay at a nearby bar is conveniently free. For the remainder of our time in Willemstad, we sit at this table – Darryl drinking beer while I experiment with the different ways of enjoying blue Curaçao. In between, I manage to get off a blog using the bar's free wi-fi while Darryl catches up with news from home. Most of it concerns the bushfires still raging throughout Australia.

"The bushfires are unprecedented," he reads. "Nearly every state has been affected, in particular New South Wales, Victoria and South Australia. Thousands have lost their homes, and 30 people have died. Parts of the country are averaging 50-degree temperatures!"

"What a nightmare summer," I answer. "I'm glad we are missing it. Imagine the heat. And the land that's been lost."

"It's the loss of wildlife that everyone is really concerned about," Darryl answers. "The number of animals killed is in the millions."

Back onboard the Arcadia and that afternoon, as I return a book to the library, I meet British born Captain Cook on the stairwell, and we get chatting. While I mention where we are from, that this is the third cruise we have taken with him and that he features in our book *Bucket Lists and Walking Sticks*, he talks about his love of Byron Bay (a town near Brunswick Heads), his family in Perth and his upcoming plans.

"I'm hoping to retire next year, spend a bit more time with the wife. Do a bit more travelling such as you are doing."

Considering he spends his time travelling the world's oceans, I take this as a compliment.

With Curaçao behind us, Venezuela, then Colombia on our port side, the Arcadia maintains a steady 22 knots westward. She is booked to traverse the Panama Canal on 17 January, and the 500,000 American dollar surcharge for doing so has already been paid.

A new guest speaker, former Panama Canal pilot Captain Kenneth Puckett has joined us, and the Palladium Theatre is crammed with guests interested in hearing him lecture on this man-made engineering marvel.

"After retiring from the army, I spent 16 years working as a canal pilot," he tells us. "I retired in 1996, wrote a book about my experiences and have been giving lectures onboard cruise ships ever since."

Traversing the Panama Canal was one of the catalysts for this entire adventure, and it's the final of the four Bucket List items we are currently chasing. Without this desire to pursue Bucket List items, to navigate one of the world's most significant waterways and compare it to the crossing of the Suez Canal, which we did in 2017, this book would not exist.

Bisecting central Panama, the Panama Canal is an 82-kilometre, man-made canal that links the Atlantic and Pacific oceans, creating an essential shipping route capable of cutting 23 days from a vessel's journey. Initially undertaken in 1880 by Ferdinand de Lesseps, the Frenchman responsible for the construction of the Suez Canal, the project was beset with financial and construction problems and epidemics of malaria and yellow fever. Declaring bankruptcy in 1888, the project was shelved until 1904 when, spying a good investment opportunity, the United States took up the gauntlet.

America, unlike the French, recognised that a flat, sea-level canal would not work in the mountainous terrain of Panama. Instead, they set about constructing a waterway that would operate using sets of locks: a short section of water with gates at either end that changed the water level when opened and closed, thus raising or lowering boats.

It took 10 years and, when combined with the French figures, suffered a loss of between 30,000-40,000 lives, but in August 1914, the Canal was opened and has been operating 365 days a year ever since. Albeit, since 1999, by the Panama Canal Authority.

Like with our Suez crossing, it's very early morning when we approach the Panama breakwaters and our pilot boards. Keen to experience every moment of the journey, we are awake and have settled ourselves into the Crow's Nest, an upper-level lounge with panoramic views where Captain Puckett will be maintaining an informative commentary of our upcoming crossing. Seated in comfortable chairs and armed with bracing cups of coffee, we watch as linesmen board the Arcadia and secure her to mules – locomotives on tracts that run alongside the canal edges and help keep a vessel centred within the tight locks. With three sets of locks that act as a staircase to traverse, it's crucial that the Arcadia stays well secured to these mules and dead steady.

Coming from the Atlantic side of the Canal, it's the narrow Gatun Lock that we enter at 8:30 am, centimetres spare on either side and are raised three times to climb the 26 metres necessary to enter Gatun Lake. There's a twin canal located alongside, almost within touching distance, designed for vessels travelling in the opposite direction, and it's surreal to find ourselves slowly rising while a sister ship unhurriedly descends.

Man-made and totalling 425 square kilometres, Gatun Lake is a true wonder to discern as we slowly ford her waters, spy semi-submerged islands and pass heavily laden cargo ships or other cruising vessels. Gatun Lake leads to Galliard Cut, a stretch of man-made canal that slices through the Continental Divide, the landmass that separates the northern and southern American continents, and eventually, five hours later, we arrive at Pedro Miguel Lock. While much of the time has been spent in the Crow's Nest listening to Captain Puckett, we have also walked most of the Arcadia's decks searching for the best photo opportunities, and lunch has been enjoyed in the Belvedere.

"There's a prison near here," Captain Puckett mentions at one point. "The prisoners would always wave to us as we passed by."

And he continues: "There are still indigenous groups that live deep in the forests here. They mainly keep to themselves although some do come out and sell their goods... The forests are full of monkeys and leopards... Two billion American dollars are collected in tolls annually... A new bigger canal for larger ships was completed in 2016... The Centennial Bridge we are just passing under can take six lanes of traffic... There's a military range nearby still full of unexploded devices."

Around 3 pm, Pedro Miguel Lock lowers us nine metres into Miraflores Lake, another man-made marvel and shortly after, we arrive at the crest of the final of our locks, the Miraflores Locks, where the Arcadia stops for a medical evacuation.

"Coincidence," I say to Darryl. "We had a medical evacuation when we traversed the Suez Canal."

Unlike the Suez evacuation, which, entangled in Egyptian bureaucracy, was a lengthy one, today's evacuation is straightforward and swift. It is spent eyeballing a purpose-built lonely hotel whose viewing platforms are currently packed with people eyeballing us. We are still all gazing at one another until the Arcadia slowly drops the 17 metres required to reach sea level, sails under the Bridge of America and is expelled into the mighty Pacific Ocean.

As we stand on the Arcadia's back deck, the swift-moving Pacific current carrying us further out into the Gulf of Panama, we gaze at the beauty surrounding us and ruminate on our day.

"That's the fourth and final Bucket List item," I murmur, as to starboard the sinking sun colours the water and distant mountains a mesmerising molten gold.

"What an incredible day," Darryl replies. "And how lucky are we to be able to compare both the Suez and Panama Canals."

"Which did you prefer?" I ask, now looking to port where Panama City, a jungle of glinting skyscrapers, scatters the last of the sun's rays like a white-hot firecracker.

"It's hard to choose but maybe the Suez. You?"

"I don't have a preference," I answer. "They were both incredible. The Suez slicing through a sandy desert and manned by armed guards every 400 metres. The Panama, a set of watery stairs created both ends of a huge man-made lake. Both so amazing."

Captivated by our surroundings, the glowing sun, the golden water, the shining city, the plethora of cargo ships waiting for their turn to enter the canal, it's well after sundown that we eventually, reluctantly, turn away and head back inside.

With two days of sailing before we reach Guatemala, our next port of call, it's comforting to be back on the Pacific Ocean. Unlike the Atlantic Ocean, an alien entity, the Pacific is our very own ocean. We live minutes from her, we visit her every day and we have swum in her waters most of our lives.

Attending a guest lecture, oceanographers Maeve and Hazel educate us on the species of dolphins and whales that live in these eastern Pacific waters.

"You are more likely to come across the blue and grey whales in these waters," Maeve tells us. "Whereas the humpback is more common off the coast of Australia."

"To spot a whale," says Hazel. "Look for a smooth patch on the ocean's surface or where the seabirds are hovering."

And they both take great pains to educate everyone on the 'Great Pacific Garbage Patch.'

"It's made of two huge islands of floating plastic that stretch between Japan and Hawaii and Hawaii and California," they tell us. "It equates to over 79,000 tons of garbage that stretches over 1.6 million square kilometres. That's over three times larger than France. And it's still growing!"

One morning, we put our watches back yet another hour, meaning Australia is even further ahead of us, and the daily newsletter that is delivered to our cabin informs us that the coronavirus is starting to appear in other countries.

"Japan and Thailand both have cases," I read. "Everyone is beginning to get a little more worried. I wonder if it will reach Australia?"

Now heading north-westerly, we parallel the Central American coast, eventually passing Costa Rica, Nicaragua and El Salvador. The water is glass-smooth and alive with small, playful dolphins. Not far from the equator, the days are hot and steamy, and I appreciate my new fake Birkenstocks, although they do stain my feet a dirty grey.

Our northerly direction draws us closer and closer to Guatemala, meaning that each afternoon we have the luxury of watching a blazing sun sink over the horizon from our private balcony. As we sit watching the burning orb sink lower and lower, I read a book while Darryl either practices his bridge moves or works on a sudoku. It's these moments that are unforgettable and bring home to us the joy of travelling.

CHAPTER 16

Guatemala

*I*T'S another sun-drenched day as I throw open the curtains of our cabin. We have arrived in Puerto Quetzal, Guatemala's largest port, and I am eager to get my first glimpse of this enigmatic, controversial country. Yesterday, the Arcadia was tailed for hours by a large naval vessel, reinforcing my view that Guatemala is an unknown entity. In front of me, I spy a vast, smoking coal refinery lying adjacent to some conical thatched huts. In the background, scrubby vegetation draws the eye to three maybe four archetypal volcanos. It looks like it's going to be a day of contrasts.

Around three and a half thousand years ago, Guatemala was inhabited by the Mayans. From 1500 BC to about 900 AD, the Mayans, one of precolonial Americas most advanced people, cultivated the land, studied the heavens and refined their construction skills. Under their rule, imposing palaces were built, a sophisticated calendar was set and huge magnificent cities with temples, pyramids and populations exceeding 100,000 people were created. One of the largest of these cities was Tikal, an urban complex of over 3,000 structures constructed deep in the rainforests of northern Guatemala, whose ruins today are one of the best surviving examples of this powerful civilisation.

For reasons not really known – however, soil exhaustion, climate change and armed conflict are a good guess – the Mayans declined rapidly as a significant influence in this area to such an extent that by the time the Spanish arrived in the early 16th century, they were a spent force, their cites abandoned, their populations dispersed.

Under the nearly 300 years of exploitive Spanish rule, Guatemala never really managed to compete with her more industrious neighbours: commerce stagnated, transportation was neglected and a satisfactory port was never built.

Unfortunately, independence saw the country fare little better. Coups, social unrest, an unscrupulous army, corrupt dictators, neglect of the indigenous population and the growing disparity between wealthy landowners and the general community saw a developing country struggle.

It's only since 1996 that Guatemala, after 36 years of civil war, has been able to focus on her people and her economy, been able to bolster civilian power while suppressing military control, and try to move into 21st century.

It's with this dismal information we have arrived in Guatemala. Suffice to say, we are eager to visit, but not expecting much.

It is, therefore, a little surprising when we step ashore mid-morning to find a brand-spanking new wharf complete with large welcoming area, efficient tour desk and small, funky post office. Nearby, under the umbrella of those conical thatched huts I noticed from my balcony earlier, a marimbula band serenades, a cheerful bar offering wi-fi with purchase beckons and an orderly souvenir market full of brightly coloured goods thrives. While keen to browse this area that glows with hand-woven rugs, gleaming silver jewellery and local jade, we have a tour to catch; for now, this area will have to wait.

Before our arrival in Guatemala, we took pains to study the tours on offer and eventually settled on visiting a coffee plantation. With our love of coffee and Guatemala being one of the top 10 coffee producers globally, a visit to a farm won out over cruising a lake or hiking a volcano.

With no clear signage, it's a little challenging finding our tour bus, but following the other lost tourists, we eventually prevail. Here, today's chatty tour guide Winston greets us and ushers us aboard. We know that this morning's first destination, the Filadelfia Coffee Estate, is a good 90-minute journey, so it's easy to sit back, admire the passing scenery and let Winston's chatter wash over us.

"Coffee is one of Guatemala's main exports; it accounts for 40% of our agricultural export revenue… It's our mild, subtropical climate along with our nutrient-rich soil that makes Guatemala the ideal environment for growing coffee… Sugar and bananas are also two of our main crops."

It's interesting that Winston has mentioned sugar and bananas because, to our right, lush sugar cane fields stretch as far as the eye can see, while to our left, thick plantations of banana trees flourish.

The road we are travelling is, surprisingly, a new dual-lane highway, and as we speed along Guatemala's flatlands, heading closer to the hills where those coffee plantations flourish, the journey feels safe and comfortable.

Always impressed by the sight of a volcano, I spend part of the journey trying to get the best shot of the few I can see ahead of me. It's as the journey progresses that I realise I need not have initially tried so hard. Our drive will disconcertingly take us to the very foot of Fuego, one of the three still active of Guatemala's 37 volcanos.

"Fuego erupted in June last year," Winston supplies. "Over 400 people died, but only the bodies of 178 were ever found. The lava flow wiped out entire villages."

Already surprised by how close we are travelling to this still active volcano, I am further nonplussed when Winston suddenly announces: "Look, see the smoke coming from the top. She's erupting now."

Apparently, Fuego is known to erupt regularly. Fortunately, today, only on a small scale.

Climbing higher, as the flatland scrub is replaced with denser, greener vegetation and cultivated coffee plantations appear more regularly, Winston continues his narrative.

"The coffee plantations provide great employment for our kids. We changed the school year so they could have a summer job picking… They also employ a lot of Canadians. They come here for six to eight months then return home... Guatemala mines the best jade. Unlike jade found in other countries, Guatemalan jade doesn't shatter when dropped!"

Eventually, 40 minutes behind schedule, we arrive at our destination. We are late because our driver has taken two wrong turns, and got us lost once – not that anyone is concerned. Stepping from the bus, I am not the only one who immediately feels the drop in temperature. While at sea level, it was a comfortable 27 degrees, here in the hills, it's a chilly 16 degrees, and I regret my shorts and thin t-shirt.

For the two hours we spend at the Filadelfia Coffee Estate, we tour gardens full of thriving coffee trees in their various stages of growth. We also walk amongst courtyards littered with the drying cream-hued beans, don hairnets to enter the aromatic bean processing plant and watch locals proudly package the final product. At the end of an enlightening tour, we visit the estate's café where reviving cups of coffee are served along with a deep-fried pastry snack.

"If you're not going to eat all yours, can I have it?" asks Darryl at some stage. "I'm not sure what they are, but they taste great, and the coffee is the best we've had in weeks."

"The coffee is incredible," I reply, dumping the remainder of my pastry onto his plate. "Especially after what's served on the Arcadia. If we get time, we should buy some beans to take home."

Unfortunately, our delayed arrival means we do not have time to visit the onsite shop; we are shortly due in Antigua, today's second stop.

Founded in the early 16th century, Antigua was once the most powerful seat of Spanish rule in this Central American region. Serving as its cultural, economic, religious, political and educational centre, it was noted for its Spanish colonial buildings, superb monuments and a gridwork of streets inspired by the Italian renaissance. In 1773, following a devastating earthquake, the capital was moved 40 kilometres to Guatemala City, and Antigua found itself virtually abandoned, a once beautiful, flourishing city left with little else but the ruins of former distinctive buildings. It was partially because of this abandonment that the city's distinct grid pattern survived, along with its cobbled streets. And although in ruins, the Baroque-style monuments, plazas and Spanish colonial architecture were salvageable. Growing prosperity resulting from increased agricultural production in the mid-1800s saw investment return to Antigua. Slowly, over time, the city was rebuilt. Today, this museum to Spanish colonial architecture is a world heritage site and, as we are about to discover, an absolute hidden gem.

Not familiar with Antigua, it's when we find ourselves bumping along these narrow 300-year-old cobbled streets, squeezing through lanes closely bordered by colourful stone buildings, that the charm of this fascinating place hits us. The sight of tiny shops, bars and businesses tucked within colonial builds painted ochre and umber, traditionally clad ladies wielding baskets of goods as headwear and full or partial remnants of impressive 17th-century buildings keep us glued to our bus windows.

Some on our tour have expressed a desire to visit a market here, myself included, and so Winston organises with the driver to depart from our scheduled tour and drop us at the Mercado de Artesanias or Artisans Market. The time we spend in this chaotic muddle of stalls overflowing with colourful textiles, woven handbags, jade jewellery, silverware, t-shirts and traditional blankets passes disappointingly fast. At a shoebox-sized booth tucked at the very back of the market, I haggle quickly but successfully over some silver earrings, a 50th birthday present for my sister, while Darryl finds himself the owner of a strange fitting t-shirt.

"No, I didn't haggle and I'm not sure if it's going to fit. But I like it."

A popular bartered item, we notice, are little animal figurines handcrafted from thousands of tiny beads. Bright and colourful, they come in various forms: the lizard and national quetzal bird are the more popular examples. Taking hours to make, they are a good source of income for the indigenous Mayan population who approach us repeatedly angling for a sale. For 20 American dollars, I purchase five of the items. This is a bargain, I later discover, but for now they are another 'travel treasure.'

From the market, we make our way to Parque Central, Antigua's leading and oldest square. Surrounded by colonial-era buildings, dominated by the 1680 San Jose Cathedral, this deeply shaded place is a popular gathering point for tourists and locals, and it's good to sit for a while, to make grateful use of its shade. Nearby, the park's central fountain known as the 'Fountain of the Sirens' gurgles happily while groups of local women in their colourful embroidered huipiles (blouses) and cortes (skirts) natter, fuss over children or work on some form of craftwork. Distracted as we are by the sheer colours on display, by the site of joyous children chasing pigeons, by locals spruiking their wares, the time passes quickly, and all too soon, it's time to reboard the bus.

As we slowly bump our way out of Antigua, passing Santa Catalina Arch, Antigua's most recognisable landmark, the talk on our tour bus is interesting.

"What an unexpected treasure," is one couple's verdict. "We were not expecting such an exciting place with so much to offer."

"It was a fascinating place," says a lady not far from me. "But those ladies desperately trying to sell their goods either from the baskets on their heads or from mats on the ground – there were so many of them, and they sold so little. They were sad to watch."

I had to agree with her. Our visit to Antigua has not only been memorable by the vibrancy of the place but by the sheer number of Mayan locals trying to sell us their wares to generate an income. Poverty is apparent here; Guatemala still has some way to go to increase the living standards of its indigenous population.

For the time it takes us to get back to port, Winston continues with his spiel.

"See that bus," he says as he points towards a colourful chrome bus coming in the opposite direction.

"They are called 'Chicken Buses.' They are former American school buses that got their name when they were used to transport chickens and other livestock. We use them for local transportation now... The Mayans produced the first-ever chocolate bar...We are the leaders in blue denim production... Only women, with their neutral pH, are allowed to handle the coffee beans."

It's fortunate that Winston's commentary is so interesting, for while this morning's journey was undertaken along a new dual lane highway, our return journey is taken along the bumpy, pothole-strewn former highway. So tragic is this road that our bus eventually gets a flat tyre, and Winston's narrative keeps everyone happy for the 40 minutes it takes for a replacement bus to arrive.

Back at port and after browsing some of the little market stalls passed earlier, admiring the intricate embroidery of the clothing and handbags, appreciating the vibrant finely woven mats, we come across the lively small bar offering free wi-fi with purchase. It appears to be doing a roaring trade, full as it is of Arcadia passengers clutching their devices, and we happily join them. Unfortunately, clutching their device is all they are doing. Struggling under the strain of so many users, the wi-fi is snail-slow and eventually crashes. While Guatemala, such a country of contrasts and an unexpectedly interesting place to visit, has given us so much, it has failed on delivering any internet. That will have to wait until we arrive in Mexico in three days' time.

CHAPTER 17

Mexico

*L*ATE evening, and with Guatemala a few hours behind us, Captain Cook issues an ominous warning.

"For those of you who have been asking for some rough seas, well, tomorrow should deliver. The Arcadia will be passing through the Gulf of Tehuantepec, an area notorious for its high winds. We have been warned to expect some heavy seas."

Unsure as to whether we appreciate the warning, we go to bed and awaken to some of the meanest seas encountered yet. Caused by winds generated in the Gulf of Mexico, these gales cut across the small isthmus that separates the Gulf from the Pacific. They gain further intensity as they cascade down the Sierra Madres and eventually blast out into the ocean bite that we are now travelling. The information channel on our television is advising that the winds are gusting at 80-plus knots per hour: hurricane-force.

Despite the mayhem occurring outside our balcony doors, the sheeting spray that soaks the decks and the cancellation of all outdoor activities, we are feeling surprisingly well. We have both suffered seasickness in the past, but today, the heaving seas and rolling floors are having little effect apart from making me slightly nervous. To negate this nervousness, I take myself off to a champagne tasting class while Darryl attends his bridge for beginners.

Booked some days earlier, the tasting class is much smaller than anticipated; no doubt many have cancelled due to the conditions, but a smaller class does mean more champagne for those who are left. Hosted by benevolent and smiling crew member Crystal, I sit alongside Maark and Lynne from Ireland while Crystal, for the full 90 minutes the class takes, keeps our glasses topped with Tattinger champagne and our conversation topped with champagne trivia.

"There are 49 million bubbles in a bottle of champagne... The only difference between sparkling wine and champagne is the area it comes from... A near-blind monk, Dom Pierre Perignon, is credited with creating champagne."

It's the perfect antidote to the dismal conditions, and I leave the class feeling pretty merry with promises to catch up with Maark and Lynne at another of Crystal's parties.

By mid-afternoon, the Gulf of Tehuantepec is behind us and the smooth ocean totally belies the morning's squall.

Wednesday, 22 January, and Captain Cook greets us with another dire announcement: "Unfortunately, due to a measles outbreak in Samoa and Tonga, these future ports have been cancelled. We will now be calling into Tahiti instead."

Although disappointed to be missing Samoa and Tonga, Tahiti sounds like an acceptable substitute, so mollified, we attend today's guest lecture given by former professional jump jockey Bob Champion. Bob makes a brilliant guest speaker with his witty memoirs and pithy quips, although, with many of the punchlines aimed at the Poms, some do go over our heads.

Outside, the Brits are happily ensconced on their loungers, dolphins are merrily frolicking in the Arcadia's wake and deep below us lies the Middle America Trench. Plummeting to depths of nearly 7,000 meters, this eerie chasm is one of Earth's deepest voids.

It's another early morning arrival at the highly popular tourist and industrial city of Manzanillo in Mexico. 'Sailfish' capital of the world; location of the 1970's Bo Derek movie *10*; and a city renowned for its offshore fishing and beautiful beaches.

Although, standing on our elevated balcony, noting the dilapidated buildings that sprawl in front of me, their shabby appearance, I am having trouble reconciling what I can see with what I have been led to expect. Located so far from many of Mexico's more famous tourist sites, like Chichen Itza (the ancient Mayan pyramids) and Mexico City (its capital), we haven't organised a tour here. We have been hoping Manzanillo alone will have enough to offer – maybe some guacamole in a little café! It will be interesting to see what our day brings.

Mexico is a country whose history parallels Guatemala's to some extent. Like Guatemala, the Mayans once thrived here until their eventual collapse, and Mexico was also similarly colonised by the Spanish, whose introduced diseases decimated millions of the indigenous population. Their post-Spaniard rule even correlates Guatemala's with overzealous presidents, harsh dictators, American interference, rebellions and always an imbalanced distribution of wealth. In recent years, Mexico's problems have been exacerbated by an ever-growing problem of drug trafficking that has contributed to police and political corruption. On the positive, foreign investment in the country's rural areas has helped with employment and wealth.

Today, Mexico – a country with a population of over 127 million people, home to more Spanish speakers than any other country – rests on a fragile economy. While its manufacturing industry is proliferating and it's the sixth-largest producer of oil globally, it equally relies on tourism to keep it afloat.

Mid-morning, and true to my expectations, we step ashore into a steamy humid Mexican climate. There's a long walk along an unshaded concrete pier, but eventually, we arrive at a scattering of market stalls offering a surprisingly scant selection of goods. Dominating the background is a considerable sculpture of a blue sailfish, reinforcing the cities 'sailfish capital' claim. With a large cluster of Arcadia passengers milling around this statue, I can only assume that many, like us, have chosen not to participate in an organised tour here. A city guide picked up at one of the market stalls displays a map, and using it, we find ourselves wandering deeper into the city's heart. The streets are narrow, busy and generally in poor condition; likewise, the footpaths and the buildings have obviously seen better days. Nothing is dissuading me from my initial impression obtained from our balcony, and I voice my surprise.

"It's hard to believe this is one of Mexico's most popular tourists spots. Everything looks so shabby, so neglected. Is this a general indication of Mexico's poverty, or are we only seeing the bad bits?"

"It's hard to tell," Darryl replies. "Maybe it's just this area. Maybe it's better a little further away from the port and city area."

In all, we spend nearly two hours exploring Manzanillo's inner city. With its fume-filled streets, lack of shade and burning sun, it's not a very enjoyable exploration, but we do come across some hidden gems. An internet joint painted avocado green and full of ancient dusty computers takes us immediately back to the late 80s, while a café speedily churning out the ever-popular tortillas on an industrial-looking conveyor belt is fascinating to watch. Eventually, hoping the area closer to the port will be cooler, we head there where a thatched café abutting a sadly, polluted harbour draws our attention. It's not yet open, but a staff member beckons us in, and it's here we remain for the time it takes us to eat three bowls of spicy guacamole, down copious heat-quenching beers and submit three blogs.

Although reluctant to leave our breezy café haven, there are only a few hours of our port visit remaining, so we use them to further explore this busy harbour area. Shops closed earlier are now open, arcades housing dozens of well-stocked stalls have thrown their shutters wide, and little booths full of ceramics, shoes and Mexican handicrafts now line the footpaths. Mexico is the world's leading producer of silver, and a few shops offer beautiful Stirling silver items. I find a cute dragonfly necklace to go with the Guatemalan earrings for my sister Michelle and grab a dangly pair of earrings for myself.

It's been an interesting visit to a not very attractive place and reboarding the Arcadia, I am still unsure as to whether this is typical of Mexico or not. It's a question I pose to Maark, Lynne and a few others later that afternoon as we attend a sailing away party organised by Crystal. Situated on one of the Arcadia's forward decks, the party attended by no more than 40 guests not only offers the most incredible departing views of Manzanillo but includes copious alcoholic beverages.

"Did any of you take a tour?" I ask, sipping my tequila sunrise drink while handing back my empty champagne glass. "Did the rest of Manzanillo look like the inner city area, pretty neglected?"

"Yes," replies Lynne, draining her dark and stormy rum cocktail. "Our tour took us further along the bay, and it was the same there."

"Is this indicative of Mexico?" I ask, commencing my long island iced tea aperitif.

Unfortunately, it's a question that no one can answer.

With three days of sailing ahead of us before we reach San Francisco, we soon settle back into our 'at sea' routine. Morning yoga is followed by a quick catch up of the world news where one morning, we learn Trump may be impeached and three American firefighters have died whilst fighting the Australian bushfires.

"Their plane, which they used to fight the fires has crashed," I read from the television screen.

Following the news, it's breakfast, which usually consists of bircher muesli or pineapple on toast accompanied by a cup of tea (the coffee is still undrinkable), and a pastry. Then, while Darryl perseveres with bridge, I head to quoits or shuffleboard. We have a great shuffleboard crew now. Jan and Rod from Essex, who are about to spend a month with family in New Zealand, Diane and David on their 10th world cruise, Carol and wheelchair-bound Laurence, friendly Val and Ian, Evonne, Dickie, Bryn and Dianne with two n's. The quoits crew are not quite so friendly. Ace player Linda who gives a short happy dance whenever she draws me as her opponent, and serious, solemn Kevin, who, after our first dismal pairing, refuses to look me in the eye.

The afternoons are spent either attending a guest lecture, reading a book or maybe even attending a ladies pamper party. Dinner is usually a three-course event taken in the Meridian restaurant before watching a show, taking a stroll or simply heading back to our cabin.

Two days out from San Francisco, as we parallel the coast of Baja California on our steep northward trajectory and the temperature starts to drop, we learn more about the coronavirus. With the number of people infected in China reaching 5,000 and the death toll jumping from three to over a hundred in six days, it's being taken seriously now. While we feel safe and out of harm's way, it's incredible to hear that Wuhan and some other Chinese provinces have been put into a total lockdown affecting nearly 56 million people.

"China has also started building a 1,000-bed hospital," people mutter in disbelief. "It's going to take only 10 days to build."

Australia Day, and it's time to put the clocks back yet again. This means that we are now 19 hours behind Australia: so far behind that it feels as if we have missed Australia Day completely.

"They celebrated Australia Day yesterday," I say mournfully to Darryl.

Overnight, the weather conditions have changed swiftly and dramatically. At 15 degrees and falling, the jeans, jumpers and jackets have made an unwelcome comeback while heavy rains have closed the outside decks. Tomorrow we are due to arrive in what I hoped would be sunny San Francisco; it will be the end of this cruise's first sector. With tours booked and new passengers arriving, I hope the current weather conditions are only temporary.

CHAPTER 18

America

*I*T's still dark when at 5 am, we open our balcony door and step outside into the eerie early morning calm. The Arcadia is due to pass under the iconic Golden Gate Bridge within the next half hour, and we want to enjoy every moment of this memorable experience. When a little before 5:30 am, we silently glide under the mist-shrouded beauty, its amber lights sketching its outline and the bluff of Battery Ridge just visible alongside us, the experience is every bit as impressive and memorable as we were hoping.

With two full days to enjoy San Francisco, today we will be using one of those convenient Hop-On buses to get an overall sense of the city, while tomorrow, a tour to Alcatraz has been booked. Before anyone can do anything, however, all 1,800 passengers and 800-plus crew members must personally meet face to face with a United States immigration officer. To avoid mayhem, each cabin has been assigned a meeting time, and fortunately, ours is an early one. Following an impatient wait in a long snaking queue, a quick chat with two talkative officers, a probing inspection of those ESTAs we had secured so many months ago, by 10:30 am, we have set foot onto American soil.

It's our first visit to America, and we are happy that San Francisco is the first place we've arrived. Whilst evidence suggests human habitation occurred in this region as early as 3000 BC, its more recent history commenced around 1769. A Spanish expedition spotted the sizeable natural bay San Francisco sits within, leading to the establishment of a Spanish mission here seven years later.

In 1821, Mexico, winning its independence from Spain, took San

Francisco and this peninsula with it, only to lose it to the Americans in 1846. Formerly called Yerba Buena, it was in 1847 that this small town of around 800 inhabitants became San Francisco and one year later, with gold discovered in the nearby Californian hills, it became the destination for those seeking their fortune. From 1849, these arriving 'forty-niners' caused the population to explode to 25,000, then later 50,000, and the city to become a violent, ungoverned place characterised by rough development and frequent, devastating fires.

By 1853, the gold rush was ending, but by then the city had been established. The discovery of silver in 1859 helped, but the impetus to grow and to develop had already been seeded. By 1900, its population was over 300,000. The first cable cars enabled the city's footprint to spread over its steep hills, and businesses such as Levi Strauss were entrenched.

Skipping forward to the 1950s, the age of the Beatniks, and then the 1960s, the 'Age of Aquarius,' means we miss the 1906 earthquake and subsequent fire which nearly destroyed the city, the 1909 plague and the 1912 building of a military prison on Alcatraz Island.

Today, San Francisco still maintains its 1970s bohemian reputation: a reputation which sits surprisingly well alongside its 1990s dot.com fame and its 2000s gay rights culture. It's a flourishing, multicultural city. Fuelled by the dot.com boom, it's also now one of Americas most expensive places to live. We can't wait to explore.

Conveniently, there's a Hop-On bus located wharf-side, and within minutes of disembarking, we have secured the upper-deck's foremost seats: the best seats. Unfortunately, with the immediate cancellation of this service, we lose them and instead must trudge a few hundred meters to board a sister bus. This trek does give us a brief insight into the Fisherman's Wharf area we have docked at, and it does introduce us to the first, of what will be many, of San Francisco's homeless.

Like on our last adventure, Darryl has conveniently left his watch at home, hoping to purchase one here in America, so today will also be about trying to locate a suitable timepiece. Union Square, San Francisco's heart and location of most of America's top department stores, is not far along our bus route, so it's here we will head to first.

With our upper-level seats and the chilly wind blasting, we gaze eager-eyed at the wide generous streets, the hilly, urban terrain, the iconic red wooden cable cars whose tracks climb steeply upwards. Earphones in, we learn a little about what we are looking at.

"The cable cars used to be hauled by horses... There are 40 hills in the city... Nob Hill used to be inhabited by the fashionable, the 'nobs'... Now, it's the Silicon Valley rich who live here."

Eventually, Union Square comes into view, discernible by its Tiffany and Co, its Saks Fifth Avenue and its Macys. Macy's reveals some watches, one of which interests Darryl, but we leave them and instead head towards Bloomingdales – such an American sounding name for a shop. Our downhill walk along more generous streets takes us past large federal structures, alongside restored Victorian buildings and between fascinating passages that lead to mews full of great restaurants and funky cafés.

"So far, I'm really liking San Francisco," I say at one point. "I wasn't expecting such wide-open streets. Such great looking buildings. Such an easy vibe. It kind of feels like a big town rather than a city. Although I am surprised by the number of homeless: the number of people, men particularly, camped in doorways, under bridges, scrounging through bins. I've never seen so many. I didn't expect this from America."

"Well, apparently," Darryl replies. "This is the good part of the city. Walk a few blocks west, and it's much worse. High crime, lots of violence and drugs, an area to really avoid."

While Bloomingdales fails to illicit a suitable timepiece, a shop next door with some original sets from the sitcom *Friends* distracts us and afterwards, a nearby pharmacy beckons. With its stock locked behind clear perspex, this chemist shop is frustrating, but it does provide some much-needed shaving cream for Darryl and headache tablets for me. Just as we are leaving the shop, we hear a lady ask for some face masks.

"Sorry we have sold out. I doubt you will find any in the whole of San Francisco," is the reply. Isolated as we have been on our floating bubble, it's our first apparent brush with the coronavirus, and it's a shock.

Hungry, we stop at a Boudins café where, after some initial confusion over their ordering system (we must help ourselves to any drinks), we manage to rest and refuel. Typical of what we were expecting regarding Americans and portion sizes, the coffees come in huge or humungous, and the simple biscuit I order is dinner-plate giant.

Realising that if he wants a watch, then maybe the one at Macy's will suffice, we return, make the purchase and head back to the Hop-On bus stop. There's an Australian lady already there – her accent gives her away – and as we wait, we chat as fellow Australian tourists tend to do.

"I'm a flight attendant," she tells us. "I work for Qantas."

"We have heard that people are worried about flying at the moment," I say. "They think they'll catch the coronavirus on the plane. Are you worried about it?"

"The planes are still full of people travelling," she replies. "And most of them are wearing masks. But it's frustrating. I find that whenever I talk to a passenger, they automatically take their mask off to reply. It defeats the whole purpose of wearing one."

Back on the bus and in-between using its free wi-fi to catch up on emails, I absorb more fascinating San Francisco titbits, observe yet more vagrants and drink in some great San Francisco sights.

"To your right is the prior home of Jimi Hendrix... Ahead is Lombard Street, the 'crookedest street in the world'... Author Danielle Steel lives just up there... There are more dogs registered in San

Francisco than kids."

At Chinatown and again at the former hippie haven of Haight-Ashbury, we alight for a quick look-round before undertaking one of the day's highlights – crossing the Golden Gate Bridge. Opened in 1937, this single-span, international orange-hued, 1.6 kilometre suspension bridge, built when many said it was unbuildable, is perhaps the world's most beautiful bridge; and certainly, its most photographed. It was deemed unbuildable due to the foggy weather San Francisco is notorious for, and the high winds and strong ocean currents that abound here. As we sit perched on the upper level of our roofless double-decker bus, which is itself travelling at 227 meters above sea level, we begin to get a better understanding of these high winds, although they are ignored in the excitement of traversing this modern-day wonder, of passing beneath its twin arches, of angling for the best photo.

It's a brief, albeit numbingly cold journey to reach Vista Point on the bridge's far side and with the option of disembarking or staying put, we remain seated. That infamous fog has decided to pay a visit and waiting for the next bus under this heavy cold blanket doesn't appeal. While it's equalling as exciting to cross back over the bridge, the cold really does begin to seep in and hurt, meaning the passing of the Lucasfilm Studios and the architecturally impressive Palace of Fine Arts do not warrant the attention they deserve. Back at port, the first thing I do is gratefully defrost under a scalding shower.

The San Francisco port area where we are currently docked includes Fisherman's Wharf, full of restaurants and souvenir shops – it's one of the city's premier attractions, along with Pier 39. That evening we explore both, but favour Pier 39. Here, the fat sea lions who have made K-Dock their home, loll languidly. The views on offer – Alcatraz Island, the Golden Gate and Bay Bridges – are beautiful. The crowded waterfront park with its carousels and game arcades is studiously avoided.

Hungry, we eventually head to a Hard Rock Café where we know we can obtain free wi-fi. Here we sit for the remainder of the evening, snacking on bruschetta with tomato and extra avocado, sipping on rosé and just enjoying being back on land, being in San Francisco.

It's a drizzly wet morning when, shortly after breakfast, we set out to explore the San Francisco foreshore a little further. With our tour to Alcatraz Island booked for mid-morning and wishing to make the most of our time, we briskly set off for another look at those captivating, chunky seals. We also revisit Fisherman's Wharf, where restaurants advertising Bubba Gump shrimp and Gumbo, a thick stew-like soup, scream to me *Forrest Gump*.

Alan and Denise, Darryl's bridge partners, have been telling him about the fantastic Irish coffees they purchased at a pub here some years back.

"It's not far from Fisherman's Wharf," says Alan. "It's called the Buena Vista."

And so, we make a concerted effort to find it. With no data, thus no internet, hence no Google Maps, we are reliant on asking for directions, which, with the surprisingly limited English-speaking shop owners here, are not always that easy to come by. Eventually, damp from the steady drizzle and numb from the cold, we stumble upon the cosy Buena Vista and proceed to enjoy some of the best Irish coffees we have had outside of Ireland.

"They have managed to get the consistency of the cream right," says Darryl. "Not many places do."

"It says here," I say, reading from a menu. "That they have been using the same recipe since 1952. They spent ages trying to get the cream to float perfectly."

Full of coffee, cream and whisky, and with the drizzle lifting, it's a leisurely and enjoyable stroll back to port. At one of the numerous tacky souvenir shops that line our way, we purchase some gifts for people back home, while at the famous Ghirardelli chocolate shop, we purchase strips of chocolate-coated bacon and chunks of creamy caramel fudge. At both places, we are surprised to discover that all goods are displayed net of tax – the 7.5% tax is annoyingly added at the register, and also that the facilities here do not have the ability to tap your credit card; it is disconcertingly taken from you and swiped elsewhere.

"It's incredible," I say with concern. "I would have thought America would have much better credit card facilities. And I still can't believe how little English is spoken here. It's been really difficult to communicate sometimes. It's America, an English-speaking country."

Located less than a few kilometres from shore, yet far enough that no prisoner ever knowingly survived an escape, from 1934 until 1963 Alcatraz was America's premier maximum-security prison. Home to infamous inmates such as Al 'Scarface' Capone and the 'Birdman' Robert Stroud, these days 'The Rock' is considered one of San Francisco's most significant tourist attractions; an assertion our afternoon tour proves absolutely correct. Commencing with a ferry ride that delivers us across the icy stretch of turbulent water that separates rugged Alcatraz Island from the mainland, we soon find ourselves arriving at this bleak, desolate place. Here we are given headsets, brief instructions, a little shove and are soon on our way to experiencing the best self-guided tour we have ever taken. Narrated by former guards and inmates, their stories ring in our ears as we wander the stark, sterile cells, scrutinise the guardhouses and gaze upon the exercise yard. It's easy to get a sense of the hardships endured here, the tedium, the fortitude required for survival.

"Cells measured five feet by nine feet... Prisoners could touch each wall if they stretched out their arms... Some went insane here... No one ever escaped, 36 tried... 23 were recaptured... Six were shot... Five are still missing, presumed dead... Only men on Alcatraz... No female prisoners nor guards."

Included in our Alcatraz tour is a visit to the former fishing village then artist colony of Sausalito, the place where Otis Redding penned '(Sittin' on the) Dock of the Bay.' Situated 12 kilometres north of San Francisco, it necessitates another trip over the Golden Gate Bridge to reach this picturesque Mediterranean-style community where the streets are full of boutique shops and the views across the bay memorable. For the time that we are here, we pop our heads into numerous creative galleries, marvel at the fog we see settling on the sharp hills behind the town and peruse the souvenir shops. At one such shop, I purchase cheeky badges for my bowling buddies, and they will forever remind me of my Sausalito visit.

It's early evening when the Arcadia, with the assistance of two tugs, manoeuvres from her berth, clears the Golden Gate and heads back out towards the Pacific Ocean. Ensconced in our cabin, we watch the lights of Point Lobos flicker in the distance and reflect on our time here.

"I regret not getting to Silicon Valley," I muse, "but I'm impressed with San Francisco. I was expecting a busy concrete jungle, but it's not like that at all."

"The amount of homeless people will probably stay with me the most," Darryl replies. "It's a great looking city with a good feel, but then you see so many people doing it tough."

"And how about the number of non-English speakers," I add. "I wasn't anticipating that. Also, I wasn't expecting to feel so safe here. With America's crazy gun laws, I thought it would feel dangerous or scary, but that wasn't the case at all."

"I hadn't thought of that, but you're right. Although we may have felt differently if we had visited some of those dodgier areas."

With our bow pointing predominately westwards, we now have four full sea days before we arrive in Honolulu, Hawaii. This morning saw us falling 20 hours behind Australia while outside the vast Pacific Ocean was pockmarked with large patches of thick soupy fog – a parting gesture from San Francisco, perhaps.

As a testament to this new sector, we have new neighbours and our guest speakers have all been renewed. Today, I forgo shuffleboard to hear Didi Conn, the actor who played Frenchy in the 1978 smash hit movie *Grease* speak. Talking predominately about how she secured her role and her life afterwards, Didi is funny and entertaining with a strangely squeaky voice that will be difficult to forget.

Like most cruise lines, P&O has a loyalty program. Called the Peninsular Club, it means the more nights you spend onboard their ships, the higher you climb within this club. Having now spent more than 50 nights aboard their vessels means we have reached the heights of Atlantis tier, the second bottommost of the six available. While it feels great to have jumped a level, and it does give us a few glasses of champagne and a larger spending discount, I come crashing back to earth when I hear some of the shuffleboard crew talking.

"We're Baltic or Ligurian tier," says Jan, Val and Diane. With 200-plus nights spent onboard, these are the top tiers. "They are throwing us lunch and drinks this Friday."

On 31 January, we awaken to the news that the coronavirus, in 24 days, has spread to India, the Philippines, Russia, Spain, Sweden, the UK, Canada, Germany, Japan, Singapore, the USA, the UAE, Vietnam and even Australia! The World Health Organisation has started calling it a world health emergency, and while there are no reported deaths outside of China, China now has 170 dead and nearly 8,000 cases. The rapid spread of this virus is so disconcerting and so widely reported that it completely overshadows the other main news story: that Britain has just left the European Union.

Sometime during the afternoon, I visit the Oasis Spa for a quick trim with Isham, the flamboyant onboard Indian hairdresser, while at dinner in the Meridian Restaurant that evening, we hear of some of the antics cruising staff can get up to.

"On our cruise last year," a British man intones. "We had two staff members jump ship in New Zealand then in Sydney, we lost three more!"

A day out from Hawaii and with an extensive low-pressure system hovering in the North Pacific, our relatively calm ocean starts to kick up a large swell. Fortunately, the chill of San Francisco is now behind us, and the days are getting warmer. Our clocks go back again, and with Australia now 21 hours ahead of us, we know that catch-up time must be imminent.

On Sunday 2 February, a little after 6:30 am, the Arcadia berths in Honolulu Harbour on the Hawaiian island of Oahu, the third largest of Hawaii's 162 islands (only seven of these are inhabited).

While initially scheduled to spend two full days in Hawaii, our altered itinerary to Tahiti has seen this shortened to one which doesn't give us long to explore this popular destination.

Forged from volcanos and titanic eruptions on the Pacific seafloor nearly 40 million years ago, the Hawaiian archipelago was first inhabited by Polynesian settlers around 500 AD. Accompanied by pigs, chickens and dogs, their journey across several thousand kilometres of open ocean in double-hulled canoes sounds genuinely remarkable. For the 1,200 years before the arrival of Captain James Cook in 1778, these early settlers appeared to do little more than fight over their kingdoms. Their fickleness and fighting prowess confirmed when Cook and his crew, warmly welcomed on their first visit, were killed a year later on their return.

Over the subsequent centuries, Hawaii saw unity within its people, bought about by the chieftain King Kamehameha's slaughter of all his opponents. Western diseases such as leprosy arrive and decimate the local population. Floods of Chinese, Japanese and Filipino settlers replace the indigenous people in increasingly thriving pineapple and sugar plantations.

In 1959, Hawaii became the 50th American state. Although its statehood brought outside investment, increased visitor numbers and booming economic growth, Hawaii's annexure and statehood have never rested well with the indigenous Hawaiian population who continue to demand land rights, autonomy and self-governance.

These days, Hawaii attracts more than 10 million visitors per year, who come to enjoy exciting volcanoes, incredible cuisine created from a fusion of diverse cultures and a near-perfect climate created by a warm equatorial location and cooling trade winds. Being exotically beautiful and the birthplace of Barack Obama must also help with drawing in the tourist crowd.

"It's a shame we have lost our second day here, but at least we haven't lost our tour," I say as we disembark the Arcadia in the early morning and head towards our coach. "I know a few who did have tours booked for tomorrow."

"I'm looking forward to Pearl Harbour," replies Darryl. "I'm glad we still get to visit."

While Honolulu, Hawaii's capital, had much to offer – including great beaches, diverse cultures and extinct volcanoes – what eventually won our patronage was a visit to Pearl Harbour, the American naval station whose bombing in World War Two propelled America headlong into war. This morning as we leave the populated port area and head the 12 kilometres out to the Pearl Harbour lagoon, I gaze at the passing high-rise buildings and note the lush green escarpment in the background.

"The scenery reminds me of the Gold Coast," I comment. "Lots of busy hotels and high-rise buildings resting beside the ocean with a mountainous, densely forested backdrop. The vegetation even looks similar."

Unlike previous tours, our driver and guide doesn't regale us with interesting facts nor witty anecdotes as we tear along the wide Hawaiian highways. He's loud and brash with cringe-worthy stories, such as the one about the big-breasted barmaid, and it's a relief to arrive at the sizeable naval station, grab our entry tickets and join the crowds entering the highly secured gates.

Inside, it takes about two hours to wander this parkland of memorials to Americans lost at war. Alongside a few masked tourists – our second unexpected confrontation with the coronavirus – we gaze upon the Battleship Missouri on whose decks Japan surrendered World War Two, view examples of downed aircraft and peruse exhibit galleries displaying war artifacts and war films. After watching one short film on the Pearl Harbour assault, we visit the most poignant memorial of all: the USS Arizona Memorial. Accessed by water aboard a sleek naval launch, this elongated, gleaming white floating memorial straddles the remains of the sunken battleship USS Arizona which was bombed here by Japanese forces on 7 December 1941. It's the final resting place for 1,102 of the 1,177 crewmen killed and represents nearly half of 2,403 Americans killed at Pearl Harbour that day.

At the shrine which sits at one end of the currently crowded memorial, a stark marble wall lists the names of the dead. Despite the beautiful day, the warming sun and the tranquil sapphire lagoon surrounding us, it is rather chilling to stand here and look at the tragically long list of names, aware that many of the bodies still rest below.

Included with our tour is a visit to some of Honolulu's more memorable sites, all of which are thought-provoking. At the 365-metre Pali Lookout we see the 'Upside-Down Waterfall,' a phenomenon caused by the constant up-draft of wind that tunnels between the mountains, and we look over the beautiful, verdant valleys to the glistening harbour where a speck of an island sits.

"You may have heard of the island," says our guide. "It's Gilligan's Island."

"Gilligan's Island?" says one tourist flippantly. "Look how close it is to the mainland. Why didn't they just walk to shore?"

While at the Punchbowl Crater National Memorial Cemetery, we walk amongst the flat marble tombstones of the 45,000 bodies buried here, feel awed by the 48 Banyan trees that stand sentinel and reflect on the underlying message of the day: to never forget the atrocities of war.

Back at port, there's a free shuttle bus to the Moana shopping centre which, we soon discover, is very reminiscent of our Australian shopping centres. With a Target, McDonald's and H&M housed within a gleaming tiled complex under a summery blue sky, we could have been shopping on the Gold Coast.

Some hours later, and heading out to find a place for dinner, another free shuttle offers us a chance to visit Walmart.

"Any idea of what a Walmart is like?"

"No idea," Darryl replies. "But it must be ok if there is a free shuttle bus."

Walmart, it turns out, is a combination of Woolworths and K-mart, only much bigger and with an added chemist. We spend our time here browsing the aisles, watching the other shoppers and picking up a few more gifts for people back home. With an hour left before our shuttle returns, we leave Walmart and head out into the balmy night, searching for some food and free wi-fi. A nearby McDonald's is mentioned, and while it does deliver the food and wi-fi, our walk to its location amongst eerily empty streets punctured by groups or lone, rambling vagrants does put me a little on edge.

At 10:30 pm, with our positions on the Arcadia's rear deck secured and a swelling moon hovering above us, we watch as the glowing lights of Honolulu slowly fade in the distance. It's a beautiful tropical night made even better by the ships gentle swaying and the music playing.

"Honolulu was interesting," I comment. "I'm not sure if I liked it though."

"Too much?" Darryl questions.

"Yes. It was a bit much," I reply. "I was expecting a more laidback place with a really mellow atmosphere. But it reminded me of a bigger, dirtier, shabbier Gold Coast. A Gold Coast on steroids."

"We only saw parts of Honolulu, and some of the outer areas," Darryl responds. "Maybe it's different elsewhere."

CHAPTER 19

Tahiti

OUR altered itinerary means we now have six full days of sailing ahead of us before reaching Tahiti, a tiny island in the vast Pacific Ocean. Never having had such a long continuous stretch at sea, I am not looking forward to it. I prefer to have solid land within easy reach. I decide to use the experience to dispel any fears, learn to trust and toughen myself up.

Now travelling in a predominately southward direction, it's not long before the Arcadia is once again buffeted by those irksome trade winds, the permanent east to west winds that flow in the Earth's equatorial region. It means that while the outside temperature is a balmy 25 degrees, the annoying high winds will not let anyone enjoy it; the Brits are once again forced to surrender their sunbeds and must, like us, seek indoor pursuits.

One afternoon we visit the Palladium Theatre where we hope to partake in an auction organised to raise funds for the devastating Australian bushfires.

"We could win dinner with the captain or a visit to the bridge," I read.

There are only six raffle prizes, and the amount raised is in excess of 15,000 Australian dollars. Suffice to say, we don't win nor even bid, but we are appreciative of those who do.

On the morning of 5 February, we awaken to news about a fellow cruise ship, the Diamond Princess, currently moored off Yokohama, Japan.

"Ten passengers of the 2,666 onboard have been diagnosed with coronavirus," the news presenter announces. "They will be taken to local hospitals in Yokohama, while the remainder of the passengers will be quarantined on board for 14 days." Hearing this announcement does make us pause. That this virus may reach us on the Arcadia was something we had not considered. It's the main topic of conversation over breakfast.

"I don't think it's likely we'll get it aboard the Arcadia," says our breakfast companion. "It may affect our future itinerary though."

The consensus is that travelling as we are through the Pacific where the virus has not yet reached, we are pretty safe. No one is really worried. Most are more concerned about the impact this virus may have on their future plans.

"Do you think they would change the itinerary?" says another of our companions with concern. "We're disembarking in Singapore."

Later that same day and marked by a 'Crossing the Line' ceremony, the Arcadia passes over the equator, meaning that after nearly four months, we are back in the southern hemisphere. Strange as it sounds, it feels great to be back in the same hemisphere as family, to view a night sky whose constellations appear just that little more familiar.

The following day we pass Malden Island, a low, arid and uninhabited atoll sitting lost in this vast, liquid realm. It's noteworthy as being the site of the first British H-bomb tests, detonated here under the name of Operation Grapple back in 1957.

At lunchtime, we hear some unfortunate news. Like shuffleboard, table tennis has its own particular crew, and this morning, during play, one of its members suffered a stroke. Currently situated too far from anywhere to organise a rescue, it casts a pall over everyone who all hope that the patient hangs on until our arrival in Tahiti in two days.

Another day and I realise as I stare out at the endless, empty ocean, with no planes, birds, nor land to be seen, that I may have reached my sailing limit.

"It's easy to understand now," I say to Darryl, "how the Pacific Ocean is larger than all the landmasses of the world put together. Five days of sailing with no sight of land. It's beginning to drive me a bit nuts. It's fine sailing for a day or so then a port stop, but I don't like these long stretches. I'm also thinking seven weeks may be just two weeks too long for a cruise."

"I love the sea days," is his reply. "Seven weeks at sea doesn't worry me at all. Lucky for you, we are not doing the full world cruise."

Despite our isolated location, it doesn't stop news of the worsening and now frightening coronavirus getting through. A daily newsletter delivered to our cabin, 'Australia Today,' advises that all arrivals into Australia, from China, are being quarantined, much to their dislike, on Christmas Island, a place notorious for being the political dumping ground of potential asylum seekers. And with the Diamond Princess coronavirus numbers rising, cruise ships are becoming destination pariahs.

Talk about changes to the Arcadia's itinerary increasingly dominates conversations.

"I doubt we will be allowed to stop at Hong Kong nor Singapore now."

"But where would we go instead? Singapore is the end of a sector. What about all the passengers disembarking or embarking?"

Finally, on the morning of 8 February, our familiar watery view is replaced by one of sharp green hills, sprawling low-rise buildings and a millpond harbour full of charming furled-sail boats. While relieved and excited to have finally reached Papeete, capital of Tahiti, the news is tempered by the reason behind our very early arrival.

"The captain got the stroke patient here as soon as he could," says our breakfast companion.

Situated halfway between Los Angeles and Sydney, Tahiti refers to both its largest island and the vast stretch of 118 other islands that make up French Polynesia. These days famous for its pure sand beaches, lush tropical mountains and warm, clear lagoons, it is believed its first inhabitants arrived from Southeast Asia between 500 BC and 500 AD in flimsy wood and fibre canoes.

European arrival occurred in 1767 when Captain Samuel Wallis claimed the islands for Britain, then less than a year later when Louis de Bougainville claimed them for France, both equally impressed by the abundance of fresh food and what they perceived as uninhibited local ladies.

Captain Cook and William Bligh visited, and it was the six blissful months spent here that later led to Bligh's downfall during the infamous 'Mutiny on the Bounty,' his crew not at all happy about leaving the idyllic isle.

Following the arrival of French missionaries, Tahiti was proclaimed a French Protectorate in 1840, a French colony in 1880 and a French territory in 1957. Gaining autonomy in 1977, Tahiti and French Polynesia are known as a French overseas collective.

Disembarking into a hot sticky climate – straight into the midst of a welcoming ukulele-strumming quartet, it feels strange that this vibrant little island, thousands of kilometres from Europe, is so French. The lush foliage and colourful hibiscus, frangipani and orchid blooms don't look French and neither do the swarthy solid locals nor the shimmering harbour waters. It will be interesting to see what other anomalies our exploration of Papeete will bring.

While initially hoping to book a tour, maybe to Tahiti's east coast to visit the Paul Gauguin Museum (Gauguin lived and painted here from 1891-1893), or its west coast to visit the Museum of Tahiti, after discovering the prohibitive cost of tours, we soon discounted the idea. We had been warned to expect high prices and that Tahiti was an expensive place to visit, but finding the tour costs to be 100-250 Australian dollars per person still surprised us.

"$200 each for a three-hour island tour," I exclaim, "and it doesn't even include the Gauguin Museum because that's been closed for years apparently. I think we'll just stick to walking around Papeete."

As Darryl agrees, it means that for the time we are in Tahiti, we stick to the confines of the town. Despite its slightly untidy appearance, its weathered buildings and its syrupy humidity, we find it to be a laidback, colourful place full of expensive French fashion, expensive local handicrafts and beautiful but expensive black pearls.

Being such a small place, we frequently run into other Arcadian passengers, and it's good to stop and compare notes.

"There's a café not far that way," mentions one couple. "If you buy something, the internet is pretty good."

"The beers cost us a fortune," says another. "Seventeen US dollars for three!"

"You should visit the Black Pearl Museum," says someone else. "It's worth the visit."

Keen to understand further the beautiful black pearl that is sold here in absolute abundance, we do as suggested and visit the centrally located museum. Surrounded by breathtaking examples, we learn that black Tahitian pearls are the world's only natural black pearl, that they come from the Black-Lipped oyster and are French Polynesia's largest export.

"I would love to buy one," I say to Darryl. "But do I really need a black pearl?"

"No," is his predictable reply.

Located within the centre of town is the local marketplace and our visit here is the most memorable of the day. Full of stalls bursting with colourful blooms or collapsing under the weight of exotic fruit, and shops swimming in local handicrafts, it's easy to lose time as we rummage the stalls, attempt to haggle and leave empty-handed.

Finally, hot and exhausted, we find a little café, negotiate some wi-fi and relax over a few cooling beers.

"I don't think Papeete is a place I need to return to," says Darryl.

"I agree," I reply. "Beautiful waters but too expensive."

Those waters are also magical when later that afternoon, as the sun slips below the horizon, we pass the beautiful island of Moorea, location of the movie *South Pacific*, and watch a glowing full moon rise. Its beams reflect like stardust on the water behind us, and the back deck is full of people just soaking in the once-in-a-lifetime view.

"Tropical island, full moon, a glass of champagne. You can't get much better than that," I hear someone say.

It's something I must agree with.

With nearly 4,000 kilometres, or four full sailing days ahead of us before we reach Tauranga in New Zealand, it's back to bridge, shuffleboard and all other onboard activities.

Judy Hinchcliffe, a forensic odontologist, gives some great lectures on her experiences with helping identify victims of catastrophic events. Sent to Indonesia after the 2004 tsunami and Christchurch after the 2019 terror attack, Judy keeps us enthralled as she explains her role in identifying the dead from their teeth.

Henry Blofeld, retired British sports journalist and another of our guest lecturers, keeps the predominately British audience happy as he talks about his years in the commentary box and takes delight in sledging our Australian cricketers.

"Anyone got a piece of sandpaper in their pocket?"

As the days pass, it becomes even less appealing to turn on the television to listen to the news. As penned in Dorothea Mackellar's poem "My Country," Australia's bushfires have given way to "flooding rains." Devastating storms have led to widespread flooding, hundreds of people have been evacuated from their homes and thousands have been left without power. The only positives we can take from these reports are that after years of drought, some regions are seeing rain for the first time in a long while, and the rain has helped extinguish fires in other areas.

Regarding the coronavirus, we learn on 11 February that it has a new name. Now called Covid-19, its death toll stands at more than

1,000 with case numbers over 33,000. It's wreaking havoc in Asia, stock markets worldwide are plummeting and countries have started closing their borders. On board, however, the mood is surprisingly upbeat. "Hong Kong is closed. So is Singapore," says one breakfast companion. "I'm not sure how new passengers will board and how others will disembark. I'm not sure where we will be going nor our route back to England. But I'm going to let P&O worry about that and just enjoy my cruise." It's a widely felt sentiment.

Although, "I'm pretty sure I wouldn't want to be visiting Asia at the moment anyway," is something I think to myself.

Dinner that evening is taken in the Meridian Restaurant, and it's an extremely interesting and informative meal. We meet Roger and his wife Anne, a lovely British couple in their early 80s. Somehow, it doesn't take long for our conversation to turn to travel, and we discover that Roger, like us, has travelled extensive prominent train routes. Like us, he has completed the Trans-Mongolian, journeyed the length of Vietnam, circled Europe and taken trains from Chiang-Mai in northern Thailand through to Singapore. With so much train travel in common, it's a fun, fact-filled conversation with Anne, unfortunately, a quiet bystander.

"Roger goes off by himself," she tells us. "And I stay at home."

One place that Roger has travelled by train that we haven't is America.

"A few friends and I spent two months travelling the US extensively by Amtrak," he tells us.

"That's on my list," I cry. "I have been doing some research, and it looks like the Amtrak network covers a good bit of America. I think it may be our next adventure."

"Will it?" says Darryl.

Later that same evening, Tuesday 11 February, we go to bed 21 hours behind Australia and awaken the morning of Thursday 13 February two hours ahead of her. We have crossed the international date line;

we have transcended time, and we will never in our life experience a 12 February 2020. It's an effortless but momentous and incredibly strange experience. To mark the occasion, we receive an additional copy of our daily Horizon newsletter dated the 12 of February and titled 'The Day That Never Was.'

Now only a day out from New Zealand and significantly further south, the temperature has cooled, I'm back in jeans and Darryl, along with most of the ship, is sniffling and sneezing with a cold. At least, we all hope it's only a cold.

One of the ship's television channels provides information on our outside conditions, and I keep myself amused using this channel to educate myself. I learn how to measure wind using the Beaufort scale (the measurement of wind speed according to its impact on the land and sea – ours is currently a slight breeze force 3), and I learn about sea state and swell.

"Sea state, for example, a light sea state, is the effect of the wind on the sea," I say to Darryl. "While swell is the description of the waves that are not caused by wind, for example, a moderate swell."

"I think it's time you got off this ship," he replies.

CHAPTER 20

New Zealand

VALENTINE'S Day, and our arrival at Mount Maunganui, a suburb of Tauranga, the largest city in New Zealand's Bay of Plenty area is tempered by the news that the stroke patient left in Tahiti has died. Aware that cruising does bear quite a high mortality rate due to its aged customers, it is disheartening. What is also disheartening is Captain Cook's announcement made shortly after breakfast.

"Due to the continuing spread of the coronavirus," Captain Cook begins. "P&O have decided to cancel the entire Asian leg of this year's world cruise. After Brisbane, we will not be heading to Manila; everyone is going to get a good look at Australia instead."

With Brisbane our disembarkation port, we consider ourselves extremely fortunate that our personal cruise hasn't been impacted, but we feel for many of the others.

"I was looking forward to Thailand," someone sighs. "Instead, we get Tasmania."

"It should only affect the Asian leg, shouldn't it?" someone else worries. "The rest of the itinerary should be fine?"

Like Tahiti, it is thought that New Zealand was first inhabited by stalwart canoeists who arrived from Polynesia around 1200-1300 AD. Isolated on the island they called Aotearoa, land of the long white cloud, they hunted, fought, fished, fought, carved fought and slowly (despite the fighting) built up their population to around 100,000. European arrival in the form of Abel Tasman in 1642, then Captain James Cook in 1769, like with Tahiti, had a detrimental effect on the locals. Calling themselves Māoris, meaning "normal," they rapidly succumbed to western disease and exacerbated fighting (especially once firearms were involved), saw their numbers decline.

In 1840, fearing the French were about to do so, the British made New Zealand a British colony and convinced the Māoris to accept annexation by the Treaty of Waitangi. Loss of their land, overwhelming increases in European arrivals combined with declining Māori numbers (by 1896, Māori population had dropped to 42,000 against over 500,000 settlers), saw a simmering resentment which still exists today.

In 1907, New Zealand declared itself a dominion or semi-independent Commonwealth realm of the British Empire, and notable occurrences since then include a rising number of Pacific Island arrivals and the 1975 Treaty of Waitangi Act from which a tribunal was formed to look at Māori land claims.

Today, New Zealand aligns itself more with Australia and Asia than it does Great Britain, and although heavily dependent on tourism, it mainly relies on agriculture for its exports.

The Bay of Plenty area we have just arrived at, bursting with kiwifruit orchards, avocado plantations and exciting tourism opportunities such as Rotorua's thermal volcanic parklands, should perfectly exemplify New Zealand.

With a tour booked, it's early morning when we disembark the Arcadia and step ashore. In front of us rises the stubby cone of the extinct Mount Maunganui volcano after which this port suburb is named, while somewhere out to sea lies White Island, site of such tragedy only a few short months back. Another cruise ship is berthed alongside us, the Voyager of the Seas, which means the town is going to be crowded.

With numerous touring options available – wine tasting at a nearby vineyard, mud pool viewing at Rotorua or even a climb of Mount Maunganui – we have elected to travel the 90-odd minutes out of town to visit 'Hobbiton' of *Lord of the Rings* fame.

Col, our coach driver/tour guide/former Brit, is chatty and eager to impress his former compatriots. He's also hyped from an event that occurred the night before.

"We had a shooting here last night," he tells us. "It was a gang shooting very close to where we will be travelling. A lot of the roads are closed."

Leaving the port area, he diverges from his shooting story.

"New Zealand exports a lot of timber, but the industry has closed down for the moment, and over 1,100 timber workers have been laid off. We have huge amounts of timber stockpiled," he says as we pass wharves and later timber yards crammed full of denuded timber logs. "It's all because of the coronavirus."

Stunned that this escalating virus has caused such significant problems even in faraway New Zealand, it's easier just to sit back, enjoy the passing scenery and let Col's words wash over us.

"House prices have quadrupled here in the past 17 years... Thirty per cent of the world's dairy comes from New Zealand... We grow avocadoes, kiwifruit, onions, maize... That bush you can see growing everywhere is gorse. Brought in by early Europeans, it's gone wild."

While outside, the scenery is becoming ever more stunning – rolling pastures dotted with cute sheep and curious cows – the gorse Col is referring to does mar the landscape, as does the hue of most of what we can see.

"We are in the middle of a terrible drought," Col informs us. "That's why everything is so brown."

In 1998, film director Peter Jackson 'discovered' the Alexander sheep and beef farm while conducting an aerial survey of potential set locations. Realising these lush green pastures and gently rolling hills falling to a perfect glassy lake would make the ideal Hobbiton, but lacking funds, he approached the New Zealand government. Helen Clark, prime minister at the time, was happy to contribute resources and sent in the New Zealand army who, armed with heavy earthmoving equipment, set to work refining the hobbit hills and building impeccable bitumen roads. While the initial *Lord of the*

Rings sets were only temporary structures, the subsequent filming of *The Hobbit* trilogy saw the designs made permanent. The entire site became one of the area's most popular tourist attractions.

We are both great *Lord of the Rings* fans and sitting in our elevated position as our coach makes its way along one of the smooth bitumen tracks, it is quite surreal, albeit fantastic, to see Hobbiton slowly come to life. From the double-arched stone bridge to the 39 perfect hobbit holes fronting a familiar lake, it's all instantly recognisable from the movies.

Commencing with coffee and fresh fruit muffins eaten in front of Sam and Rosie's Green Dragon pub, our 90-minute tour covers a generous portion of the 12-acre former film set before finishing with hearty ales back at the Green Dragon. Along the way, we pass some of the most stunning pastoral scenery I have ever seen: gentle green hills coated in lush swaying grass dotted with vibrant blazing flowers and humming with lazy bees; tempting wooden hobbit holes, round and colourful like Smarties; a silvery lake graced by elegant swans and happy quacking ducks. Throw in 'Bag End' – home of Bilbo and Frodo Baggins, the thatched mill, the fibreglass oak tree under which Bag End sits, and it's both an incredible tour and site, the attention to detail unbelievable.

While promised a visit to a kiwifruit farm on our return journey, the promise must, unfortunately, be broken.

"Sorry folks," says Col. "It looks like we are about to get caught up in the road closures caused by last night's shooting." Sitting in the slow-moving traffic, Col continues: "It's a gang-related shooting. Ever since Australia started kicking out all Kiwis (Kiwi can refer to a bird, a fruit or a New Zealander) with criminal records, we have been having increased problems with gangs. Those returning from Oz try and assert their authority which leads to trouble."

That afternoon, after a quick late lunch aboard the Arcadia, we set out and explore the small town of Maunganui. Full of exclusive gift and boutique shops, hip cafés and trendy pubs, it's an unassuming but great place where we frequently run into fellow Arcadian passengers.

"It's funny," I say to Darryl. "We come across more people that we know here than we do when walking around Brunswick Heads."

It's an easy 250-kilometre sail overnight to reach Auckland, our next port of call. Along the way, we hear that the Diamond Princess cruise ship, still stuck in Japan, unbelievably now has 300 passengers testing positive to the coronavirus. Worldwide, the figures are growing, with over 1,400 dead and 60,000 infected. Despite this grim news, the realisation of just how susceptible the Arcadia, and other ships are to coronavirus, all on board remain positive. Although, sometimes our dinner conversations do have cause for concern.

"What would happen if it came on board?" and even more worrying, "how would we know if it came aboard?"

To explore Auckland, New Zealand's largest metropolis, a city that straddles the isthmus between two large harbours, we have decided to use the Hop-On buses once again. Aboard this bus, it's easy to see the small, chic yachts that dot the numerous bays and to understand how Auckland earned itself the nickname 'City of Sails.' It's also fascinating to observe at least four of the 48 volcanic cones that punctuate this Auckland region.

Sitting on the edge of two tectonic plates, the Australian and the Pacific, it is the movement of these two landmasses slowly pushing against each other that has created New Zealand's volcanoes and caused the thousands of earthquakes for which the country is notorious. Travelling the hilly terrain, marvelling at the sprawling city landscape, it is quite a novel experience to view these friendly extinct volcanoes and to admire the lush parklands that have been made of them.

With 17 stops on our bus run, we decline to alight at any, content instead just to observe and complete the circuit. It's a circuit that includes Albert Park – its manicured greenery an inner-city oasis – the 180-metre Mount Eden volcanic cone and the Eden Park sports stadium: a highlight for Darryl. Long winding stretches of road take us through small, residential areas out to the Auckland Zoo.

"It's the first Hop-On bus I think we have done," Darryl comments, "that takes us through so many residential suburbs, past so many private homes. We're really in suburbia."

As usual, as our bus progresses, we learn a little more about the city and country we are visiting.

"Auckland has become the largest Polynesian city in the world," the commentary coming through our earphones advises. "The zoo has kiwis, but they mainly come out at night… With nine sheep per person, New Zealand has the highest sheep ratio in the world… Auckland's most famous resident is Sir Edmund Hilary of Mount Everest fame."

Back in the city and we eventually alight at the top of Queen St, Auckland's main shopping thoroughfare. Orderly and spacious with a great selection of shops and beautiful old buildings, we follow its downhill trajectory until a McDonald's lures us in for coffee and wi-fi. Surprisingly, both are quite strong.

"There's no problem with the internet here."

"There's no tourists from Asia," I reply. "I noticed it back on the Hop-On bus. Normally the bus would be full, but it wasn't. And usually there are heaps of tourists fighting for the wi-fi but there isn't."

"Do you think it's because of the coronavirus?"

"It must be. I can't think of any other reason. But it's incredible how it's already making such an impact. Hopefully, it won't affect us much in Australia."

"Surely it won't affect us in Brunswick Heads."

Situated towards the pointy end of New Zealand's north island, the 144 islands that make up the Bay of Islands are famous for their rolling beauty. They are equally well-known for their secluded bays, long silvery beaches and abundant wildlife which includes dolphins, marlin, whales and penguins.

It's also a region that faced a fair share of the conflict between early British settlers and indigenous Māoris which cumulated in the Waitangi Treaty – a treaty signed a stone's throw from the tiny tourist town of Paihia, our next arrival point. With a mother who hails from New Zealand, I spent many of my early childhood holidays in this country and have, in fact, visited this region, explored Paihia and inspected the Waitangi Treaty grounds. For these reasons, any tours offered have been eschewed; instead, today will be a leisurely one with a stroll around Paihia before a visit to Russell, a 20-minute ferry ride across the bay.

Accessible only by tender, Paihia's population of around 1,500 disconcertingly more than doubles with the mid-morning arrival of the Arcadia. Lightly sprinkled with café and souvenir shops, there is little to see and do, and so after a quick browse, an expresso affogato and wi-fi scrounged from the famous Movenpick ice cream shop, we board a ferry to Russell. It's a choppy ride brought about by a developing low, and I'm grateful to step ashore, pull out my travel umbrella and start to explore.

Being one of the oldest towns in New Zealand and one of the country's first permanent European settlements, there's a fair bit of history here, and as we walk, we learn a little more.

"Russell used to be known as the 'hellhole of the southwest pacific,'" I read from my tourist guide. "The Māoris burnt the town to the ground at one stage. Christ Church, the Anglican church here, is New Zealand's oldest church and has musket-ball holes in the walls, a reminder of the Māori Wars."

In all, it's a brief but enjoyable visit cut short by increasing rain. Back on board the Arcadia, it's a relief to get out of our damp clothes, to settle back into our cosy little cabin, but also a little depressing.

"There's only Sydney left," I mourn. "Then up to Brisbane. Our global adventure is nearly over."

CHAPTER 21

Australia

O UR crossing of the international date line just a few days ago actually had us leapfrogging over Australian time. It means that on the morning of 17 February, two days out from Sydney and for the 18th occasion, we rewind our watches.

"It's something I hadn't thought about before we left home," Darryl's says as he unstraps his watch for the final time. "All this passing through different time zones at ground level. Having to put our watches back every few days or so."

"There's definitely more to it this way than just flying through a heap of zones at once," I reply.

Today, Australian customs officials who conveniently boarded the Arcadia in Auckland spend most of the day checking visas, passports and customs declarations. When it's our turn to front the efficient and jovial officers, one of them looks up in surprise.

"You're the first Australians we have come across."

"Yes. We are a rare species on this ship," we reply.

Although excited to be so near home, to once again be in Australian waters, our arrival in Sydney will mean that this global adventure will be nearing its end. Following a two-day hiatus in Sydney, the Arcadia will spend a further day travelling north tracing Australia's eastern coastline before arriving in Brisbane on 22 February, marking the end of our journey. I am not unhappy to be leaving the Arcadia – seven weeks at sea is a few weeks too many (for me at least) – but I love this life of travel. Of touching on different countries and places and learning a little of their history. Of being judged by where you are going, not by what you do for a living. The thrill of waking and experiencing a new place. It will be sad to see it come to an end.

Others who are melancholy are the numerous passengers due to disembark, most of them Poms who will be heading back to England.

"We only have a few days here," says Val mournfully. "Then back to wet, wintery England."

"We booked our flights with P&O," says Daphne. "We have two days in Sydney then we were supposed to spend a few days in Singapore. That's been cancelled now due to the virus, but P&O haven't told us what the change of plans are. We have no idea what's happening."

"We're going the whole way around," says Diane and David. "But who knows what's going to happen after Australia. We're expecting our itinerary to change again. It's turning into the Captain's 'Mystery Tour.'"

Outside, and that rain-inducing low felt in Paihia is still hovering. Only the most stalwart British sunbathers are braving the sunbeds, while the Tasman Sea we are now traversing is a see-sawing mass of white-capped water. It stays this way until our early morning arrival at the 2-kilometre entrance to Sydney Harbour, the headlands known as North or Quarantine Head to the north, and South or Dunbar Head to the south.

Having once lived in Vaucluse, a Sydney suburb very close to these headlands, Darryl is keen to view their passing from the elevated position of our cabin; thus, we are both awake early. Still dark, we watch the forbidding headlands slide past, the light of Hornby Lighthouse winking, and feel the turbulent swell ease the further into the harbour we advance. Still early and with hours left before sunrise, we return to bed and awaken to a motionless ship moored right in the middle of beautiful Sydney Harbour.

It will cost P&O close to 100,000 Australian dollars per day to moor at the Circular Quay passenger terminal, with two full days in Sydney; our first day will instead be spent more cheaply tethered to

Athol Buoy before moving to the more expensive location late tonight. Waking to see the iconic cream sails of the famous Opera House, the familiar iron curve of the Sydney Harbour Bridge, an incredible blue Australian sky all visible from my bed is not only breathtaking but also very welcoming.

This morning, knowing that we would probably never again have the opportunity of indulgently lounging and eating while surrounded by some of Australia's most captivating and iconic landmarks, we have pre-ordered a room service breakfast. We savour our Danish pastries, enjoy our orange juice and shudder at our coffees while sitting on our balcony, all the while marvelling at our incredible location and pinching ourselves that we are back in Australia. Our phones, so long silent, have recognised their homeland and it's great when breakfast is over to insert old sims, phone family members and reconnect with 'our' world.

Somewhere between 50,000 and 70,000 (or even more) years ago, Aboriginal people arrived in Australia by sea and land-bridge from Southeast Asia. Infiltrating this vast, flat, dry continent, they learnt to live with her idiosyncrasies, to tame her desert centre, her icy south and her humid tropical north. In April 1770, when Captain Cook first stepped ashore, this most ancient and oldest living cultural civilisation numbered anywhere between 300,000 and a million people distributed over 500 tribes.

In what is now a familiar story with European arrival, the natives once again received the poorer end of the stick. From the 1788 arrival of Australia's First Fleet – carrying the first of the 162,000 convicts that would eventually be sent from Great Britain to Australia – through to the 1850s gold rush that saw an explosion of immigrants, to federation in 1901, Aboriginal people were ostracised and demonised. Australia, today a sovereign state of Great Britain, the worlds 14th largest economy and a country rich in resources, unfortunately still has a poor relationship with her forebearers, and although this relationship is strengthening, it's at an unforgivably slow pace.

With two days to spend in Sydney, Australia's oldest European settlement, a city we used to know quite well, today will be about rediscovering and catching up on any tasks, while tomorrow we will once again become tourists. My sister Michelle is celebrating her delayed 50th birthday party next week, while Darryl's sister Petria is getting married the week after. One of my more enjoyable tasks will be to purchase an outfit for each event.

"It makes sense to try and purchase something here," I cajole. "There will be a lot more choice, and this way I won't have to give it any thought once we arrive home."

"But I'm not interested in spending my time in Sydney shopping," Darryl replies with a shudder. "I think I'll prefer to do my own thing. I've never explored the area behind the Opera House – the Botanic Gardens. I've never even walked to Mrs Macquarie's Chair."

"And I would prefer to shop on my own. So, let's meet up later?" I happily reply.

Leaving Darryl still planning his day's route – his visit to the sandstone bench hand-carved by convicts in 1810 known as Mrs Macquarie's Chair – I am one of the first to board a tender that will deposit me at a pier alongside the Sydney Opera House. As I sit chatting with some Poms, here on their first visit, it feels strange to be arriving in Sydney as a foreign tourist.

"No, we haven't booked a tour," I answer the couple sitting next to me. "We used to live here and have done nearly everything that's on offer. Tomorrow we may catch the Hop-On bus and have a look around. What have you got planned?"

"We have booked a tour," the gentleman replies. "But we have no idea where it goes. We booked it over six months ago now and can't remember."

The following hours pass incredibly quickly and enjoyably as I refamiliarise myself with the Sydney CBD, traipse Pitt Street mall and note the new light rail that now runs down George Street. David

Jones and Myer are every bit as good as I was hoping and provide two great outfits; my search made easier by familiar clothing brands, easy communication and affordable prices. Finally, footsore and laden with carrier bags, I phone Darryl.

"I got lost," he tells me. "But then I found an old pub, so I've just been sitting here."

Meeting up, more time passes as we meander back through the city, noting how good and clean it looks in comparison to so many other cities, stroll the Circular Quay precinct and eventuate at the boardwalk fronting the iconic UNESCO-listed Sydney Opera House. It is an area packed with bars and tourists.

"Coronavirus doesn't seem to be having much impact on the tourists here," I comment.

"It is busy," Darryl agrees.

With a little bar providing $5 beers and $10 margaritas, it's an easy decision to join the crowds and sit and enjoy the late afternoon sun. In front of us is the majestic Opera House, alongside us the commanding Harbour Bridge, while over the sparkling harbour, the gapped-toothed face of Luna Park leers. With such beauty and entertainment surrounding us and having experienced such a great day, it's entirely understandable how Sydney consistently ranks as one of the best cities in the world to live.

Sometime during the night, the Arcadia is smoothly and silently moved from her buoy and equally stealthily moored alongside the Sydney Overseas Passenger Terminal. It means that a little after 10 am, we simply have to cross a gangplank and walk a few hundred metres before finding ourselves in the Rocks area of Sydney and in front of a Hop-On Bus.

Like in so many other cities where we have used them – Dubai, Berlin, Paris, Heraklion, Budapest, San Francisco and Auckland – the Hop-On Bus is unbeatable as it gives us a comprehensive, affordable taste of Sydney.

While we pass by the 1821-built Gothic St. Mary's Cathedral, seedy

King's Cross and the odorous fish market, we do alight at iconic Bondi Beach and the vast precinct of Darling Harbour.

Darling Harbour is a bit of an eye-opener for us. Only really developed 35 years ago when we lived in Sydney, it has changed twofold since even then. It's fascinating to see how the 35-year-old convention centre has been rebuilt, the entertainment centre gone and to note the attention now given to parklands and walkways.

One such walkway allows us to pass through an eerily empty Chinatown – "This *must* be an effect of the virus," says Darryl – and towards a completely new harbourside development Barangaroo, before guiding us through The Rocks area and back to our terminal.

"Sydney is much more pedestrian-friendly than I remember," I comment in bemusement.

"I agree. I didn't think we would be able to walk so easily from Darling Harbour right back to Circular Quay," Darryl replies. "I've been impressed with Sydney."

"Me too. I was sceptical about it living up to some of the other places we have visited, but it definitely holds its own against any of them."

With the Arcadia not due to depart until the early hours of the morning, that evening we had planned to do as most of the other passengers were doing – to head back out onto the Sydney streets in search of food and entertainment. As we stand on the Arcadia's back deck and enjoy a drink from the nearly empty Aquarius Bar, I look down upon the throngs choking the harbourside bars and restaurants far below.

"Why do we want to get back off again?" I question. "To put up with those crowds? If we stay here, not only do we have our own barman to bring us drinks which we can book to our room and free food, but we probably have the best view of the bridge, the harbour and the Opera House in the world."

As Darryl agrees, what eventuates is an incredible and unforgettable night as, unhindered by madding crowds and surrounded by breathtaking monuments, we stand on our elevated platform and watch as the sinking sun melts and glowing stars come out to dance their way across the interminable sky. To watch the Harbour Bridge twinkle and glow like a curved firestick and the Opera House gleam like an incandescent shell. When it's time for a drink, a friendly barman is always on hand, and when it's time to eat, we simply pop into the adjacent Belvedere restaurant, feast on the buffet, then return to our picturesque position.

Tired from a busy few days, I return to our cabin a little before midnight, but Darryl stays up and watches as, in the darkest hours of the morning, the Arcadia once again slips her mooring and backtracks through Sydney Harbour.

Sydney was the end of the second leg of the Arcadia's world cruise and is the leg that sees the most departures. It means when we awaken on what will be our final full day aboard the Arcadia, the last full day of this incredible adventure, that many new faces are mingling about and there's a noticeable absence of old ones.

This final day was always going to be a highlight for us: to gaze from a ship that has bought us halfway around the world on Australia's familiar coastline, passing the well-known townships of Newcastle, Port Macquarie and Coffs Harbour. It's a day that will merge our 'itchy feet' life and our 'global adventure' world with our everyday life when we closely pass Brunswick Heads and see the familiar beacon of Byron Bay lighthouse welcoming us.

As expected, it's a joyful but sad day. Joyful to be so nearly home, to once again be able to catch up with family and friends, sad to farewell new acquaintances. Joyful to soon be back in our own bed, our own space. Sad that this adventure is nearly over. Although Darryl is sorry to be farewelling Alan and Denise, his bridge partners, he is not sad that his bridge lessons are coming to an end. "We are all sick of bridge," he tells me.

That afternoon over one last decadent high tea in the Meridian Restaurant, our conversation, naturally, turns to our travels.

"I've worked out that we have visited four continents, travelled through 24 countries including Belarus, Slovakia and Panama, and caught 28 trains, although that doesn't include the tubes in London," I say, reading from my phone.

"Did you work out how far in kilometres?"

"By air over 8,000 kilometres. By land, nearly 16,000 and by sea, over 32,000. Nearly 57,000 kilometres in all."

"What did you like best?"

"That's impossible to answer. The journey was incredible. We did and saw so much. But I'll never forget sitting in the shadow of the Matterhorn watching the sun go down. Seeing the snow turn the wind visible as it swirled around its peak."

"I'll never forget Mongolia," Darryl replies. "Those endless sandy plains. It's a place that looks like it's in for some major change. It's been a different trip this time. Do you think you have learnt anything?"

"To make sure your pre-existing injuries are insured," I quip instantly. "I had a lot of anxious moments there. But really, I think the entire journey has just reinforced how incredible and educational travel can be. How small, despite the huge kilometres travelled, and accessible the world really is. I've learnt a lot – to have Google Translate on stand-by, to not always believe the media (look at Moscow), and to check our guide's name before jumping in with him – remember China. But more importantly I have learnt, as a result of this virus so badly affecting the onward itinerary of this cruise, that it may be prudent to use a travel agent for parts of a trip in future. Let them handle any catastrophes, any rescheduling. Or at the very least, have excellent cancellation insurance. You?"

"I've learnt that the time of year you travel is important. Travelling in winter has been good – cheaper and with far fewer crowds. I've also learnt not to have too many expectations, especially regarding food," Darryl laughs. "I can't believe there was no lemon chicken in China, no Madeira cake in Madeira."

Early evening and on the clearly visible coastline, Yamba slips past as we locate our passports, pack our bags one final time and eye our copious dirty washing.

"You know, on our next trip, I'll make sure there are more washing machines. I also think that we should stay a little longer in some places. Rest up a bit. This one may have been a little too fast."

"Can we just get home from this one first?" Darryl cries.

Around 9 pm, with the flashing beacon of Byron Bay lighthouse behind us and the glowing lights of Ocean Shores shortly ahead, we stand on our familiar balcony, aware that Brunswick Heads, our journey's starting point, must lie close alongside. Although we have yet to reach Brisbane, yet to catch a train to the Gold Coast where Pierce will be meeting us, passing this point means, in effect, the circuit has been completed, our 'global adventure' is over. It means there will be no more time zones to traverse, no more languages to cope with, no more watches to adjust. That despite food poisoning, train accidents, itinerary adjustments and a looming world pandemic, we have just done something that neither of us thought we would ever do. We have together, successfully and happily, circumnavigated the entire world. Our itchy feet, for now, are content.

EPILOGUE

I WRITE this epilogue in late January 2021, Jo Biden's inauguration day, thankful that Trump (while he was in power at least) didn't blow up the world.

In hindsight, we were incredibly fortunate to have completed our entire amazing 'global adventure.' To get back when we did. Covid-19 declared a pandemic on 11 March 2020 (20 days later), destroying most travel plans since then. With no idea of what the remainder of 2021 will bring, I can only reflect on the crazy year that was 2020.

After dropping us in Brisbane on 22 February 2020, the Arcadia, following its adjusted itinerary, turned around and spent the following weeks exploring the southern length of Australia. Initially, most onboard and indeed, most Australians were unaware of just how serious and disruptive coronavirus would become. The feeling on board the Arcadia was that it was still, mainly, an Asian problem. In the time it took the Arcadia to reach Perth, however, this had all changed. The virus had well and truly taken hold globally, health systems were struggling, and countries were slamming their borders closed, especially to cruise ship passengers. Unable to continue its original itinerary, the Arcadia (thankfully coronavirus-free) was forced to return to Southampton via Durban and Tenerife, stopping only to refuel and replenish supplies. Passengers were unable to disembark. They spent the entire 33 days, from Perth to England, confined to the ship.

Regarding the shocking 'apocalyptic' fires that ravaged Australia while we were on our journey, figures reveal that over 3,000 houses were razed, 33 people killed and more than a billion animals lost. Total land destroyed was estimated at 12.6 million hectares, an area nearly the size of Spain. While Australia has experienced horrendous bushfires before, few were proceeded by the hottest and driest conditions in Australia's history, nor so widespread.

In November 2020, a New Zealand workplace safety probe into that White Island tragedy that killed 22 people, 14 of them Australian, recommended charging 10 organisations and three individuals. It is still inconceivable that an accident like this could happen, that tourists were allowed to visit an area of such heightened risk.

Covid-19 knocked the assassination of Iranian commander Qassem Soleimani from the world's headlines. But with the 3 January first anniversary just passing and rumblings continuing in the Middle East, this story may not be over yet.

Today, 20 January 2021, Covid-19 has reached every country, every continent. Over 98 million people have contracted the disease, and nearly 2,100,000 people have died from it. We have been fortunate in Australia, our isolated location meaning we have been able to lock down our borders and keep the worst of the virus out. Apart from practising social distancing, our lives have pretty much continued as usual. We feel lucky to have escaped the horror that continues to unfold in countries like the UK and America.

Reflecting on all the fantastic places we travelled during our incredible four-month journey, the adventures we had, then looking at the state of the world today, I am so grateful that we braved the unknown, ignored the expense and took off when we did. It looks to be quite some time before a journey such as this can be undertaken again. Before it is safe to travel. It certainly lends weight to the phrase *carpe diem*: seize the day.

Bucket Lists
and
Walking Sticks

^{by} Emma Scattergood

A terrible accident.
Forced retirement.
An excuse to pull out the bucket list!

After a motorbike accident leaves her husband with life-changing injuries, author Emma organises a worldwide adventure based on the contents of an old, laminated bucket list.

It will be the journey of a lifetime ticking off list items: from viewing ancient Petra and treading Greece's Parthenon to traversing the Suez Canal and hunting down Doc Martin.

Taking seven months and spanning Asia and Europe, this journal, told in mouth-watering detail, will pull you headlong into the sights, life, culture and beauty of each place visited.
It will make you want to follow in their footsteps.

Printed in Great Britain
by Amazon

76052641R00159